'Arabiyyat al-Naas (Part One)

'Arabiyyat al-Naas (Part One) offers a groundbreaking introduction to Arabic as it is written and spoken by native speakers. It combines a progressive and rigorous grounding in Modern Standard Arabic (MSA) – the form employed for reading, writing and formal speaking – with an innovative integration of the spoken Levantine variety used in everyday situations in Syria, Lebanon, Jordan and Palestine. Introducing the two simultaneously, *'Arabiyyat al-Naas (Part One)* uses each in its proper context: Levantine for conversations and MSA for reading and writing activities. In this way, the course efficiently prepares students for the practical realities of learning and "living" Arabic today.

Features include:

- a broad range of stimulating activities and exercises fostering active engagement with the course and comprehensively covering the 5 Cs: communication, culture, connections, comparisons and communities
- a free DVD filmed on location in Jordan, presenting over 40 videos and incorporating a wide variety of entertaining and realistic scenarios
- a free companion website (**www.routledge.com/cw/younes**) offering a wealth of additional instructor and student resources, including a teacher's guide, an introduction to the letters and sounds of Arabic (with audiovisual aid and writing demonstrations), audio recordings of songs and listening passages, video clips, sample tests, an answer key and language games
- clear explanations of grammatical structures and concepts as they occur in the reading and listening materials to encourage progressive learning and active interaction with the text.

Written by a dynamic author team and tested over a number of years at Cornell University, *'Arabiyyat al-Naas (Part One)* is an essential resource for students beginning to learn Arabic. While primarily designed for classroom use, the accessibility of the course and website also renders it highly suitable for independent study.

This volume is the first in an exciting three-part series of Arabic textbooks which together provide a complete three-year undergraduate language program.

Munther Younes is Reis Senior Lecturer of Arabic Language and Linguistics and Director of the Arabic Program in the Department of Near Eastern Studies at Cornell University, USA.

Makda Weatherspoon is a Lecturer in Arabic Language in the Department of Near Eastern Studies at Cornell University, USA, where she is the Coordinator of the Elementary Arabic Program.

Maha Saliba Foster is a Lecturer of Arabic in the Department of Languages and Literatures at the University of Denver, USA. Prior to that, she taught Arabic at Colorado College and the Air Force Academy.

Other titles in the 'Arabiyyat al-Naas series:

'Arabiyyat al-Naas (Part Two): An Intermediate Course in Arabic
Munther Younes and Hanada Al-Masri
978-0-415-50908-4

'Arabiyyat al-Naas (Part Three): An Advanced Course in Arabic
Munther Younes and Yomna Chami
978-0-415-50901-5
Forthcoming – spring 2014

"This program is a bold, honest, and compelling presentation of how Arabic is actually used by native speakers. It is thoughtfully presented by seasoned and passionate Arabic teachers and will take the novice Arabic language student to the solid Intermediate Mid level in all four language skills."
Maher Awad, Senior Lecturer of Arabic, Certified ACTFL and ILR Tester, Rice University, USA

"A truly excellent textbook; comprehensive in its coverage of language skills; uses wide-ranging and up to date material; a good balance between classical and contemporary material; coherent across units and focused in each lesson. Choice of material is careful, closely matching the use of Arabic in social context and maintaining a good balance between narratives, news reports and current affairs. The icing on the cake for me is the element of humour that runs throughout the passages and dialogues. The language learner and the teacher will find this material a joy to work with."
Enam Al-Wer, University of Essex, UK

"Arabiyyat al-Naas is a game-changing series that embodies a pioneering approach to Arabic language teaching and learning. By integrating formal and colloquial Arabic, Arabiyyat al-Naas presents the language as it is used in real life. The demand for this approach is now increasing exponentially around the world. Arabiyyat al-Naas is the result of years of creative thinking and innovative teaching."
Jeremy Palmer, American University of Sharjah, UAE

"*Arabiyyat al-Naas (Part One)* is one of the best Arabic books that I have ever encountered. I have waited for years for this type of book, and it is finally here. This book teaches the Arabic spoken and formal languages. Could you imagine teaching your foreign student the written language and the colloquial at the same time? Usually, Arabic textbooks only teach one colloquial language. So, you may ask, which colloquial language does *Arabiyyat al-Naas (Part One)* teach? All of them! Each chapter the actor/hero/player travels to a new Arabic country and talks with the people in the colloquial day-to-day language native to that country. Then she goes and writes in her diary about her experiences and what she learned from that culture. The conversations are absolutely wonderful and sometimes funny. Students will learn to read and speak both dialects without too much trouble. I highly recommend this book to any institution or university, and especially government employees who want to pass their OPI, ACE, DLPT and other standardized tests. I encourage all the Arabic teachers in the USA and the rest of the world to use this long awaited book. This three-level book series includes videos, translated conversations, a variety of exercises which are fun, unique and challenging and much, much more. Arabiyyat al-Naas is the answer to the questions asked in every educational conference meeting: Which Arabic dialect should we teach? Should teachers teach colloquial at the same time as the formal language? Thank you to all who participated in creating this long awaited, fabulous book."
Ferial Demy, Arabic Instructor at Diplomatic Language Services, Washington D.C., USA

ʻArabiyyat al-Naas (Part One)

Munther Younes
Makda Weatherspoon
Maha Saliba Foster

Routledge
Taylor & Francis Group

LONDON AND NEW YORK

Supplementary Resources Disclaimer

Additional resources were previously made available for this title on DVD. However, as DVD has become a less accessible format, all resources have been moved to a more convenient online download option.

You can find these resources available here: www.routledge.com/9780415516938

Please note: Where this title mentions the associated disc, please use the downloadable resources instead.

First published 2014 by Routledge

2 Park Square, Milton Park, Abingdon, Oxon OX14 4RN
711 Third Avenue, New York, NY 10017, USA

Routledge is an imprint of the Taylor & Francis Group, an informa business

First issued in hardback 2017

British Library Cataloguing in Publication Data
A catalogue record for this book is available from the British Library

Library of Congress Cataloging in Publication Data
Younes, Munther Abdullatif, 1952–
    Arabiyyat al-naas / by Munther Younes, Makda Weatherspoon, Maha Saliba Foster, Hanada Al-Masri, Yomna Chami.
        volumes cm.
    Volume 2 has subtitle: Intermediate course in Arabic
    Volume 3 has subtitle: Advanced course in Arabic
    Includes index.
    1. Arabic language–Textbooks for foreign speakers–English.   I. Title.   II. Title: Intermediate course in Arabic.
III. Title: Advanced course in Arabic.
    PJ6111.Y68 2014
    492.7'82421–dc23
                                                                                                2013001630

ISBN: 978-0-415-51693-8 (pbk)
ISBN: 978-1-138-43770-8 (hbk)

Typeset in Scala
by Graphicraft Limited, Hong Kong

All images, with the exception of the maps and clock line drawings (© Routledge) and the photo of Rasheim Wright (p. 251, © FIBA), were sourced from Shutterstock (www.shutterstock.com).

Audio recording credits: Rahaf al-Masri, Ahmad Alswaid, Muna Barghout, Munther Younes

Audio content recorded at Cornell University, USA. Video content filmed and edited by Bashar Studio, Jordan, and re-edited and formatted at Cornell University, USA. DVD menu interface created by Tom, Dick + Debbie Productions, www.tomdickanddebbie.co.uk.

Visual Tour of the Textbook

Throughout the text you will see icons in the margin, which indicate where further multimedia resources are available. These stimulating online exercises are exclusive to purchasers of the textbook and provide a rigorous grounding in Modern Standard Arabic (MSA) while also seamlessly integrating the spoken Levantine variety.

Multimedia resources include:

Video Material

Over 40 videos provide students with a variety of entertaining and realistic scenarios to help build up a diverse vocabulary and effective speaking and listening skills.

Video material can be found on the accompanying DVD and the companion website.

Audio Material

Extensive audio recordings of songs and listening passages will help students to develop their listening and speaking skills.

Audio material can be found on the accompanying DVD and the companion website.

Writing Demonstrations

These videos show the learner how to write Arabic numbers, individual letters and whole words. They have been skilfully designed to accompany the first unit of the textbook.

Writing Demonstrations can be found on the companion website only.

PowerPoint slides with audio

This set of PowerPoint slides introduces the reader to Arabic letters and sounds using the vocabulary of the first unit of the textbook. Each word in the unit is presented on a slide, along with an image and an audio recording of its pronunciation.

PowerPoint slides with audio can be found on the companion website only.

All rich and interactive multimedia resources can be found in the student resources section of the companion website (**www.routledge.com/cw/younes**) and follow the layout of the textbook with resources listed by unit.

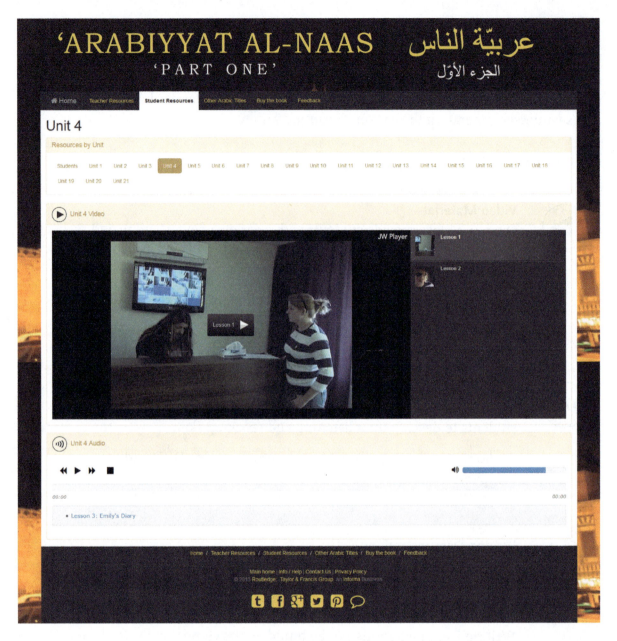

To access the student resources please follow the instructions on the inside front cover of this textbook.

The DVD features all audio and video files. Click on "Audio" on the DVD menu to access the audio files, which follow the structure of the textbook (e.g. "Unit 2, L1, Ex2" corresponds with Unit 2, Lesson 2, Exercise 2). For video files, click on "Video" on the DVD menu and you will find them in the order they correspond with the textbook (again clearly named, e.g. "Unit 10 Lesson 1 Part 1").

Contents

Acknowledgments

Much of the material in this book appeared in two previous versions, one called *Elementary Arabic: An Integrated Approach* (Yale University Press, 1995) and the other *Living Arabic* (The Language Resource Center, Cornell University, 2007). We remain eternally grateful to all who have contributed to these earlier versions. Their contribution lives on in this new edition.

This revised version has been expanded to include several new elements, which required the involvement and participation of a large number of people. Many of these new features were added at the suggestion of colleagues and friends whose continuous support and appreciation for this unorthodox way of introducing Arabic to the foreign learner have kept us going in our determination to bring the project to completion. In particular, we would like to express our deepest gratitude to the following colleagues and friends (in alphabetical order): Enam Al-Wer, University of Essex; Hanada Al-Masri, Dennison University; Jeremy Palmer, the American University in Sharjah; Jonathan Featherstone, Edinburgh University; Kassem Wahba, Georgetown University; Kirk Belnap, Brigham Young University; Maher Awad, Rice University; Mohammad al-Masri, University of Oklahoma; and Salah El-Dine Hammoud, Air Force Academy, Colorado.

Two independent learners whom we've never met but whose comments on *Living Arabic* have been particularly helpful as we worked on this edition are Jason J. Kilborn, Professor of Law at the John Marshall Law School in Chicago, and Chris Stuebner, Cornell '91, with her tutor Sarah Ramadan.

A special word of thanks goes to Mr Nicholas LaVerne of the Language Resource Center at Cornell University who has graciously and patiently given us so much of his time with this and many other projects involving audio and video technology. Thank you, Nick.

We would like to take this opportunity to thank the following people for their participation in the creation and production of the video component that accompanies the book: Rahaf al-Masri, Project Manager in Jordan, who also played the role of Fadwa, Emily's roommate in Jordan; Emily Koppelman, who played Emily's role; and the following members of the crew: Muhammad Amayreh, Hamza al-Sawa'ir, Sameer Mahrous, Dina al-Ukur, Adiyy Haddad, Jihad Yousif Muhammad, Ismail al-Masri, Riyad Ziyade, Mirna Tashman, and Abdallah al-Masri.

We were assisted in the preparation of the audio recordings by Rahaf al-Masri, Ahmad Alswaid and Muna Barghout, to whom we are very grateful.

Words fail to describe the dedication, professionalism and efficiency of the Routledge team who have worked with us tirelessly on this and other Arabic projects. In particular, we are very grateful to the following people who have been involved at the different stages of the publication process: Andrea Hartill, publisher in Language Learning; Isabelle Cheng, Senior Editorial Assistant, Colloquials and Language Learning; Samantha Vale Noya, Associate Editor, Colloquials and Language Learning; Rebecca Shillabeer, Textbook Development Editor; and Sarah May, Deputy Production Editorial Manager, Humanities. We could not have done it without you!

Last but not least, we would like to offer our sincerest gratitude to all the students who have patiently worked with the different versions of these materials. This book and accompanying media would not be the way they are without their valuable comments and positive feedback.

Makda Weatherspoon would first and foremost like to thank God for granting her wisdom, guidance and perseverance during this project, and indeed throughout her life. She would also like to express her gratitude to her husband and best friend, Hakim, for his constant support and expert advice with the different computer programs used for developing the media material for this book. She would also like to acknowledge her kids, Menelik, Saba and Elsa, for their love, contagious energy and unique ability to serve as a wonderful distraction when she is not working. And last but not least, she would like to dedicate all her work to the memory of her father, Sisay, and the unceasing support and encouragement of her mother, Hiwet.

يهدف كتاب "عربية الناس" الى تقديم اللغة العربية للمتعلم الأجنبي بوجهيها المكتوب والمنطوق في نفس الوقت. المكتوب يعني العربية الفصحى، التي يستعملها العرب في الكتابة والقراءة والمناسبات الرسمية، والمنطوق يعني ما يستعمله العرب في حياتهم اليومية للتفاهم الشفهي مع بعضهم البعض. السبب في اختيار هذا الطريق واضح وبسيط وهو أن الكتاب يهدف الى إعداد الطالب لاستعمال العربية كما يستعملها أهلها فعلاً. ويسعى الكتاب الى تطوير المهارات اللغوية الأربع من استماع ومحادثة وقراءة وكتابة، ولا يسعى الى تطوير مهارة متخصصة واحدة كقراءة القرآن أو دراسة قواعد اللغة العربية.

من أصعب الأمور التي يواجهها مَن يدعو الى منهاج كهذا هو عدم وجود لهجة محكية يعترف بها العرب ويعتبرونها لهجة رسمية مقبولة لأكثر الناس، كما هو الحال في الانجليزية والفرنسية والألمانيّة مثلاً. اللهجات العربية المحكيّة كثيرة، فأيها نختار؟

للمشكلة في رأينا وجهان؛ وجه يتعلق بالطالب ووجه يتعلّق بالمدرّس. فمن وجهة نظر الطالب الذي يريد أن يتعلّم العربية ليفهمها ويتحدّثها ويقرأها ويكتبها، ليس هناك فرق في أية لهجة محكية يتعلّم، فإنه اذا تعلّم لهجة معيّنة وأتقنها، أيا كانت تلك اللهجة، فسيتمكن من استعمالها في التفاهم مع العرب الذين يستعملون لهجات أخرى، كما يتفاهم العرب أنفسهم الذين يتحدثون لهجات مختلفة مع بعضهم البعض وكما يتكلم غير العرب الذين تعلموا لهجة عربية محكية مع عرب يتكلمون لهجات أخرى. وإذا استثنينا بلاد المغرب العربي، فإن المصري يتفاهم مع السعودي والعراقي مع السوداني، وهكذا، دون أية مشاكل تُذكر. وفي حالة بلاد المغرب العربي فإن المشكلة في أكثر الأوقات هي مشكلة مستوى تعليمي ووقت وتعوّد، فالمتعلمون من المشرق والمغرب (اذا لم يلجأوا الى لغة غير العربية) يتفاهمون مستعملين لهجاتهم المحكية التي قد تكثر فيها كلمات مأخوذة من الفصحى، وبعد مرور وقت قصير يعتاد متحدّثو اللهجات الشرقية والغربية على بعضهم ويسهل التفاهم.

أما من ناحية المدرّس ففي رأينا أن يستعمل ما يمكننا وصفه بالعربيّة المحكيّة العامّة، وهي ما يستعمله المثقّفون العرب من البلاد العربيّة المختلفة في التفاهم فيما بينهم، وهي العربيّة المستعملة في هذا الكتاب كما ينطقها مثقّفو الشرق العربي وخصوصاً ما يعرف ببلاد الشام. عندما يستعمل العرب هذه الصيغة من لغتهم فإنّهم يركّزون بشكل تلقائي على تلك الكلمات والتعابير والتراكيب التي تجمعهم بغيرهم من متحدّثي اللغة لتسهيل عمليّة التفاهم. وتزداد نسبة المشترك والمفهوم بارتفاع مستوى التعليم، لأنّ لغة التعليم، وهي الفصحى، واحدة في كلّ البلاد العربيّة.

وقد استُعملت طبعات سابقة من هذا الكتاب من قبل مدرّسين من العراق والكويت ومصر والسودان وتونس والمغرب، بالإضافة إلى مدرسين من كافّة أنحاء بلاد الشام. ولم تلاحظ أيّة اثار سلبيّة لاختلاف اللهجات على الطلاب.

مع ذلك نحن ندرك كلّ الإدراك أنّه ليس من الطبيعي للمدرّس المصري مثلاً أن يستعمل كلمات مثل "بدّي" أو "شو" أو "وين"، وما شابهها من الكلمات التي تميّز لهجة بلاد الشام، ولكنّنا نريد تذكير ذلك المدرّس أنّ آلاف الكلمات الأخرى هي مشتركة بين اللهجتين الشاميّة والمصريّة، وندعوه للنظر إلى قائمة الكلمات الموجودة في نهاية الكتاب للتأكّد من صحّة ما نقول. كذلك، وإذا أخذنا مصلحة الطالب بعين الاعتبار، فإنّه لا يعنيه الفرق بين "شو" و "أيه"، ولكن يعنيه إتقان أحدهما أو اثنيهما للتعامل مع العرب، وليس الحلّ من وجهة نظرنا في تعليمه "ماذا" التي لا يستعملها عربيّ في الحديث مع عربيّ آخر. في الحالات التي قد يجد المدرّس صعوبة في استعمال كلمة أو تعبير لاختلافه عن ما يستعمله في حياته اليوميّة، نقترح عليه أن يستعمل الكلمات والتعابير التي يرتاح لاستعمالها عندما يتكلّم مع طلابه بالإضافة إلى ما هو موجود في الكتاب، وليس من الضارّ أن يتعلّم الطلاب بضع كلمات إضافيّة يستعملها ملايين العرب في التفاهم اليومي مع بعضهم البعض.

أخيراً نودّ التذكير أنّ مقدّمة الكتاب المكتوبة باللغة الإنجليزية والتي تلي هذه المقدّمة تحتوي على شرح مفصّل لمواد الكتاب والموقع الإلكتروني المرافق له واقتراحات لتقديم تلك الموادّ.

General Introduction

'Arabiyyat al-Naas is a comprehensive Arabic-as-a-foreign-language program that consists of three textbooks and accompanying instructional materials. It integrates Modern Standard Arabic, known as فصحى with Levantine Arabic, the Arabic spoken in Syria, Lebanon, Jordan, and Palestine, in a way that reflects the use of the language by native speakers. Arabs communicate in a spoken variety in everyday situations, and use فصحى for reading, writing, and formal speaking. Being two varieties of the same language, فصحى and Levantine, known in Arabic as شامي, share most of their vocabulary and grammatical structures. This book introduces the two simultaneously, building on their shared features and using each in its proper context: شامي for conversation and discussion and فصحى for reading and writing activities. We believe that this is the most effective way to prepare students to function in Arabic. We also believe that if a student masters a major spoken variety such as شامي well enough, he/she will be able to function in other spoken varieties, just as native speakers from different areas of the Arab world do.

Native language usage is also reflected in the fact that as the program progresses from the beginning to the advanced levels of proficiency, the ratio of فصحى materials in the form of listening and reading passages is increased relative to the شامي materials. In the first volume of the series, emphasis is on the familiar, concrete, and informal, for which the spoken variety is particularly appropriate. فصحى materials occupy an increasingly more prominent role in the program with the progression towards the less familiar, less concrete and more formal, but integration remains an important feature of the whole program. Following common practice by native speakers, material presented in فصحى is discussed in شامي, which helps the continuous skill building of the two varieties.

The texts, activities, exercises, and accompanying media in the three textbooks have been designed with the goal of developing all language skills simultaneously. Humor, illustrations, maps, pictures, and different types of vocabulary-building activities are used to help make the acquisition and retention of language elements both enjoyable and effective.

'Arabiyyat al-Naas (Part One)

Part One of the 'Arabiyyat al-Naas series consists of this textbook, the accompanying DVD (which includes the audio recordings and video clips described below), and a companion website. The material is designed to be covered in two 15-week academic semesters at the college level or about 120 to 140 hours of classroom instruction.

Structure of the textbook

The textbook consists of 21 units, two glossaries, and a grammar index. The first two units introduce the Arabic letters and sounds. Units 3–21 build on these two units through the introduction of carefully designed video and reading materials and activities with the goal of developing the four skills of listening, speaking, reading, and writing. The common thread among the units is the story of an American student, Emily, who travels to the Arab world and experiences situations that the foreign learner of Arabic is likely to encounter: arriving at the airport, having her passport checked, taking a taxi, going to a hotel, eating at a restaurant, and so on. The video material shows her interacting with Arabic speakers in these situations, while most of the reading materials consist of a written diary of her experiences.

The Arabic–English glossary includes all the words introduced in the book arranged mostly by root, while the English–Arabic glossary is arranged alphabetically.

As mentioned above, the majority of words and structures are shared by فصحى and شامي. However, the forms that are used in one but not the other are identified in the comprehensive glossary: forms used exclusively in فصحى are marked with a diamond (◆) and forms used exclusively in شامي are marked with a star (*).

The companion website

The book's companion website (www.routledge.com/cw/younes) contains the following materials:

Teacher resources

These include a Teacher's Guide with suggestions on how to use the textbook and accompanying materials, the texts of the listening and video materials, oral grammar drills, and language games.

Student resources

1. Introduction to the letters and sounds

A set of PowerPoint slides introduces the Arabic letters and sounds using the vocabulary of the first unit of the textbook. Each word in the unit is presented on a slide, along with an image and an audio recording of its pronunciation.

2. Writing demonstration

This video shows the learner how to write Arabic numbers, individual letters, and whole words. It has also been designed to accompany the first unit of the textbook.

3. Audio recordings (also on the DVD that accompanies the book)

The audio recordings consist of the listening materials of Units 1 and 2, a number of songs designed to be introduced with certain units, as well as a recording of Emily's Diary (Units 3–21), which forms the bulk of the reading material in the book.

4. Video clips (also on the DVD that accompanies the book)

The video clips accompany Units 3–20. Each video clip is about 1–2 minutes long and tells a part of Emily's story.

5. The texts of the listening and video materials

It is strongly recommended that these materials be used by students only as a reference and not as a convenient short-cut. It is crucial that students spend enough time and effort listening and watching the videos to adequately develop their listening comprehension skills.

6. Answer key

The crossword puzzles are designed as a fun way for students to master the unit vocabulary. The key is provided to help learners check their answers after completing the puzzles.

Units 3–21

Whereas in Units 1 and 2, the teacher introduces the material in class first which students review and practice at home, in Units 3–21 students prepare the material for each class meeting ahead of time and class time is used for discussions and activities based on the material prepared.

Each unit in this part consists of five lessons. The first three lessons introduce video and reading materials; the fourth lesson focuses on the grammatical structures introduced in these materials; while the fifth lesson is a wrap-up lesson, which includes activities and exercises to recycle the vocabulary of the unit and to use the learned material in spoken and written production.

The units are theme-based: Unit 3 focuses on travel and self-identification, Unit 4 on taking a taxi and checking into a hotel, Unit 5 on losing and finding things, and Unit 6 on eating in a restaurant, and so on. The texts and the activities in the unit revolve around the same theme and most words are recycled in varying contexts to help the learner build up a solid vocabulary base relatively easily and fast.

Each of the video clips and reading activities is accompanied by a list of new words and a set of comprehension questions. Only the texts of the reading selections, written in فصحى, are presented in the main body of the book; the texts of the listening materials and the video clips, written in شامي, are found in the Teacher's Guide for reference only.

Video clips (مشاهدة)

The goal of these clips is to help develop the listening and speaking skills. Students watch the clip as a whole before coming to class as many times as needed with minimal help from the vocabulary lists, which should be used only to aid comprehension and not as an exercise in memorization. In class, the teacher initiates a discussion about the dialogue in the clip: asking comprehension and discussion questions (in Arabic) and answering questions about vocabulary and structure. A useful group activity in class is for students to create a dialogue based on the one in the clip using similar vocabulary and structures.

Reading (قراءة)

The reading activities of Unit 1 consist mainly of numbers, words, and short phrases. In Unit 2, a transition is made to the sentence and short paragraph level. Starting with the third unit, the reading activity, found in the third lesson, consists mainly of a diary of Emily's experiences in Jordan and neighboring Arab countries, written in paragraph form. The diary helps the unity of the theme and offers a chance to recycle the vocabulary and structures introduced in the dialogues of the video clips.

The reading activities have been prepared with the goal of developing the skill of silent reading comprehension, not the skill to read aloud or to translate from Arabic into English. Questions that aid comprehension are provided in English first, then in both English and Arabic, and in the last seven units, in Arabic only. However, discussion of the material in class should always be conducted in Arabic only. Listening to the selections on the audio recording before, during, or after reading them will help make it easier to understand them.

Fourth lesson: grammar notes

The grammar notes and written exercises, included in the fourth lesson of units 3–21 cover the main grammatical structures in the audio, video, and reading activities of each unit and include a number of drills, oral and written, to help master them. They are intended for the student to work on outside of class, except for the oral drills, which require teacher involvement.

Most grammar lessons include a "sociolinguistic corner", which focuses on issues related to فصحى and شامي, (and, in one unit, Egyptian) particularly where differences are observed between the two language varieties in the material presented in the relevant unit.

Fifth lesson: "wrap-up" activities

The activities of this lesson bring together the material introduced in the rest of the unit with the ultimate goal of taking the student's productive skills of speaking and writing to a higher level. The lesson starts with an alphabetic listing of all the new vocabulary items introduced in the unit. This is followed by activities of different types to recycle the vocabulary and to provide an element of enjoyment. These activities include songs, crossword puzzles, fill-in the blanks, selecting the correct form of the word, opposites, synonyms, plural formation, roots and families, and اختبر معلوماتك (see below). Instructions for these activities are given with the individual exercises as needed or on the companion website. The lesson ends with suggested production activities in the form of dialogues, presentations, and written compositions on the main theme of the unit.

Songs and games

The textbook includes six songs and a number of games: a Jeopardy-type game (اختبر معلوماتك), M & M, and Bingo, among others. The song lyrics are found in the textbook, while the corresponding audio recording is found on the accompanying DVD and companion website. The games with instructions on how to play them are found on the companion website. The songs have been introduced for their relatively simple language and relevance to the themes of the book. In addition to helping the development of the various language skills, songs and games can play an important role as a source of variety and fun in the classroom. The teacher is encouraged to introduce other songs and games that are appropriate for a specific theme in the book which can help make his/her instruction more effective and the student's classroom experience more enjoyable.

Culture

There are no separate sections dealing with Arab culture in the textbook, but culture is an integral part of it. In addition to the notes on Arab geography and descriptions of some Arab cities, culture is reflected in Emily's dealings with Arabic speakers of different ages and backgrounds and her experiences with airport officials, hotel employees, restaurant waiters, taxi drivers, a roommate and the roommate's family, and Arab friends.

Lesson 1 الدرس الأوّل

Exercise 1 (Listening)

Listen to the numbers 1–10 and memorize them.

Exercise 2 (Listening and Reading)

Listen to the numbers 1–10 again and read them as you hear the audio recording. Remember that, unlike English, Arabic is written and read from right to left.

١. ٩ ٨ ٧ ٦ ٥ ٤ ٣ ٢ ١

Exercise 3 (Reading)

The following are the numbers 1 through 10. They are in the correct order in the first line, and scrambled in the second and third lines. Read each number.

١٠ ،٩ ،٨ ،٧ ،٦ ،٥ ،٤ ،٣ ،٢ ،١

١ ،٣ ،٥ ،٧ ،٩ ،١٠ ،٨ ،٦ ،٤ ،٢

١٠ ،١ ،٧ ،٥ ،٦ ،٩ ،٢ ،٣ ،٨ ،٤

Exercise 4 (Listening and Reading)

Arabic letters are connected when forming words. Of the 28 letters, 6 are one-way connecters, i.e. they connect only to a preceding letter not to a following one. These will be identified as they are introduced.

New Letters:

ـل	ط	ت	كـ	بـ/ب	ا
l	T (emphatic)*	t	k	b	aa

Emphatic consonants have a "thicker" or "deeper" pronunciation than their non-emphatic counterparts. To listen to their correct pronunciation and the pronunciation of other sounds not found in English and marked with a "*", refer to the audio of the table of letters in Lesson 9 of this unit.

Look at the pictures and listen to the recording of each of the following four words and identify the letters each word is made up of.

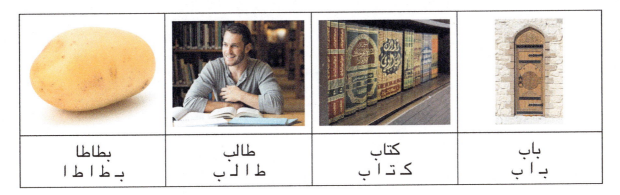

بطاطا بـ ط ا ط ا	طالب ط ا لـ ب	كتاب كـ تـ ا ب	باب بـ ا ب

Note that ـل and ا are differentiated by the fact that ا is a one-way connector while ـل connects on both sides.

Exercise 5 (Listening and Reading)

Circle the word you hear. (In class with the teacher.)

٤. باب/بنات   ٣. طالب/بطاطا   ٢. باب/كتاب   ١. باب/طالب

٧. كتاب/كاتب   ٦. بطاطا/بنطلون   ٥. كتاب/كتب

Exercise 6 (Listening and Reading)

Circle the letter you hear. (In class with the teacher.)

٧. ا/ل	٦. ط/ا	٥. ب/ل	٤. ط/ت	٣. ت/ك	٢. بـ/ت	١. بـ/ك

Exercise 7 (Reading)

Circle the letters you recognize in each of the following words and write their English equivalents.

بيروت

ليبيا

بيت

كبير

لبنان

بنات

Exercise 8 (Watch and Write)

Watch the video or your teacher and practice writing the following numbers and words in your notebook.

١٠	٩	٨	٧	٦	٥	٤	٣	٢	١

باب	كتاب	طالب	بطاطا

Lesson 2 الدرس الثاني

Exercise 1 (Listening)

Listen to the numbers 11–20 and memorize them.

Exercise 2 (Listening and Reading)

Listen to the numbers 11–20 and read them as you hear the audio recording.

٢٠   ١٩   ١٨   ١٧   ١٦   ١٥   ١٤   ١٣   ١٢   ١١

Exercise 3 (Reading)

١.   ١، ٢، ٣، ٤، ٥، ٦، ٧، ٨، ٩، ١٠.

٢.   ١١، ١٢، ١٣، ١٤، ١٥، ١٦، ١٧، ١٨، ١٩، ٢٠.

٣.   ١٢، ١٤، ١٦، ١٨، ٢٠، ١١، ١٣، ١٥، ١٧، ١٩.

٤.   ٣، ٨، ١٤، ١٢، ١٦، ١٩، ١٠، ٦، ٥، ٢.

٥.   ٢، ٣، ٧، ٨، ٦، ٩، ١٧، ١٩، ٥، ٢٠، ١.

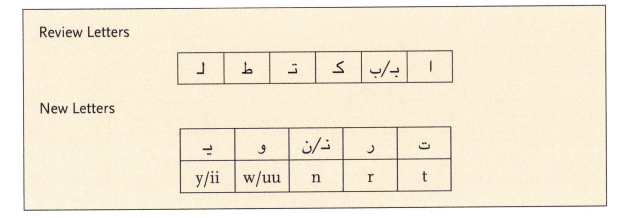

Review Letters	ا	ب/بـ	كـ	تـ	طـ	لـ

New Letters	ت	ر	نـ/ن	و	يـ
	t	r	n	w/uu	y/ii

Exercise 4 (Listening and Reading)

Look at the pictures and listen to the recording of each of the following words and identify the letters each word is made up of.

Kuwait	House	Lebanon	Libya	Beirut
الكويت	بيت	لبنان	ليبيا	بيروت
ا لـ كـ و يـ ت	بـ يـ ت	لـ بـ نـ ا ن	لـ يـ بـ يـ ا	بـ يـ ر و ت

Exercise 5 (Listening and Reading)

Circle the word or phrase you hear. (In class with the teacher.)

١	ليبيا	لبنان
٢	باب	كتاب
٣	باب	بيت
٤	بيت	بنت
٥	بنت	بنات
٦	كبير	الكويت
٧	باب كبير	بيت كبير

Exercise 6 (Listening and Reading)

Circle the letter you hear. (In class with the teacher.)

٦. ر/لـ	٥. ا/لـ	٤. ت/يـ	٣. ت/ن	٢. ب/ن	١. ب/ت
	١١. ت/ط	١٠. و/يـ	٩. ط/كـ	٨. ا/و	٧. ر/و

Exercise 7 (Reading)

Circle the letter you recognize and write its English equivalent.

سوريا

صغير

الرياض

العراق

بغداد

السودان

Exercise 8 (Watch and Write)

Watch the video or your teacher and practice writing the following numbers and words in your notebook.

٢٠	١٩	١٨	١٧	١٦	١٥	١٤	١٣	١٢	١١

بيت	باب	لبنان	ليبيا	بيروت

الدرس الثالث Lesson 3

Exercise 1 (Listening)

Listen to the numbers 10–100 and memorize them.

Exercise 2 (Listening and Reading)

Listen to the numbers 10–100 and read them as you hear the audio recording.

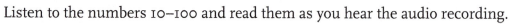

١٠، ٢٠، ٣٠، ٤٠، ٥٠، ٦٠، ٧٠، ٨٠، ٩٠، ١٠٠

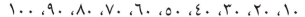

Exercise 3 (Reading)

١.   ١٠، ٢٠، ٣٠، ٤٠، ٥٠، ٦٠، ٧٠، ٨٠، ٩٠، ١٠٠

٢.   ٢٠، ٤٠، ٦٠، ٨٠، ١٠٠، ٩٠، ٧٠، ٥٠، ٣٠، ١٠

٣.   ٢، ١٢، ٢٠، ٣، ١٣، ٣٠، ٤، ١٥، ٥٠، ٧، ١٩، ٩٠، ١٠٠

Review Letters									
يـ	و	نـ/ن	لـ	كـ	ط	ر	تـ/ت	بـ/ب	ا

New Letters					
مـ	ق/ـق	شـ	سـ/س	د	
m	K (emphatic)*	sh	s	d	

Exercise 4 (Listening and Reading)

Look at the picture and listen to the recording of each of the following words.

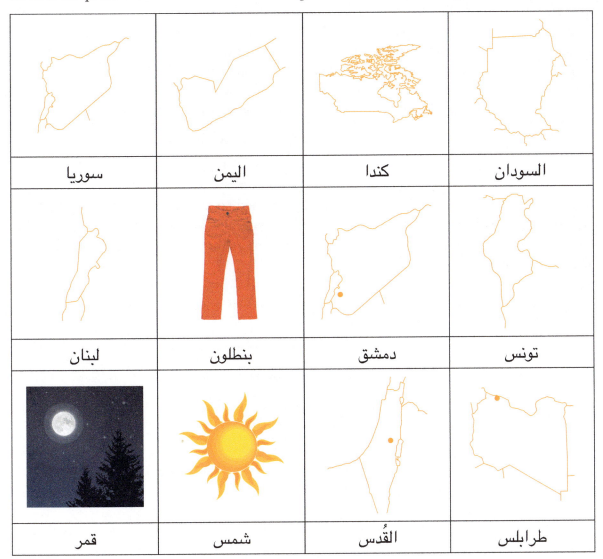

سوريا	اليمن	كندا	السودان
لبنان	بنطلون	دمشق	تونس
قمر	شمس	القُدس	طرابلس

قواعد (Grammar)

The definite article

Definiteness in Arabic is expressed by attaching the prefix الـ "the" to nouns and adjectives:

the student الطالب	student طالب
the door الباب	door باب
the book الكتاب	book كتاب

The definite article appears in the names of some Arab countries and cities but not others. At this point, try to remember the name of the country or city as coming with الـ or without it. For example:

Without the definite article	*With the definite article*
سوريا، لبنان، بيروت، طرابلس، دمشق	السودان، الكويت، اليمن، القُدس

Sun and moon letters

You may have noticed that in words like السودان, the لـ is not heard in the pronunciation. This is because the سـ is known as a "sun" letter. The لـ of the الـ is *assimilated* (becomes the same as) to a following sun letter, which results in a doubled consonant in pronunciation but not in writing. لـ remains unchanged before "moon letters".

لـ *followed by a moon letter*	لـ *followed by a sun letter*
الباب	الطالب
الكتاب	السودان

The following table shows the letters you have learned so far divided into sun letters and moon letters. The pronunciation of sun letters generally involves the front part of the tongue, while the pronunciation of moon letters involves the back of the tongue or does not involve the tongue at all.

Sun letters	*Moon letters*
ت/ت	ا
د	بـ/ب
ر	قـ/ق
سـ/س	كـ/ك
شـ/ش	مـ/م
ط	و
لـ/ل	يـ/ي
نـ/ن	

Exercise 5 (Reading)

Read the following words while paying special attention to the sun and moon letters. (و means "and".)

والسودان، والكويت، واليمن، والقُدس، والشمس، والقمر، والكتاب، والبنطلون، والبيت

Exercise 6 (Listening and Reading)

Circle the letter you hear. (In class with the teacher)

٧. ن/ت	٦. ب/ن	٥. لـ/ن	٤. ت/ط	٣. س/ش	٢. ك/ط	١. ب/ت
	١٣. د/لـ	١٢. د/ر	١١. ا/و	١٠. ا/لـ	٩. و/يـ	٨. س/و

Exercise 7 (Listening and Reading)

Circle the word you hear. (In class with the teacher.)

٤. شمس/تونس	٣. السودان/سوريا	٢. كندا/الكويت	١. بنطلون/طرابلس
	٧. اليمن/قمر	٦. لبنان/ليبيا	٥. قمر/دمشق

Exercise 8 (Watch and Write)

Watch the video/your teacher and write the following numbers and words as many times as needed in your notebook.

١٠٠	٩٠	٨٠	٧٠	٦٠	٥٠	٤٠	٣٠	٢٠	١٠

لبنان	تونس	سوريا	بنطلون	اليمن	كندا	السودان

ليبيا	طرابلس	قمر	شمس	دمشق	القدس

الدرس الرابع Lesson 4

Exercise 1 (Listening)

Listen to the numbers 21–30 and memorize them.

Exercise 2 (Listening and Reading)

Listen to the numbers 21–30 again and read them as you hear the audio recording.

٣٠	٢٩	٢٨	٢٧	٢٦	٢٥	٢٤	٢٣	٢٢	٢١

Exercise 3 (Reading)

١.   ٢١، ٢٢، ٢٣، ٢٤، ٢٥، ٢٦، ٢٧، ٢٨، ٢٩، ٣٠

٢.   ٢١، ٢٣، ٢٥، ٢٧، ٢٩، ٣٠، ٢٨، ٢٦، ٢٤، ٢٢، ٢٠

٣.   ٣١، ٤٢، ٥٣، ٦٤، ٧٥، ٨٦، ٩٧، ٩٨، ٩٩

٤.   ١١، ٣، ٨، ١٤، ٢١، ١٢، ١٦، ٢٦، ١٧، ١٠٠

٥.   ٣، ٨، ٢٨، ٨٢، ٣٨، ٦٧، ٦٦، ٤١، ٦٢، ٨٥

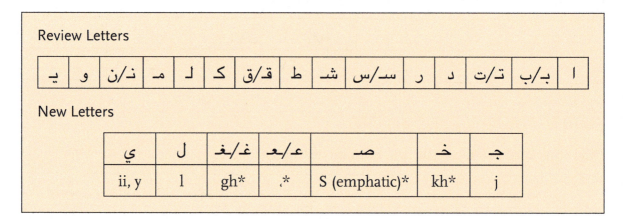

Review Letters													
ي	و	ن/ن	مـ	لـ	ك	ق/ق	ط	شـ	سـ/س	ر	د	تـ/ت	ب/ب	ا

New Letters						
ي	ل	غـ/غ	عـ/عـ	صـ	خـ	جـ
ii, y	l	gh*	*،	S (emphatic)*	kh*	j

Exercise 4 (Listening and Reading)

Look at the following pictures and read the word or words associated with each one as you listen to the recording.

Iraq	Baghdad	Egypt
العراق	بغداد	مصر
خمسين	صغير كبير	north شمال / شرق / غرب / جنوب

Exercise 5 (Listening and Reading)

Circle the number you hear. (In class with the teacher.)

٦٢ ،٢٦	.٥	٧٢ ،٦٢	.٤	٤٠ ،٤٥	.٣	٥٠ ،١٥	.٢	٣٠ ،٢٣	.١
٨٨ ،٧٧	.١٠	٧٣ ،٣٧	.٩	٨٧ ،٨٦	.٨	٦٨ ،٨٠	.٧	١٢ ،٢	.٦

Exercise 6 (Listening and Reading)

Circle the letter you hear. (In class with the teacher.)

٦. كـ/ق	٥. خـ/جـ	٤. عـ/غـ	٣. مـ/صـ	١. صـ/سـ ٢. سـ/شـ
	١١. عـ/ا	١٠. ر/و	٩. ر/د	٨. لـ/ا ٧. د/لـ

Exercise 7 (Listening and Reading)

Circle the word you hear. (In class with the teacher.)

٤. تونسي/سوداني	٣. كويتي/الكويت	٢. الكويت/كبير	١. مصر/صغير
٨. مصر/مصري	٧. جنوب/خمسين	٦. يمني/مصر	٥. سوري/سوريا

Exercise 8 (Reading)

Word search: find the following words. You can go down or right to left.

قطر، مصر، اليمن، العراق، بيروت، الكويت، دمشق

ن	ـمـ	ي	ل	ا	ل
ق	ا	ر	عـ	ل	ا
ط	ق	ش	ـمـ	كـ	ل
ر	ط	ق	ص	و	ي
ض	ت	و	ر	ي	ب
ق	ش	ـمـ	د	ت	ي

Exercise 9 (Watch and Write)

Watch the video/teacher and write the numbers and the words several times in your notebook.

٣٠	٢٩	٢٨	٢٧	٢٦	٢٥	٢٤	٢٣	٢٢	٢١

كبير	صغير	بغداد	العراق	غرب	شرق	جنوب	شمال	خمسين	مصر

Write the four directions in the spaces provided around the compass below.

_____

_____ _____

_____

Lesson 5 الدرس الخامس

Exercise 1 (Listening)

Listen to the numbers 100–1000 and memorize them.

Exercise 2 (Listening and Reading)

Listen to the numbers 100–1000 again and read them as you hear the audio recording.

١٠٠، ٢٠٠، ٣٠٠، ٤٠٠، ٥٠٠، ٦٠٠، ٧٠٠، ٨٠٠، ٩٠٠، ١٠٠٠

Exercise 3 (Reading)

Read the following numbers:

١٠٠، ٢٠٠، ٣٠٠، ٤٠٠، ٥٠٠، ٦٠٠، ٧٠٠، ٨٠٠، ٩٠٠، ١٠٠٠

١٠١، ٢٠٢، ٣٠٣، ٤٠٤، ٥٠٥، ٥٥٥، ١١١، ٢٢٢، ٧٦٦، ٨٧٧، ٩٩٩، ١٩٩٩

٩١، ١٩١، ٧٢، ٩٧٢، ١٩٧٢، ١٩٦٧، ١٩٥٦، ١٩٧٣، ١٩٨٢، ١٩٩٠

Exercise 4 (Listening and Reading)

Circle the number you hear. (In class with the teacher.)

٣٠٤/٤٠٣	٥.	١١٩/١٩٠	٤.	٨٣٠/٣٨٠	٣.	٦٢٠/٧٢٠	٢.	٢١٠/٢١١	١.
١٣١٠/١٣٢٠	١٠.	٦٨٠/٨٧٠	٩.	٩٠٩/٩٩٠	٨.	١٧١٦/١٨١٧	٧.	٥٥٠/٦٥٠	٦.

Review Letters

ا	ب/ـب	ت/ـت	ج	خ	د	ر	س/ـس	ش	ص/ـص	ط	ع/ـع	غ/ـغ
ق/ق	ك	ل/ـل	مـ	ن/ـن	و	ي/ـي						

New Letters

هـ/ـه [1]	ـة/ة [2] (تاء مربوطة)
h	a(t)

[1] ـه is the shape the letter takes in initial position or after a non-connecting letter. ـه is the shape in medial position.

[2] taa' MarbuuTa (تاء مربوطة, see below) is found only in final position: ـة after a two-way connector, ة after a one-way connector.

Exercise 5 (Listening and Reading)

Look at the following pictures and read the word or words associated with each one as you listen to the recording.

طبيبة	طبيب	مهندسة	مهندس	طالبة	طالب

مدينة القاهرة

Grammar

١. طالب ـ طالبة ، مهندس ـ مهندسة

Arabic nouns are generally made feminine by attaching the suffix ـة, called تاء مربوطة (taa' marbuuTa) to the masculine form, as shown in the following table:

	Feminine	Masculine
student	طالِبة	طالِب
doctor, physician	طبيبة	طبيب
engineer	مهندسة	مهندس

Not only nouns can end in تاء مربوطة; adjectives agree with the nouns they modify in terms of gender, as shown in the following:

	Feminine	Masculine
new student	طالِبة جديدة	طالب جديد
new doctor	طبيبة جديدة	طبيب جديد
new engineer	مهندسة جديدة	مهندس جديد

Exercise 6 (Listening and Reading)

Circle the word you hear. (In class with the teacher.)

٤. قهوة/القاهرة	٣. طبيبة/طبيب	٢. طبيب/طالب	١. مهندسة/مهندس
	٧. الخميس/خمسة	٦. البحرين/كبير	٥. مصر/قطر

Exercise 7 (Listening and Reading)

Circle the letter you hear. (In class with the teacher.)

٦. ـه/ا	٥. ق/ك	٤. شـ/سـ	٣. د/ر	٢. مـ/ن	١. هـ/خـ
	١١. ط/ت	١٠. صـ/سـ	٩. صـ/غـ	٨. عـ/غـ	٧. يـ/ت

2. The *Nisba* (relative) adjective

Many adjectives in Arabic are derived from nouns by suffixing the ending ي to the noun from which they are derived. If the noun ends in a vowel or تاء مربوطة, the ending is dropped when the adjectival suffix is added. If the noun has a definite article, that is dropped too.

	Feminine	Masculine	Country
Egyptian	مصريّة	مصري	مصر
American	أمريكيّة	أمريكي	أمريكا
Sudanese	سودانيّة	سوداني	السودان

Exercise 8 (Reading)

Fill in the empty cells in the following table with a nisba adjective and the English translation.

Lebanon-Lebanese		لبنان
	سوري	سوريا
		الكويت
		ليبيا
		العراق
north-northern		شمال
	يمني	اليمن
		جنوب
		شرق

Exercise 9 (Watch and Write)

	بيت كبير
	مدينة كبيرة
	مدينة صغيرة
	القاهرة مدينة كبيرة
	جرش مدينة صغيرة
	بيروت مدينة كبيرة
	صيدا مدينة صغيرة

الدرس السادس Lesson 6

Review Letters

غ/ـغ	ع/ـع	ط	صـ/ص	شـ	س/ـس	ر	د	خـ خ	جـ ج	ت/ـت	بـ/ب	ا
		تاء مربوطة	يـ/ي	و	هـ/ـهـ	ن/ـن	مـ	لـ/ل	ك	ق/ق		

New Letters

ء (همزة)	لا	ز	ذ	حـ	ثـ
hamza (glottal stop)	laa	z	th (as in *then*)	H*	th (as in *thin*)

Exercise 1: Days of the week (Reading)

Identify the day of the week for each of the dates in the following calendar. (In class with the teacher.) For example, what day falls on the 4th of the month? Or on which dates does Saturday fall?

الجمعة	الخميس	الأربعاء	الثلاثاء	الإثنين	الأحد	السبت
٣	٢	١				
١٠	٩	٨	٧	٦	٥	٤
١٧	١٦	١٥	١٤	١٣	١٢	١١
٢٤	٢٣	٢٢	٢١	٢٠	١٩	١٨
٣١	٣٠	٢٩	٢٨	٢٧	٢٦	٢٥

The glottal stop (ء – *hamza* همزة)

When you pronounce an English word that begins with a vowel, like *apple*, *orange*, etc., there is a short blocking and release of air in your Adam's apple area at the very beginning of the sound. This "consonantal" element in the *a* of *apple* and *o* of *orange* is called *a glottal stop*. The glottal stop is automatic in English and is not represented regularly in the English alphabet like *a*, *p*, *o*, *l*, and other English sounds. In Arabic, the glottal stop, called همزة (*hamza*), has its own symbol, or rather, symbols. In fact, it has six different shapes determined mainly by adjacent vowels. These shapes are: أ، إ، ـئـ، ئ، ؤ، ء. When followed by ا the همزة is merged with it, and the two appear as a prolonged ا, represented by the symbol آ, called مدّة (*madda*). More on همزة in Lesson 9 below. For now, remember that أ، إ، ـئـ، ئ، ؤ، ء all represent the same sound and are orthographic variants of the same letter and that آ is made up of همزة and ا.

لا (لـ + ا)

When the letter لـ is followed by ا, whether it has همزة or not, the two letters are joined together forming one special symbol, written لا or لأ, as in ثلاثة "three" and الأردن "Jordan". لا is often considered another letter of the Arabic alphabet.

Exercise 2 (Listening and Reading)

Circle the letter you hear. (In class with the teacher.)

٧. أ/هـ	٦. س/صـ	٥. غـ/عـ	٤. هـ/عـ	٣. هـ/حـ	٢. حـ/جـ	١. حـ/خـ
١٤. ءـ/عـ	١٣. ذ/ث	١٢. د/ذ	١١. ن/مـ	١٠. لا/مـ	٩. ق/ك	٨. حـ/هـ

Exercise 3 (Listening and Reading)

Circle the letter you hear. (In class with the teacher.)

٤. خمسة/الخميس	٣. أربعة/الأردن	٢. واحد/الأحد	١. أسبوع/السبت
٨. ثلاثة وأربعين/ أربعة وثلاثين	٧. الثلاثاء/ثلاثة	٦. سبعة وسبعين/ سبعة وأربعين	٥. بغداد/هذا

Exercise 4 (Reading)

Match the number with the word by copying the word under the corresponding number.

١٠	٩	٨	٧	٦	٥	٤	٣	٢	١
							ثلاثة		
ستة	واحد	عشرة	خمسة	تسعة	سبعة	ثلاثة	ثمانية	أربعة	اثنين

Exercise 5: Months of the year, birthdays

In many parts of the Arab world, people often use numbers to refer to the months of the year. So instead of نيسان "April", people say شهر أربعة "month four". For example, if you were born on October 25, 1992, you could say that your birthdate is:

٢٥/١٠/ ١٩٩٢

Now say your birth date in Arabic.

Exercise 6 (Watch and Write)

الجمعة	الخميس	الأربعاء	الثلاثاء	الإثنين	الأحد	السبت

Exercise 7 (Reading and Writing)

Complete the following without looking at exercise 6 above!

السبت، _____، الإثنين، _____، _____، _____، الجمعة.

الدرس السابع Lesson 7

Review Letters

ا	ب/بـ	ت/ت	ث	ج جـ	ح حـ	خ خـ	د	ذ	ر	ز
سـ/س	شـ	صـ	ط	عـ/ع	غـ/غ	ق/قـ	ك	لـ/ل	مـ	نـ/ن
هـ/ـه	و	يـ/ي								
همزة		لا	تاء مربوطة							

New Letters and Diacritics

فـ	ضـ/ض	ك	فتحة ـَ	كسرة ـِ	ضمّة ـُ	شدة ـّ	سكون ـْ
f	emphatic ذ*	k	short ا	short ي	short و	doubling	no vowel following

You must have noticed by now that short vowels are not represented by letters of the alphabet. Native speakers are so familiar with most Arabic words that they can easily recognize them and pronounce them correctly without having to rely on short vowels. A novice learner, on the other hand, could conceivably read an unfamiliar word like دمشق as *damashq, dumashq, dimashq, damshaq, damshiq, damshuk* or something else. That is why in addition to the 28 letters of the alphabet, Arabic has a system of "diacritics", which are symbols written above or below the letters. These diacritics include symbols for the short vowels, as well as a symbol for indicating the absence of vowels and another for doubling letters. In this lesson only those diacritics that are essential for helping you pronounce words correctly will be introduced. These include the following five, which are shown as they would appear on or under the letter ب.

فتحة	ـَ (fatHa)	بَ	ba
كسرة	ـِ (kasra)	بِ	bi
ضمّة	ـُ (Damma)	بُ	bu
شدّة	ـّ (shadda)	بّ	bb
سكون	ـْ (sukuun)	بْ	b

Exercise 1 (At home: Reading)

Now read the following words, paying special attention to the diacritics:

طَرابُلْس/طَرابِلْس	الرياض	حَلَب	إرِبد	القاهرة	القُدس	عُمان	عَمّان	دِمَشْق
فِلِسطين/فِلَسطين/فَلَسطين	بُيوت	بَيْت	مُدُن	مَدينة	طُلّاب	طالِب	كُتُب	كِتاب

Exercise 2 (In class: Listening and Reading)

Circle the phrase you hear. (In class with the teacher.)

سوريا وليبيا	سوريا ولبنان	١
بيروت قريبة	باب كبير	٢
هو من سوريا؟	هو من مصر؟	٣
ليبيا أكبر من تونس	ليبيا قريبة من تونس	٤
العراق شرق سوريا	الأردن جنوب سوريا	٥
ثلاثة وخمسين	الثلاثاء والخميس	٦
اثنين وأربعين	الإثنين والأربعاء	٧
أربعة وتسعين	تسعة وأربعين	٨

Exercise 3 (In class: Listening and Reading)

Circle the word you hear, paying special attention to the diacritics.

٤. كِتاب/كُتُب	٣. طالِب/طُلّاب	٢. عَمّان/عُمان	١. كتبَت/كتبْت
	٧. أنتَ/أنتِ	٦. كتبتْ/كتبتِ	٥. كتابَك/كتابِك

Exercise 4 (In class: Listening and Reading)

Circle the letter you hear.

٦. د/ض	٥. فـ/غـ	٤. ثـ/ت	٣. طـ/ت	٢. ثـ/ذ	١. ق/ك
١٢. سـ/صـ	١١. غـ/عـ	١٠. عـ/حـ	٩. حـ/عـ	٨. حـ/خـ	٧. جـ/حـ
	١٧. فـ/ق	١٦. ص/ض	١٥. هـ/حـ	١٤. مـ/صـ	١٣. ن/ل

Number in Arabic: the singular, the dual, and the plural

A noun in Arabic can be singular, dual, or plural.

The singular

A book or one book is expressed as كتاب واحد or simply كتاب, with the number following the noun it refers to or no number at all. (Note that واحد كتاب* is ungrammatical.)

The dual

The dual is expressed by attaching the suffix ين (*een*) to the noun. If the noun ends in التاء المربوطة, then the t of التاء المربوطة is pronounced when the dual suffix is added.

two books	kitaabeen	كتابين	كتاب
two female students	Taalibateen	طالبتين	طالبة

(Note that اثنين كتاب* is ungrammatical.)

The plural

Nouns are pluralized in a variety of ways, but for the most part they follow general patterns. At this stage, try to remember the plurals of individual nouns as they are introduced; you will develop a feel for the plural patterns later.

One Arabic grammar rule that might strike you as strange or counterintuitive is the following: with the numbers 3–10 the plural form of the noun is used, and with 11 and above, the singular form is used:

three books	٣ كُتُب
four male students	٤ طُلّاب
five female students	٥ طالِبات
ten houses	١٠ بُيوت

But,

11 books (literally 11 book)	١١ كِتاب
40 male students (literally 40 male student)	٤٠ طالِب
200 female students (literally 200 female student)	٢٠٠ طالبة
1000 houses (literally 1000 house)	١٠٠٠ بيت

Exercise 5 (Watch and Write)

كتابَك	كتابَك	انتِ	انتَ	كِتابِ	كتبتِ	كتَبْتْ	كتَبَتْ	كُتُب	كَتَب
	بُيوت	بَيت	مُدُن	مَدينة	طُلاب	طالِب	عُمان	عَمّان	

Exercise 6

Fill in the empty cells in the following table using the singular, dual or plural form of the noun as appropriate.

		بيت	مهندس	بنت	طالب	صفحة
Singular						
Dual					طالبين	
Plural		١٧	٦ مهندسين	٣ بنات	٩	٣
		١٠	٣	٩	١٥	١٣ صفحة
		٧٠	٩	١٩	٦١	١٠٠٠

الدرس الثامن Lesson 8

Review Letters and Diacritics

		ز	ر	ذ	د	خ/ـخ	ح	ج	ث	ت/ـت	ب/ـب	ا
ـن/ن	م/ـم	ل/ـل	ك/ك	ق/ق	ف	غ/ـغ	ع/ـع	ط	ض/ض	ص	ش	س/ـس
							ي/ي	و	هـ/ـه			

			تاء مربوطة		لا		همزة	
		ـْ سكون	ـّ شدة	ـُ ضمّة	ـِ كسرة		ـَ فتحة	

New Letters and Diacritics

fatH or accusative nunation (تنوين الفتح) اً	ـم	م
an	h	m

Note that ـﮭ is the shape of ـﻪ if it is preceded by a two-way connector, whereas ﻩ is the shape seen after a one-way connector.

You will notice that many Arabic words end in ﺍ with a double فتحة on top of it: ﺍً. The combination is pronounced *an*. Many of these words are adverbs of time, place, or manner:

Thanks	shukran	شُكراً
You're welcome	'afwan	عَفواً
Welcome	'ahlan wa sahlan	أهلاً وسهلاً
Sometimes	'aHyaanan	أحياناً

Listen to the following greetings and practice them with your classmates. ﺍ is the greeting and ب is its response.

ب		أ	
On you peace.	وعليكم السلام[1]	Peace be on you.	السلام عليكم.[1]
Good morning.	صباح النور	Good morning.	صباح الخير.
Good evening.	مساء النور	Good evening.	مساء الخير.
Hello, Welcome.	أهلاً وسهلاً	Hello, Hi.	مرحبا.
Thank God. Good, fine.	الحمد لله، كويّس. الحمد لله كويّسة.	How are you?	كيف حالَك (to a man)؟ كيف حالِك (to a woman)؟
Good-bye.	مع السلامة.	Good-bye.	مع السلامة.
You're welcome.	عفواً.	Thank you.	شكراً.

[1] This greeting is generally more formal than the following three and is used at all times particularly when greeting a group of people.

Possession

Possession in Arabic nouns is expressed by attaching a pronoun suffix to the noun:

his book	kitaab-uh	كتابُه	كتاب+ـه
her book	kitaab-ha	كتابها	كتاب+ها
your (m.s.) book	kitaab-ak	كتابَك	كتاب+َك
your (f.s.) book	kitaab-ik	كتابِك	كتاب+ِك
my book	kitaab-i	كتابي	كتاب+ي

If the noun to which the pronoun suffix is attached ends in التاء المربوطة (ـة), then a ت replaces التاء المربوطة:

his city	madiina-t-uh	مدينتُه	مدينة+ه
her city	madiina-t-ha	مدينتها	مدينة+ها
your (m.s.) city	madiina-t-ak	مدينتَك	مدينة+ك
your (f.s.) city	madiina-t-ik	مدينتِك	مدينة+ك
my city	madiina-t-i	مدينتي	مدينة+ي

Exercise 1 (In class: Listening and Reading)

Circle the letter you hear. (In class with the teacher.)

٦. ف، ق	٥. لا، ر	٤. و، د	٣. ك، ل	٢. ج، ح	١. ن، ي
١٢. ض/ط	١١. ص/ض	١٠. ث، ت	٩. س، ش	٨. ع، ح	٧. خ، ج
				١٤. هـ/م	١٣. هـ/ح

Exercise 2 (Watch and Write)

	عفواً		شكراً
	كيف حالَك		أهلاً وسهلاً
	الحمد لله		كيف حالَك
	صباح النور		صباح الخير
	مساء النور		مساء الخير

Exercise 3 (Writing)

Fill in the empty cells in the following table by adding each of the possessive pronouns to each of the nouns:

apartment شقّة	condition حال (How is he, etc.?)	house بيت	
	حالُه		his
		بيتها	her
			your (m.s.)
		بيتِك	your (f.s.)
شقّتي			my

الدرس التاسع Lesson 9

Review Letters and Diacritics

		ز	ر	ذ	د	خ/ـخـ	ح/ـحـ	ج	ث	ت/ت	ب/ـب	ا
ن/ـن	م/ـم	ل/ل	ك/ك	ق/ق	ف	غ/ـغ	ع/ـع	ط	ض/ض	ص	ش	س/ـس
						ي/ـي	و				هـ/ـه	
				ة/ة تاء مربوطة		لا				ء همزة		
اً (تنوين الفتح)	اً	ـْ سكون		ّ شدة		ُ ضمّة		ِ كسرة		ـَ فتحة		

New Letter Shapes and Diacritics

ألف مقصورة (ى)	ه	ف	غ/ـغ	ع/ـع	ص	ش	خ	ح	ج	ظ
aa (word final only)	h	f	gh*	'*	emphatic s*	sh	kh*	H*	j	emphatic ذ*

More on همزة (hamza – ء)

As was mentioned in Lesson 6 of this unit, همزة has six different shapes determined mainly by adjacent vowels. The rules that determine where each shape is used are quite complicated and native speakers of Arabic have a lot of trouble with them. At this stage, you need to recognize the different shapes of hamza as you see them in the reading passages of the book and to be familiar with the basic rule about which shape of hamza is used in which position: همزة takes the shape ـئ and ئ next to ي and كسرة, ؤ next to و and ضمّة, and ا at the beginning of the word.

The basic shape of همزة is identical to that of ع, but smaller ء. In fact, when the writing of همزة was introduced, which came later in the development of the Arabic alphabet, it was written as a small ع because of the similarity in pronunciation between the two sounds.

If همزة is accompanied by a ضمّة or فتحة at the beginning of a word, it is written above the ألف, as follows:

أستاذ، أنا

If it is accompanied by a كسرة it is written underneath the ألف:

إيران

The ئ/ـئ shape is identical to that of ي/ـي with the همزة symbol replacing the two dots, but above the letter,

ـئ، ئ

For the ؤ shape you just write the و with the همزة symbol above it.

ى (الف مقصورة, *alif maqsuura*)

This letter is found only at the end of words and is pronounced like the letter ١. When suffixes are attached to the word that ends in الف مقصورة, the letter generally changes to ـي. For example,

على on عليه on him

الى to اليها to her

The emphatic group

You may have noticed that some Arabic consonants sound "thicker" or "deeper" than others, such as the sound of the letter ط in طالب. These consonants are known in Arabic as emphatic and contrast with a set of more familiar, non-emphatic, consonants. The following table shows the two sets. Listen to the audio and notice the difference between the members of each pair.

Non-emphatic	Emphatic
س	ص
د	ض
ت	ط
ذ	ظ
ك	ق

Families of letters

You may have noticed by now that most Arabic letters come in groups or families with the same shape but with a difference in the number and placement of dots or vertical strokes.

١. ب/ت/ث

To this family, the letters ن and ي, when in non-final position, can be added: ب، ت، ث، نـ، يـ

٢. ج، ح، خ

٣. د، ذ

٤. ر، ز

٥. س، ش

٦. ص، ض، ط، ظ

٧. ع، غ

٨. ف، ق

٩. ك، ل

The basic movement in writing the members of each family and the way the letters are connected to adjacent letters is the same for all members. You learn the technique for writing ج, for example, and you use the same technique for writing ح and خ, and so on.

Exercise 1 (Watch and Write)

	ثـ		تـ		بـ
			يـ		ـنـ
	ث		ت		ـب
			ي		ن
	خـ		حـ		جـ
	خ		ح		ج
			ذ		د
			ز		ر
			شـ		سـ
			ضـ		صـ
			ض		ص
			ظ		ط
			غـ		ـعـ
			ـغـ		ـعـ
			غ		ع
			ـغ		ـع
			قـ		فـ
			ق		ف
			لـ		كـ
			ل		ك

One-way connectors

Of the 28 Arabic letters, 6 connect to a preceding letter, but not to a following one; the rest connect to both a preceding and a following letter. The non-connecting letters are:

ا، د، ذ، ر، ز، و

Exercise 2 (Writing)

Now write the following words underlining the one-way connectors:

	العراق		لُبنان		باب
	الكويت		حُزيران		طرابلس
	بيروت		آذار		بغداد
	طالب		السودان		سوريا

Exercise 3 (Reading and Writing)

The following list includes the names of Arab countries and cities with the letters scrambled. Rearrange the letters and connect them to match the correct spelling of these names. The countries and cities listed are:

بغداد، مصر، بيروت، تونس، لبنان، اليمن، عمّان، الخرطوم، جدّة، دمشق.

	ا خ ر ط ل م و
	س ن ت و
	م ا ي ن ل
	ا ب د غ د
	ص ر م
	ة دّ ج
	ت ر ب و ي
	ش ق د م
	مّ ن ا ع
	ن ب ل ن ا

Exercise 4 (Reading)

Read aloud in class.

إسم	انتِ	انتَ	أنا	أخت	أخ	أم	أب	١
إلى	علي	عَلى	عَن	في	مِن	كَم	لا	٢
كانون ثاني	صَغير	كبير	كِتاب	شهر	بيت	يوم	باب	٣
سوريا	لُبنان	طالِب	بارِد	بَنات	بِنت	وَلَد	عائِلة	٤

The Arabic alphabet (summary)

Listen to the audio recording and memorize the names of the letters (not the diacritics and other symbols) and their order.

Shape(s)	Letter name
ا	ألف
بـ/ب	باء
تـ/ت	تاء
ثـ/ث	ثاء
جـ/ج	جيم
حـ/ح	حاء
خـ/خ	خاء
د	دال
ذ	ذال
ر	راء
ز	زاي
سـ/س	سين
شـ/ش	شين
صـ/ص	صاد
ضـ/ض	ضاد
ط	طاء
ظ	ظاء
عـ/ـعـ/ع/ـع	عين
غـ/ـغـ/غ/ـغ	غين
فـ/ف	فاء
قـ/ق	قاف
كـ/ك	كاف
لـ/ل	لام
مـ/م	ميم
نـ/ن	نون
هـ/ـهـ/ـه/ه	هاء
و	واو
يـ/ي	ياء

Note that of the 28 letters, 8 have one shape each, 17 have two basic shapes (one at the beginning of the word and after one-way connectors and one word-finally), and 3 have four shapes each: (1) at the beginning of a word and after one-way connectors, (2) in the middle of a word, (3) at the end of the word after one-way connectors, and (4) at the end of the word after two-way connectors. This is shown in the following table:

	Other letters in the category	*Final after two-way connector*	*Final after one-way connector*	*Medial*	*Initial and after one-way connector*
One shape	د، ذ، ر، ز، ط، ظ، و	ا			
Two shapes	ت، ث، ج، ح، خ، س، ش، ص، ض، ف، ق، ك، ل، م، ن، ي	ب			بـ
Four shapes	غ، هـ	ع	ع	ـعـ	ع

Secondary letters and diacritics

Shape(s)	
ء، أ، إ، ـؤ/ئ، وؤ	همزة
ـة/ة	تاء مربوطة
لا	لام ألف
ى	ألف مقصورة
ـَ	فتحة
ـِ	كسرة
ـُ	ضمّة
ـّ	شدّة
ـْ	سكون
اً	تنوين الفتح

الدرس العاشر Lesson 10

Common problems with the alphabet

١. Confusing د، ر، ل

It is sometimes difficult to distinguish between ل and د and between د and ر. There are two differences between د and ل: First, the vertical line of the ل forms a 90-degree angle with the horizontal line, while the two lines of the د form an acute angle. Second, ل is a two-way connector while د is a one-way connector.

Exercise 1 (Watch and Write)

د and ل (the vertical line in ل is at a 90 degree angle and is taller.)

الحمد	السودان	boy/child/son ولد

ر and د
ر is generally flatter and less angular than د.

إربد	الأردن

2. Connecting letters

Exercise 2 (Watch and Write)

a. Writing ج، ح، خ when not connected to a previous letter.

خ	ح	ج

Connected to a previous letter:

الخميس	فتحة	الجُمعة

b. Writing ص، ض، ط when not connected to a previous letter:

ط	ضـ	صـ

Connected to a previous letter:

الطالب	بطاطا	الضمّة	مصر

c. The loop in م ، ق ، ف

Remember when writing م that it is "looped" under the line of writing, not above it, while both ف and ق are looped above it:

مـ	ف	ـق

القاهرة	إفريقيا	الفتحة	الخميس	الضمة	الجمعة

d. The four shapes of ـهـ

Initial and following a non-connector	ـه
When connected on both sides	ـهـ
Word-finally when preceded by a one-way connector	ه
Word-finally when preceded by a two-way connector	ـه

Note that ـهـ is simplified to ⫫ when writing by hand. The top half is not written. Now write the following words a few times in your notebook.

أهلاً وسهلاً	كتابه	أستاذه

Shortcuts

There are a few shortcuts that writers of Arabic use when writing by hand. These include writing س and ش with a straight line and no teeth, using a short line in place of the two dots and a circumflex in place of the three dots (and removing the top half of ـهـ).

Now copy the following letters in the space provided under each one.

ـكي	⫫	ـشـ	ـسـ	ـئـ	ـتـ

Grammar: the construct (الإضافة)

When two nouns are closely associated, as in the case of possession or something being part of something else, they form a special grammatical construction called *the construct* (إضافة). In an equivalent English phrase, the two nouns are joined by the possessive "'s" or the preposition "of", as in *the capital of Egypt* or *Egypt's capital*:

the student's book كتاب الطالب

the capital of Egypt, Egypt's capital عاصمة مصر

The following two points about the إضافة are important to remember. First, if the first word in the إضافة construction ends in تاء مربوطة, the تاء مربوطة is pronounced as a ت and not just a vowel:

the University of Texas	*jaami'at Texas*	جامعة تكساس
the capital of Syria	*'aaSimat suurya*	عاصمة سوريا

Second, the first part of the إضافة never takes the definite article; it is made definite by association with the second part. So الجامعة تكساس* and العاصمة سوريا* are ungrammatical.

Exercise 3 (Reading, Writing, and Pronunciation)

Study the following table which shows the Arab countries and their capitals and complete the sentences below. Then read the completed sentences aloud. The first sentence is given as an example. Notice that in some Arabic fonts when ل is followed by م, the two are combined to form ﻟﻢ.

دَوْلة country
عاصِمة capital

	The Arab countries الدول العربية			
العاصمة	الدولة		العاصمة	الدولة
الخرطوم	السودان		القاهرة	مصر
الرباط	المغرب		الجزائر	الجزائر
الرياض	السعودية		بغداد	العراق
صنعاء	اليمن		دمشق	سوريا
مغاديشو	الصومال		تونس	تونس
عمّان	الأردن		طرابلس	ليبيا
القدس	فلسطين		بيروت	لبنان
مسقط	عُمان		نواكشوط	موريتانيا
الكويت	الكويت		أبو ظبي	الإمارات العربية
المنامة	البحرين		الدوحة	قطر
جيبوتي	جيبوتي		موروني	جزر القمر

١. مدينة الجزائر عاصمة دولة الجزائر.

٢. مدينة_____عاصمة دولة مصر.

٣. مدينة_____عاصمة_____العراق.

٤. _____دمشق_____دولة_____.

٥. _____تونس _____ _____ _____.

٦. _____ _____ _____ ليبيا.

٧. _____بيروت _____ _____.

٨. _____ _____ السودان.

٩. _____ الرباط _____ _____ _____.

١٠. _____ _____ _____ السعوديّة.

١١. _____صنعاء _____ _____.

١٢. _____ عمّان _____.

١٣. _____ القدس _____.

١٤. _____ مسقَط _____.

١٥. _____ _____ الكويت.

١٦. _____ _____ البحرين.

١٧. _____جيبوتي _____ _____.

Crossword puzzle

With reference to the table of Arab countries and their capitals above, do the following crossword puzzle. Read each clue and fill in the letters in the empty cells as indicated by the numbers. For example, the first clue under أفقي says عاصمة لبنان "the capital of Lebanon". The answer is بيروت, which you fill in in the first five spaces across.

Please note that if one row or one column has two clues (and two answers), the clues are separated by a semi-colon ('').

The following words will help you complete the puzzle:

across أَفُقي	vertical, down عَمودي	capital عاصمة
country دولة	big كبير	small صغير
Asia آسيا	Africa إفريقيا	north شمال
south جَنوب	east شَرق	west غَرب

	١	٢	٣	٤	٥	٦	٧	٨	٩	١٠
١										
٢										
٣										
٤										
٥										
٦										
٧										
٨										
٩										
١٠										

أفقي

١. دولة عربيّة صغيرة في غرب آسيا؛ دولة عربيّة كبيرة في شمال شرق إفريقيا.

٣. دولة عربيّة في غرب آسيا، شمال الأردن.

٥. عاصمة سوريا؛ دولة عربيّة صغيرة في غرب آسيا، جنوب غرب سوريا.

٨. عاصمة عُمان.

٩. عاصمة تونس.

عمودي

١. دولة عربيّة كبيرة في إفريقيا.

٣. عاصمة الأردن.

٥. دولة عربيّة صغيرة في غرب آسيا، شرق السعوديّة.

٧. عاصمة المغرب.

١٠. دولة عربيّة في غرب آسيا، غرب جنوب السعوديّة.

الكلمات الجديدة Unit 1 Vocabulary

teacher/professor (m./f.) أُستاذ/أُستاذة		door باب	
doctor (m./f.) طبيب/طبيبة		book/s كِتاب/كُتُب	
engineer (m./f.) مُهندس/مُهندسة		student (m./f.) طالب/طالبة	
north شمال		potatoes بطاطا	
south جنوب		big (m./f.) كبير/كبيرة	
east شرق		small (m./f.) صغير/صغيرة	
west غرب		girl/s بنت/بنات	
city/cities مدينة/مُدُن		house/s بيت/بيوت	
capital عاصمة		pants بنطلون	
nation/s دولة/دول		sun شمس	
Asia آسيا		moon قمر	
Africa إفريقيا		you (m.s.) إنتَ	
day/s يوم/أيام		you (f.s.) أنتِ	
week/s أسبوع/أسابيع		I أنا	

Review exercises

1. Write the correct word under each picture

كتاب   بيت   بطاطا   باب   طالب

2. Write down the missing numbers

١، ___ ،٣ ،___ ،٥،٦ ،___ ،___ ،٩ ،___ ،١١ ،___ ،___ ،___ ،١٥ ،___ ،___ ،___ ،١٩، ٢٠

3. Matching: match the word with the corresponding number.

خمسة	١
عشرة	٢
ثمانية	٣
واحد	٤
ثلاثة	٥
اثنين	٦
ستة	٧
تسعة	٨
أربعة	٩
سبعة	١٠

4. Matching: match the days of the week in Arabic and English.

Tuesday	السبت
Thursday	الأحد
Sunday	الإثنين
Friday	الثلاثاء
Saturday	الأربعاء
Monday	الخميس
Wednesday	الجمعة

5. Grammar: fill in the following empty cells by adding the possessive pronoun.

	بنت	أُستاذ
his		
her		
your (m.s.)		أستاذَك
your (f.s.)		
I		

6. Complete the following puzzle based on the pictures and their corresponding numbers.

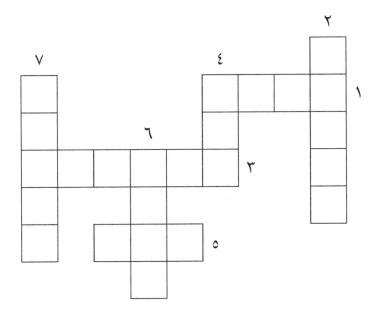

الدرس الأوّل: الصفّ

تمرين رقم ١: قراءة (Exercise 1: Reading)

(وافق بين الصورة والكلمة)

Match each of the following words with the corresponding picture by copying the word in the space provided under the picture.

أُستاذ	باب	شُبّاك	صَفّ	صَفحة	طالِب	طالِبة	كِتاب

تمرين رقم ٢: استماع (Exercise 2: Listening)

You will hear seven sentences. Each sentence contains one of the words in the previous exercise. Write the word in the space provided below.

_____ .٢   _____ .١

_____ .٤   _____ .٣

_____ .٦   _____ .٥

                              _____ .٧

تمرين رقم ٣: استماع

أسئلة (Questions)

١.   كم (how many) باب؟ _____

٢.   كم شُبّاك؟ _____

تمرين رقم ٤: استماع

سؤال (Question)

1.   Which page should Nadia open the book to? _____

تمرين رقم ٥: استماع

Listen to the dialogue and complete the table below.

	طالِب
٩	طالِبة
	أُستاذ

تمرين رقم ٦: قراءة

هذا الصفّ صغير. فيه باب واحد وشُبّاك واحد. في الصفّ ستّة طُلّاب وسبع طالِبات وفيه أُستاذ واحد.

أسئلة (Questions)

١.   كم شُبّاك في الصفّ؟ _____

٢.   كم طالِب؟ _____

٣.   كم طالِبة؟ _____

٤.   كم أُستاذ؟ _____

تمرين رقم ٧: قراءة وكتابة (read and copy the following two sentences)

هذا كتاب كبير. فيه ألف صفحة.

_____

سؤال (Question)

كم صفحة في الكتاب؟ _____

الدرس الثاني: دول وعواصم عربيّة

تمرين رقم ١: قراءة (Exercise 1: Reading)

(وافق بين الصورة والكلمات)

Match each of the following phrases with the corresponding map by copying the phrase in the space provided under the map. Some phrases fit in more than one place.

سوريا شمال شرق لبنان	تونس شمال غرب ليبيا	السودان جنوب مصر
مصر شمال السودان	مصر شرق ليبيا	لبنان جنوب غرب سوريا

تمرين رقم ٢: استماع

Write down in Arabic the names of Arab countries and cities you hear in each sentence. Some sentences contain more than one name.

٣.	٢.	١.
٦.	٥.	٤.
٩.	٨.	٧.

تمرين رقم ٣: استماع

أسئلة

١.   من وين وليد؟ (Where is Waleed from?) _____

٢.   حلب عاصمة سوريا؟ _____

تمرين رقم ٤: استماع

أسئلة

١.   من وين يوسف؟ _____

٢.   ايش نادية بتعمل؟ (What does Nadia do?) _____

تمرين رقم ٥: استماع

Complete the table.

What does he/she do? ايش يعمل/تعمل؟	From where? من وين؟	الإسم
		سامي
		نادية

تمرين رقم ٦: قراءة وكتابة

Read the short paragraph and complete the table below.

مريم طالبة وسليم أستاذ. مريم من مدينة صيدا في جنوب لبنان. وسليم من مدينة الإسكندريّة في شمال مصر. مدينة الإسكندريّة كبيرة، لكن مدينة صيدا صغيرة.

	in في from مِن (pronounced لاكِن) لكِن	
مكان المدينة *Location of city*	من أي مدينة؟ *From which city?*	الإسم

تمرين رقم ٧: قراءة وكتابة

Read the paragraph and complete the table.

اسمي سليم. أنا طالب. أنا من مدينة الدمّام. الدمام مدينة كبيرة في شمال شرق السعوديّة. هذا علي. هو أستاذ من طرابلس عاصمة ليبيا. تقع طرابلس في شمال غرب ليبيا. وهذه فاطمة. فاطمة طالبة من مدينة الرباط عاصمة المغرب. تقع مدينة الرباط في غرب المغرب.

hو هُو   she هِي   it is located تقع

مكان المدينة	مِن أي مدينة؟	العمل *Work*	الاسم
		طالب	سليم
شمال غرب ليبيا			
			فاطمة

تمرين رقم ٨: قراءة وكتابة

Read and label each name with one of the following words. Some names can have more than one label.

دولة   مدينة   عاصمة   ولاية

٢. القاهرة ــــــــــــــــــــ   ١. الأردن ــــــــــــــــــــ

٤. فلوريدا ــــــــــــــــــــ   ٣. سان فرانسيسكو ــــــــــــــــ

٦. عُمان ــــــــــــــــــــ   ٥. الكويت ــــــــــــــــــــ

الدرس الثالث : الساعة وأيّام الأسبوع

الجمعة	الخميس	الأربعاء	الثلاثاء	الإثنين	الأحد	السبت
٥	٤	٣	٢	١		
١٢	١١	١٠	٩	٨	٧	٦
١٩	١٨	١٧	١٦	١٥	١٤	١٣
٢٦	٢٥	٢٤	٢٣	٢٢	٢١	٢٠
			٣٠	٢٩	٢٨	٢٧

تمرين رقم ١: قراءة وكتابة (Reading and Writing)

Working with your neighbor, match the Arabic and English word lists by copying the Arabic word under its English translation. Four words are given as examples.

السبت، الأحد، الإثنين، الثلاثاء، الأربعاء، الخميس، الجُمعة، ساعة، دقيقة، نُصّ، رُبع، ثُلث، و، إلا، أوّل، آخِر

clock, watch, hour	Wednesday	Sunday	except, minus, to	first	last
	الأربعاء			أول	
	quarter	minute	one-third (20 minutes)	Saturday	Thursday
			ثُلث		
	and	half (30 minutes)	Friday	Tuesday	Monday
					الثلاثاء

تمرين رقم ٢: استماع (أيّام الأسبوع)

Write in Arabic the name(s) of the day(s) you hear in each sentence. Some sentences do not contain names of days.

	٢.		١.
	٤.		٣.
	٦.		٥.
	٨.		٧.
			٩.

تمرين رقم ٣: استماع (الساعة)

Match the picture with the sentence or phrase you hear by writing the number of the sentence under the corresponding picture.

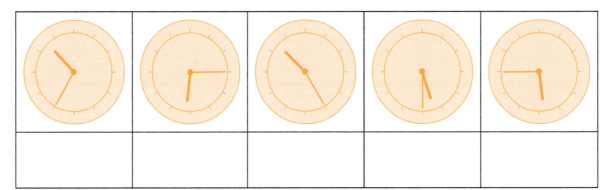

تمرين رقم ٤: استماع

أسئلة

١.   مين بيحكي (?Who is speaking) _____

٢.   كم الساعة؟ (?What time is it) _____

تمرين رقم ٥: استماع

Listen and complete the table.

	وليد
٨:٣٥	نادية

تمرين رقم ٦: استماع

أسئلة

١. كم يوم بتروح (goes) الطالبة للجامعة؟[1] _____

٢. إيش الأيّام؟ _____

٣. ايش اليوم؟ _____

[1] Note that if the preposition ل "to, for" is attached to a word starting with the definite article, like الجامعة (the university), then the ا of the definite article is deleted. So ل+الجامعة is written as للجامعة (to the university).

تمرين رقم ٧: قراءة وكتابة

Match the time phrases with the times on the clock by writing the phrase under the correct time.

ثلاثة إلّا رُبع، ثلاثة إلّا عشرة، ثلاثة ورُبع، سبعة إلّا عشرة، سبعة وعشرة، ستّة وعشرة

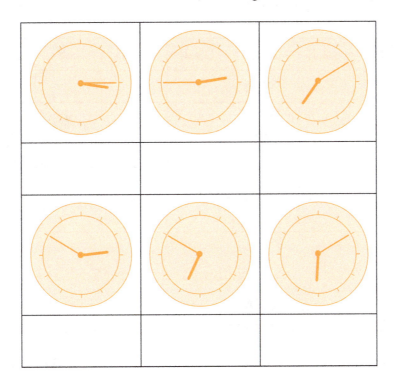

تمرين رقم ٨

Working in pairs rearrange and write down the following days of the week in their correct order.

الجُمعة الأحد الثلاثاء السبت الخميس الإثنين الأربعاء

١. _____   ٢. _____   ٣. _____   ٤. _____

٥. _____   ٦. _____   ٧. _____

الدرس الرابع : شهور السنة

الجمعة	الخميس	الأربعاء	الثلاثاء	الإثنين	الأحد	السبت
شهر أيّار						
٣	٢	١				
١٠	٩	٨	٧	٦	٥	٤
١٧	١٦	١٥	١٤	١٣	١٢	١١
٢٤	٢٣	٢٢	٢١	٢٠	١٩	١٨
٣١	٣٠	٢٩	٢٨	٢٧	٢٦	٢٥

الجمعة	الخميس	الأربعاء	الثلاثاء	الإثنين	الأحد	السبت
شهر نيسان						
٥	٤	٣	٢	١		
١٢	١١	١٠	٩	٨	٧	٦
١٩	١٨	١٧	١٦	١٥	١٤	١٣
٢٦	٢٥	٢٤	٢٣	٢٢	٢١	٢٠
			٣٠	٢٩	٢٨	٢٧

تمرين رقم ١: قراءة وكتابة (Reading and Writing)

Working with a partner, match the Arabic and English word lists by copying the Arabic word under its English translation. Four words are given as examples.

آب، آذار، أيار، أيلول، تشرين أوّل، تشرين ثاني، تمّوز، حُزيران، شباط، كانون أوّل، كانون ثاني، نيسان

June	May	April	March	February	January
	أيّار				كانون ثاني
December	November	October	September	August	July
		تشرين أوّل		آب	

تمرين رقم ٢: استماع

Write in Arabic the name of the month you hear in each sentence.

	.٢		.١
	.٤		.٣
	.٦		.٥
			.٧

تمرين رقم ٣: اسمع وترجم للإنجليزية (Listen and translate into English.)

.١
.٢
.٣
.٤
.٥

تمرين رقم ٤: في الصفّ (in class)

Ask your classmates about their birth dates and write each one down in Arabic following this format: اليوم/الشهر/السنة.
For example, June 12, 1991 will be يوم ١٢، شهر حُزيران، سنة ١٩٩١
Report your dates to the class and figure out which month has the most birthdays! (أي شهر فيه أكثر أعياد ميلاد).

تمرين رقم ٥: قراءة

اسمي نبيل حسن. أنا أستاذ لغة عربيّة في مدينة نيويورك في ولاية نيويورك. أنا من مدينة جرش في الأردن. جرش مدينة صغيرة. في الأردن كنت أستاذ لغة إنجليزيّة.

أنا جئت لأمريكا سنة ١٩٩٨، قبل ١٣ سنة. جئت من مدينة عمان عاصمة الأردن لأوستن عاصمة ولاية تكساس في شهر آب.

لُغة language   قَبْل before (ago)   جئت I came

أسئلة

1. What does Nabeel Hasan do?
2. Where is he from?
3. When did he come to America? (Specify month and year.)
4. Which city did he come to in America?

تمرين رقم ٦: قراءة

قُنصليات السعودية ومصر في الولايات المتحدة				
مصر			السعودية	
رقم التلفون	المدينة		رقم التلفون	المدينة
(٣١٢) ٦٧٠-٢٦٣٣	شيكاغو		(٢١٣) ٢٠٨-٦٥٦٦	لوس انجلس
(٢١٢) ٦٥٩-٧١٢٠	نيو يورك		(٢٠٢) ٣٤٢-٣٨٠٠	واشنطن دي سي
			(٢١٢) ٧٥٢-٢٧٤٠	نيو يورك
			(٧١٣) ٧٨٥-٥٥٧٧	هيوستن-تكساس

كلمات جديدة

consulates قنصليات

the United States الولايات المتحدة

zero صِفر

number رَقم

أسئلة

١. ايش (what) رقم القنصليّة السعوديّة في هيوستن وواشنطن دي سي؟

_____

٢. ايش رقم القنصليّة المصريّة في نيويورك وفي شيكاغو؟

_____

الدرس الخامس: فصول السنة والطقس

تمرين رقم ١: قراءة وكتابة (وافق بين الصورة والكلمة)

Match each of the following words with the corresponding picture by copying the word in the space provided under the picture.

بارد، ثلج، حامي، خريف، ربيع، شتاء، شمس، صيف، مطر

 تمرين رقم ٢: استماع

حسب الحوار (according to the dialogue) ،

١.   العراق دولة كبيرة؟ _____

٢.   ايش أنواع (types, kinds) الطقس في العراق؟ _____

٣.   وين المناطق (areas) الحامية في العراق؟ _____

٤.   كيف الطقس في شمال العراق؟ _____

٥.   وين فيه مطر؟ _____

 تمرين رقم ٣: استماع

أسئلة

١.   كيف الطقس في الرياض؟ _____

٢.   كيف الطقس في الشمال والغرب؟ _____

٣.   وين أبها؟ _____

٤.   كيف الطقس فيها؟ _____

 تمرين رقم ٤: استماع

أسئلة

١.   كيف الطقس في سوريا في الصيف؟ _____

٢.   امتى (when) فيه ثلج في سوريا؟ _____

٣.   فيه شمس كثير في سوريا؟ _____

٤.   كيف (how) الطقس في كاليفورنيا؟ _____

تمرين رقم ٥

ترجم إلى الإنجليزيّة

فصول السنة: الصيف، الخريف، الشتاء، الربيع.

ترجم الى العربيّة

1.   The weather in Lebanon is cold in the winter.
2.   The weather in Alaska is cold in the winter, fall, and spring and moderate (مُعتدِل) in the summer.

تمرين رقم ٦: قراءة

سوريا دولة عربية كبيرة في غرب آسيا. هي غرب العراق وجنوب تُركيا وشمال الأردن وشرق لبنان. من المُدن الكبيرة في سوريا دمشق (العاصمة) وحلب. تقع مدينة دمشق في جنوب سوريا وتقع مدينة حلب في شمال سوريا. دمشق قريبة من لبنان، وحلب قريبة من تركيا. الطقس في سوريا بارد في الشتاء وحارّ (حامي) في الصيف.

آسيا Asia   مُدُن (مدينة plural of) cities   تقع is located

أسئلة

1.   What borders Syria from the west and north? _____
2.   Which city is located in southern Syria? _____
3.   To which country is the city of Aleppo (حلب) close? _____
4.   What is the weather like in Syria in the summer? _____

تمرين رقم ٧: اكتب واحكي عن نفسك

Write a short paragraph at home and then speak about yourself in class. Use the outline below.

اسمي (My name is) ... أنا من مدينة ... في ولاية.... مدينة ... كبيرة/صغيرة ... هي في شمال ... الولاية. الطقس في.... حامي ... الصيف ... ، مطر، شمس ...

أغنية: كيف الطقس في نيسان؟

(كلمات: منذر يونس، غِناء: جواد إياد قبها)

Listen to the song as many times as you need to and write down the missing words. Then try to memorize it.

كيف _____ في نيسان؟	
_____ كويّس _____ بيروت،	
حامي شويّة في _____ ،	
_____ كثير في إربيل،	
شمس _____ في أسوان.	

الدرس السادس: البيت والمواصلات

تمرين رقم ١: قراءة وكتابة (وافق بين الصورة والكلمة أو العبارة)

Match each of the following words and phrases with the corresponding picture by copying the word or phrase in the space provided under the picture.

باص، بيت، جامِعة، حمّام، سيّارة، شارع، شَقّة، طيّارة/طائِرة، غُرفة أَكِل، غُرفة جلوس، غُرفة نوم، مَشي، مطبخ

تمرين رقم ٢: استماع

أسئلة

١. وين "وليد" ساكن (living) ؟ _____

٢. بيته كبير؟ _____

٣. كم غرفة نوم في بيت "وليد"؟ _____

٤. البيت بعيد؟ كم دقيقة أو ساعة بالسيّارة؟ _____

تمرين رقم ٣: استماع

أسئلة

١. كم غرفة نوم في شقّة عبدالله؟ _____

٢. المطبخ كبير أو صغير؟ _____

تمرين رقم ٤: استماع

أسئلة

١. كم غرفة نوم بدّه (he wants)؟ _____

٢. بدّه غرفة أكل؟ _____

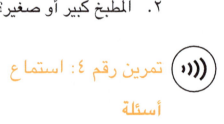

تمرين رقم ٥: استماع

أسئلة

١.   كيف راح (he went) _____ لنيويورك؟

٢.   كم دقيقة أو ساعة أخذت (took) _____ الطيّارة؟

٣.   كم دقيقة أو ساعة بياخذ (takes) _____ الباص؟

تمرين رقم ٦: استماع

أسئلة

١.   البيت قريب أو بعيد؟ _____

٢.   على أيّ (on which) _____ شارِع؟

تمرين رقم ٧: قراءة

يوسف أستاذ في الجامعة الأمريكيّة في بيروت. هو ساكن في بيت كبير بعيد عن الجامعة. في
بيت يوسف أربع غرف نوم وغرفة جلوس وحمام واحد ومطبخ كبير. بيت يوسف على شارع
صغير. اسم الشارع "شارع دمشق".

عَن from   عَلى١ on

أسئلة

1.   What does Yousef do? _____

2.   How many bedrooms does Yousef's house have? _____

3.   What is the name of the street that Yousef's house is on? _____

4.   Is Yousef's house on a big or small street? _____

¹ Remember that the word على is pronounced 'alaa: the final letter, called ألف مقصورة, is pronounced
exactly like ا.

قواعد Grammar

When the إضافة was introduced in the first unit, two points were mentioned as important
to remember. First, if the first word in the إضافة construction ends in تاء مربوطة, the
تاء مربوطة is pronounced as a ت and not just a vowel; and second, the first part of the
إضافة never takes the definite article.

Now with these two points in mind, do the following two exercises:

تمرين رقم ٨: قراءة وترجمة

Read the following phrases aloud and then translate them into English. One sentence has two meanings. Give the two meanings.

١. غرفة نوم ــ

٢. غرفة نوم صغيرة ــــــــــــــــــــــــــــــــــ

٣. غرفة جلوس كبيرة ــــــــــــــــــــــــــــــــ

٤. غرفة الجلوس كبيرة. ــــــــــــــــــــــــــــ

٥. سيّارة الطالب الأمريكي ــــــــــــــــــــــــ

٦. سيّارة الطالب الأمريكيّة ــــــــــــــــــــــــ

٧. سيّارة الطالبة الأمريكيّة ــــــــــــــــــــــــ

تمرين رقم ٩: ترجم الى العربيّة

Translate the following phrases and sentences into Arabic and then read them aloud.

1. A small dining room _____
2. The small dining room _____
3. The dining room is small _____
4. The student's house _____
5. The American student's house _____

الدرس السابع: العائلة والمهن

تمرين رقم ١: قراءة وكتابة (وافق بين الصورة والكلمة)

أخ، أُمّ، بنت/أُخت، جامِعة، سكرتيرة، طبيب، عائلة، مَدرسة، مُستشفى، مطعم، مُهندِس، ولد وأب

تمرين رقم ٢: استماع

أسئلة

١. مين يوسف؟ ـــــــــــــــــــــ

٢. كم بيت عند يوسف؟ ـــــــــــــــــــــ

٣. وين يوسف هلأ؟ ـــــــــــــــــــــ

٤. امتى بيرجع لدمشق؟ ـــــــــــــــــــــ

تمرين رقم ٣: استماع

أسئلة

١. كم أخ وأخت عند يوسف؟ ـــــــــــــــــــــ

٢. كم أخ وأخت عند البنت؟ ـــــــــــــــــــــ

تمرين رقم ٤: استماع

أسئلة

١. من وين "سعيد"؟ ـــــــــــــــــــــ

٢. سعيد عنده بيت في عمّان؟ ـــــــــــــــــــــ

٣. كم شخص (person) في العائلة؟ ـــــــــــــــــــــ

٤. ايش اسم أمّ سعيد؟ ـــــــــــــــــــــ

٥. ايش أبو سعيد بيشتغل (he works)؟ ـــــــــــــــــــــ

٦. ايش أمّ سعيد بتشتغل؟ ـــــــــــــــــــــ

تمرين رقم ٥: استماع

أسئلة

١. كم ولد عند أُختي؟ ـــــــــــــــــــــ

٢. كم أعمارهم (their ages)؟ ـــــــــــــــــــــ

٣. مين ساكن قريب من بيت أُختي؟ ـــــــــــــــــــــ

تمرين رقم ٦: استماع

أسئلة

١. ايش أبو يوسف بيعمل؟ وين؟ ـــــــــــــــــــــ

٢. ايش بيعمل أخو يوسف؟ ـــــــــــــــــــــ

٣. ايش بيعمل أبو البنت؟ ـــــــــــــــــــــ

تمرين رقم ٧: قراءة

ليلى طالبة في الجامعة الأمريكيّة في القاهرة. عائلة ليلى كبيرة. عند ليلى أب وأمّ وأخوين وأُختين. ليلى ساكنة مع عائلتها في بيت كبير. أبو ليلى مُهندس وأمّ ليلى أستاذة في مدرسة بنات. أخو ليلى الكبير يعمل في بنك والصغير طالب في مدرسة. أخت ليلى الكبيرة سكرتيرة في مكتب وأختها الصغيرة تعمل في مطعم.

أسئلة

1. What does Layla do and where?
2. How many people are in Layla's family?
3. What do Layla's brothers do and where?
4. What do Layla's sisters do and where?
5. What do Layla's parents do?

her family عائلتها	Layla has عِند ليلى	Layla's family عائلة ليلى

قواعِد

Number

As was pointed out in Unit 1, a noun in Arabic can be singular, dual, or plural. The following three rules concerning number are particularly important to remember at this stage because they involve frequently used constructions and because they might be counter-intuitive to speakers of other languages.

A. For the numbers 3–10, the plural form of the noun is used and the noun follows the number. (Note that the تاء مربوطة of the number is dropped before the noun.)

three books	thalath kutub	ثلاث كتب
four books	'arba' kutub	أربع كتب
ten books	'ashar kutub	عشر كتب
three pages	thalath SafHaat	ثلاث صفحات
seven pages	sabi' SafHaat	سبع صفحات
ten pages	'ashar SafHaat	عشر صفحات

B. For the number 11 and above, the singular form of the nouns is used. (Note the addition of the suffix ـر ar to the numbers 11–19 when a noun follows them.)

eleven books	iHdaashar kitaab	احداشر كتاب
twenty books	'ishriin kitaab	عشرين كتاب
a thousand books	'alf kitaab	ألف كتاب
fifteen pages	khamisTaashar SafHa	خمسطاشر صفحة
a million pages	malyoon SafHa	مليون صفحة

C. After كم "how many", only the singular form of the noun is used:

How many boys (children) do you have?	كم ولد عندَك؟
How many rooms are in your house?	كم غرفة في بيتكم؟
How many brothers and sisters do you have?	كم أخ وأُخت عندك؟

الدرس الثامن: الملابس والألوان

تمرين رقم ١: قراءة وكتابة (وافق بين الصورة والكلمة)

بنطلون، جاكيت، فُستان، قَميص، كُنَدَرة

تمرين رقم ٢ (الألوان colors): قراءة وكتابة (وافق بين الصورة والكلمة)

Working with your neighbor, match the Arabic and English word lists by copying the Arabic word under its English translation.

أبيض، أحمر، أخضر، أزرق، أسود، أصفر، بنّي

Brown	Blue	Yellow	Green	Red	Black	White

تمرين رقم ٣: قراءة وكتابة

Match the feminine form of the color with its masculine counterpart, by copying the feminine form in the space provided under the masculine form. Follow the example.

حمراء، بنّية، خضراء، بيضاء، صفراء، زرقاء، سوداء

بُنّي	أزرق	أصفر	أخضر	أحمر	أسود	أبيض
						بيضاء

تمرين رقم ٤: استماع

سؤال

أكمل الجدول (complete the table)

	فستان	البنت
أسود		الولد
	قميص	

تمرين رقم ٥: استماع

ابن son   دينار/دنانير (dinar(s)

أسئلة

١. امتّى راح للسوق (market, mall)؟ ــــــــــــــــــــــــــــ

٢. ايش اشترى (bought)؟ ــــــــــــــــــــــــــــ

٣. لمين (for whom)؟ ــــــــــــــــــــــــــــ

٤. بكم (for how much) كانت (was) الكُندرة؟ ــــــــــــــــــــــــــــ

تمرين رقم ٦: استماع

سؤال

أكمل الجدول

	قميص	الأم
	بنطلون جينز	
أسود		الأب
	قميص	

تمرين رقم ٧: استماع

أسئلة

١.   ايش لون بنطلونه؟ ـــــــــــــــــــ

٢.   ايش لون قميصه؟ ـــــــــــــــــــ

٣.   ايش لون السيّارة؟ ـــــــــــــــــــ

تمرين رقم ٨: قراءة وكتابة

Locate the following seas on the map below by writing the name of each sea next to or inside it.

البحر الأبيض المتوسّط   البحر الأحمر   البحر الأسود

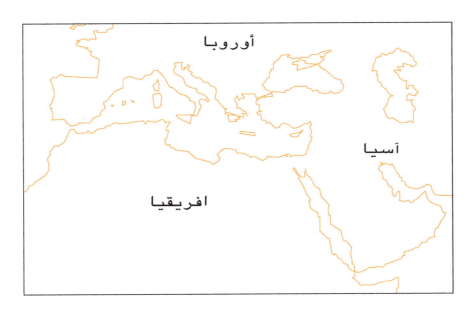

تمرين رقم ٩: ترجم الى العربيّة

1. Saudi Arabia (السعوديّة) is east of the Red Sea.

   _____

2. Turkey (تركيا) is south of the Black Sea.

   _____

3. The Mediterranean Sea is large, and the Red Sea is small.

   _____

4. The city of Jedda (جدّة) is in the west of Saudi Arabia.

   _____

5. Egypt is north of Sudan and west of the Red Sea.

   _____

6. Libya is south of the Mediterranean Sea and east of Tunisia (تونس) and Algeria (الجزائر).

   _____

تمرين رقم ١٠: احكي (في الصفّ) Speaking (in class)

Take turns describing someone in the class based on the type and color of their clothing. The rest of the class will try to guess the right person by asking questions....

مين هو، هي؟
لابس قميص أسود وبنطلون جينز؟ الخ.

الدرس التاسع: الأكل

تمرين رقم ١: قراءة وكتابة (وافق بين الصورة والكلمة)

تُفاح، موز، برتقال، بطاطا، بندورة، دجاج، لحم، سمك، بيض، خُبْز، جِبن، ميّة، قهوة، شاي، عصير، حليب، فواكه، خضار، مطعم

تمرين رقم ٢: استماع

أسئلة

١.   نادية بتحبّ (she likes) بيت الطلاب؟ ـــــــــــــــــــــــــــــــــــــ

٢.   ليش (why)؟ ـــــــــــــــــــــــــــــــــــــ

٣.   شقّة أخت وليد كبيرة؟ ـــــــــــــــــــــــــــــــــــــ

٤.   وين أخته بتاكل؟ ـــــــــــــــــــــــــــــــــــــ

))) تمرين رقم ٣: استماع

أسئلة

١.   وين وليد بياكل؟   ـــــــــــــــــــــــــــــــ

٢.   ليش؟   ـــــــــــــــــــــــــــــــــــ

٣.   وين البنت بتاكل؟   ـــــــــــــــــــــــــــــ

))) تمرين رقم ٤: استماع

أسئلة

١.   بكم كيلو التفّاح؟   ـــــــــــــــــــــــــــــ

٢.   بكم كيلو الموز؟   ـــــــــــــــــــــــــــــــ

٣.   كم كيلو بندورة بدها (she wants)؟   ـــــــــــــــــــــــــ

))) تمرين رقم ٥: استماع

أسئلة

١.   فيه سمَك؟   ـــــــــــــــــــــــــــــــ

٢.   بكم كيلو اللحم؟   ـــــــــــــــــــــــــــــ

٣.   كم كيلو لحم بدها (she wants)؟   ـــــــــــــــــــــــــ

))) تمرين رقم ٦: استماع (استمع واملأ الفراغات Listen and fill in the blank spaces)

أفطرت you had breakfast   تغَدّيت you had lunch

تعَشّيت you had dinner, supper

أكمل الجدول

العشاء dinner	الغداء lunch	الفطور breakfast
ـــــــــــ،	سندويشة ـــــــــــ،	بيض، ـــــــــــ،
و ـــــــــــ،	و ـــــــــــ، وقهوة	برتقال، و ـــــــــــ،

تمرين رقم ٧: استماع

أسئلة

١.   أيّ ساعة الغداء اليوم؟

٢.   كم الساعة هلأً؟

تمرين رقم ٨: قراءة وكتابة

مِثل like

Join the letters to make up words and sentences, then read what you have written and translate it into English.

١.   ف ي—ا ل م ط ب خ—ف و ا ك ه—م ث ل—ت ف ا ح—و م و ز—و ب ر ت ق ا ل.

في المطبخ ...

In the kitchen ...

٢.   س م ك—و د ج ا ج—و ل ح م—ب ق ر.

_____

_____

٣.   ف ي—ا ل م ط ب خ—خ ض ا ر—م ث ل—ب ن د و ر ة—و ب ط ا ط ا.

_____

_____

٤.   ل ح م—خ ر و ف—و ل ح م—ب ق ر.

_____

_____

٥.   ع ص ي ر—ب ر ت ق ا ل—و ع ص ي ر—ت ف ا ح—و ع ص ي ر—ب ن د و ر ة.

_____

_____

٦.   ع ص ي ر—و ح ل ي ب—و ش ا ي—و ق ه و ة.

_____

_____

الدرس العاشر: مراجعة

كلمات الوحدة الجديدة

بَنطلون	pants, trousers	أب	father
بيت	house	أخ (إخوان)	brother
بيت طُلاب	dormitory	أُخت (أخوات)	sister(s)
بيض	eggs	أُكل	food
تعشّيت	I had dinner	أكلت	I ate
تغدّيت	I had lunch	أُم	mother
تُفّاح	apples	أوّل مبارح	the day before yesterday
تَقع	it is located	أيش؟	what?
ثُلث	third	أيوا	yes
ثَلج	snow	إلّا	minus, to
جاكيت	jacket	إسم	name
جامِعة	university	أفتَح	open
جِبن	cheese	أفطرت	I had breakfast
جيت	I came	البحر الأبيض المتوسط	the Mediterranean Sea
حامي	hot	البحر الأحمر	the Red Sea
حَليب	milk	البحر الأسود	the Black Sea
حَمّام	bathroom	طقس	weather
خُبز	bread	اليوم	today
خُضار	vegetables	بسُكّر	with sugar
دَجاج	chicken	بارِد	cold
درّاجة/بُسُكليت (بِسِكليت)	bicycle	باص	bus
دقيقة	minute	بدون	without
رُبع	quarter	بُرتُقال	orange
ساحِل	coast	بَعد بُكرة	the day after tomorrow
ساعة	hour, time, watch, clock	بَعيد	far
سَكِّر	close	بُكرة	tomorrow
سِكرتير	secretary	بِنت	girl, daughter
سَمَك	fish	بَندورة	tomato

قميص shirt		سيّارة car	
كثير a lot/very		شارع street	
كَم؟ how many?		شاي tea	
كُندرة shoes		شُبّاك window	
كويّس good		شربت I drank	
لأ no		شَقّة apartment	
لَحم meat		شَمس sun	
لون (ألوان) color(s)		شويّة a little	
ما فيه there is not, there are not		صَفّ class	
مبارح yesterday		صَفحة page	
مَدرسة school		طبيب (دكتور) doctor	
مُستشفى hospital		طيّارة plane	
مِش not		عائلة family	
مطبخ kitchen		عشاء dinner	
مَطر rain		عصير juice	
مَطعم restaurant		عصير بُرتقال orange juice	
مُعتدل moderate		عُمر age	
مَكتب office		عمل–يعمل he worked–he works	
مُهندس engineer		عيد ميلاد birthday	
موز banana		غداء lunch	
ميّة water		غُرفة room	
نُصّ half		غُرفة أَكِل dining room	
هذا/هذه this m./f.		غرفة جلوس living room	
هلّا now		غُرفة نوم bedroom	
و and		فُستان dress	
وَلاية state		فصل (فصول) season(s)	
وَلَد boy, son		فُطور breakfast	
يحُدّ it borders		فواكه fruits	
يوم (ج. أيّام) day		فيه there is, there are	
		قريب close (distance)	

فصول السنة	أيام الإسبوع
summer الصيف	الأحد Sunday
fall, autumn الخريف	الإثنين Monday
winter الشتاء	الثلاثاء Tuesday
spring الربيع	الأربعاء Wednesday
	الخميس Thursday
	الجُمعة Friday
	السبت Saturday

الألوان

	feminine	masculine		feminine	masculine
yellow	صفراء	أصفر	white	بيضاء	أبيض
orange	بُرتقاليّة	بُرتقالي	black	سوداء	أسود
blue	زرقاء	أزرق	red	حمراء	أحمر
brown	بنّيّة	بُني	green	خضراء	أخضر

أغنية: البيت الأبيض بابه أحمر

(كلمات: منذر يونس، غِناء: جواد إياد قبها)

The white house,	البيت الأبيض
Its door is red,	بابه أحمر،
The red house,	البيت الأحمر
Its door is green	بابه أخضر،
The green house,	البيت الأخضر
Its door is brown,	بابه بنّي،
The brown house?	البيت البنّي؟
...	...
Its door is shut.	بابه مسكّر.

تمرين رقم ١: قراءة (جمع/مفرد، plural/singular)

The following nouns are all plural. Write under each one its meaning in English and its singular form. Follow the example.

شهور	بنات	إخوان	أولاد	ساعات	آلاف	غُرَف	سنوات	أخوات	بيوت	ولايات	أيّام	طُلاب
												students
												طالب

تمرين رقم ٢: قراءة (العكس opposites)

Write the opposite of each of the following words under it.

قبل	أبيض	صيف	بعيد	أوّل	جنوب	شرق	كبير

تمرين رقم ٣: قراءة

مصر دولة عربية كبيرة في شمال شرق إفريقيا. يحدّها من الشرق البحر الأحمر ومن الجنوب السودان ومن الغرب ليبيا ومن الشمال البحر الأبيض المتوسّط.

من المُدُن المصريّة الكبيرة مدينة القاهرة (العاصمة) ومدينة الإسكندريّة ومدينة أسوان. تقع مدينة الإسكندرية في شمال مصر على ساحل البحر الأبيض المتوسّط، وتقع مدينة أسوان في الجنوب.

coast   ساحِل   borders it, it is bordered by   يحدّها

أسئلة

اكتب صحّ (√) أو خطأ (x)

١. تقع (is located) مصر على ساحل البحر الأبيض المتوسّط وساحل البحر الأحمر.

٢. مصر غرب البحر الأحمر.

٣. مصر غرب ليبيا.

٤. السودان جنوب مصر.

٥. الإسكندريّة مدينة مصريّة كبيرة.

٦. تقع مدينة الإسكندريّة في جنوب مصر.

٧. تقع مدينة أسوان على ساحل البحر الأبيض المتوسّط.

تمرين رقم ٤: كتابة

ايش أكلت وشربت مبارح؟ (What did you eat and drink yesterday?)

العشاء	الغداء	الفطور

تمرين رقم ٥: قراءة وكتابة

Join the letters to form words, phrases, and sentences. Then translate the phrases and sentences into English.

١. ا ل ص ي ف ـ و ا ل خ ر ي ف ـ و ا ل ش ت ا ء ـ و ا ل ر ب ي ع.

_____

_____

٢. ا ل ي م ن ـ ق ر ي ب ـ و ا ل ع ر ا ق ـ ب ع ي د.

_____

_____

٣. ع ل ي ـ ط ا ل ب ـ و أ ح م د ـ م ه ن د س.

_____

٤. الأردن دولة صغيرة و مصر دولة كبيرة.

_____

_____

٥. الجامعة الأمريكية في بيروت.

_____

_____

تمرين رقم ٦: ترجم الى العربيّة.

Translate the following paragraph on a separate piece of paper.

Syria is a large Arab country in West Asia (آسيا). It is bordered from the west by the Mediterranean Sea and Lebanon, from the south by Jordan, from the east by Iraq, and from the north by Turkey. Among the big Syrian cities are Damascus, the capital, Aleppo (حلب), HimS (حمص), and Latakia (اللاذقيّة). Damascus is located in the south, Aleppo is located in the north close to the Turkish borders, and Latakia is located on the Mediterranean Sea.

تمرين رقم ٧: اكتب واحكي عن نفسك

Write a short paragraph and then speak about yourself. The following words and phrases will help you construct your paragraph.

اسمي (My name is) ...

عندي (أخ واحد/أخوين/ثلاث إخوان ...) و (أخت واحدة، أختين، ثلاث أخوات ...)

اسم أبي ...، واسم أمي ... أبي (طبيب، مهندس، أستاذ، سكرتير، يعمل في مكتب، مستشفى، مدرسة ...) وأمّي (طبيبة، مهندسة، أستاذة، سكرتيرة، تعمل في مكتب، مستشفى، مدرسة ...)

أنا ساكن (ة) في بيت/شقّة/غرفة كبير(ة)/صغير(ة) في مدينة ... في ولاية ...

مدينة ... كبيرة/صغيرة ... هي في شمال ... الولاية.

تمرين رقم ٨: كلمات مُتقاطعة (crossword puzzle)

	١	٢	٣	٤	٥	٦	٧	٨	٩	١٠
١										
٢										
٣										
٤										
٥										
٦										
٧										
٨										
٩										
١٠										

عمودي down	أفقي across
١. عاصمة العراق	١. عاصمة لبنان
٢. مُفرَد (singular) طُلّاب	٢. عكس أسود
٣. عكس جنوب	٣. عاصمة سوريا
٤. اسم شهر	٤. عكس آخِر
٦. دولة عربيّة كبيرة في شمال افريقيا	٥. دولة عربيّة صغيرة في غرب آسيا
٧. عَكس صغير (معكوسة، backwards)	٧. دولة عربيّة كبيرة في غرب آسيا
٨. دولة عربيّة صغيرة في غرب آسيا	٨. عكس بارد
٩. عكس بعيد	٩. عكس قريب
١٠. اسم حرف عربي	١٠. عكس حامي

الوحدة الثالثة: في المطار

أهمّ الكلمات والتعابير الجديدة
Key words and expressions of the unit

she traveled سافرت		أُجرَة fare, rent	
airplane طائرة=طيّارة		أهلاً (وسهلاً) فيكِ welcome to you	
it, she flew طارَت		تأشيرة visa	
address عُنوان		تاريخ date	
hotel فُندُق		جِنسيّة nationality	
airport مَطار		جَواز سَفَر passport	
place مَكان		رَقَم number	
birth وِلادة		زِيارة visit	
		سافر he traveled	

تمارين تحضيريّة (Preparatory exercises)

Fill in the blanks by choosing the appropriate word (املأ الفراغات) :١ تمرين رقم

١.   _____ _____ (رقم، جنسيّة، ولادة) أبي مصريّة وجنسيّة أمي أُردنيّة.

٢.   _____ (أُجرة، سافر، مكان) للسودان بـ _____ (المطار، الفندق، الطيّارة).

٣.   _____ (سافرت، ساكنة، طارت) الطائرة من _____ (العنوان، الزيارة، المطار) الساعة ٨:٣٠.

٤.   _____ (أهلاً وسهلاً فيكِ، عنوان، شكراً) في الأردن!

٥.   _____ (عنوان، فندق، زيارة) البيت ٢٩٤ شارع بغداد.

٦.   _____ (تأشيرة، مكان، جواز السفر) الولادة القاهرة و _____ (أجرة، أسبوع، تاريخ) الولادة ١٩٨٨/٨/٨.

تمرين رقم ٢: وافق بين الصورة والكلمة. أكتب الكلمة أو العبارة المناسبة تحت الصورة.

Copy each word or phrase in the space provided under the corresponding picture.

جواز سفر   فندق   مطار   طائرة/طيّارة

تمرين رقم ٣: رتب الحروف وكوّن كلمات مُفيدة

Unscramble the letters to form some of the words you have seen above.

١.   خ ا ر ت ي   _____

٢.   ج ة أ ر   _____

٣.   يّ ن ج س ة   _____

٤.   ر ق م   _____

٥.   ط ر م ا   _____

الدرس الأوّل

النصّ الأوّل–مشاهدة: إملي في المطار

كلمات جديدة

يَعني it means	عُنوان address
مُدرّس=أستاذ teacher	فُندُق hotel
	مِهنة profession

تعبير Expression

مع السلامة good-bye

أسئلة

١.   أيش اسم أبو إملي؟ _____

٢.   كم عُمر إملي؟ _____

٣.   أيش عنوان إملي في الأردن؟ _____

٤.   أيش إملي بتعمل (بتشتغل)؟ (أيش مهنتها)؟ _____

النصّ الثاني–قراءة: تأشيرة دخول

المملكة الأردنية الهاشميّة وزارة الداخلية تأشيرة دخول	
إسم الأب: هنري	الإسم: إملي
إسم العائلة: وليمز	إسم الأم: اليزابث
مكان الولادة: نيو يورك، أمريكا	تاريخ الولادة: ١٩٨٧/٢/٢٧
رقم جواز السفر: ٣٥٢٦٧	الجنسية: أمريكية
تاريخ ومكان الصدور: ٢٠١١/٧/٦ واشنطن دي سي	المهنة: طالِبة
مدّة الزيارة: ٤ شهور	العنوان في الأردن: فندق "الأندلس"، عمّان

كلمات جديدة

صدور issue	تاريخ date
مدّة period	مكان place
زيارة visit	وِلادة birth
	جنسية nationality

تعابير Expressions

تأشيرة دخول entry visa

جواز سفر passport

أسئلة

1. What is Emily's father's name? _____
2. When was she born? _____
3. What is the place and date of issue of her passport? _____
4. What is Emily's address in Jordan? _____
5. How long is she staying in Jordan? _____

كتابة (في البيت)

Pretend that you are traveling to Jordan to take an Arabic summer course that will last two months. Fill out the following form accordingly. Remember that in order to make a noun "dual", you just add the suffix ين.

	المملكة الأردنية الهاشميّة وزارة الداخلية تأشيرة دخول		
	إسم الأب:		الإسم:
	إسم العائلة:		اسم الأم:
	مكان الولادة:		تاريخ الولادة:
	المهنة:		الجنسية:
	تاريخ ومكان الصدور:		رقم جواز السفر:
	مدّة الزيارة:		العنوان في الأردن:

Note on writing English names

When Arabs write foreign words with sounds that have no correspondences in their language, they generally use the Arabic letter that represents the Arabic sound closest to the foreign one. The following table shows some of the English sounds that have no Arabic equivalents and what Arabic speakers generally substitute for them:

English	Arabic substitute		
g	ج، غ، ك	انجليزي، كونغرس، كراج	English, Congress, garage
p	ب	بيبسي	pepsi
v	ف	فيتامين	vitamin
ch	تش	ماتش	match

What Arabs perceive as short vowels are not normally written:

Bill	بل
Rebecca	ربكا

They represent what they perceive as an *o* sound with و:

Theodore	ثيودور
Morgan	مورغان
Paul	بول
Robert	روبرت

They represent what they perceive as *ay*-sounds with ي:

Casey	كيسي
Rachel	ريتشل

الدرس الثاني

النصّ الأوّل–مشاهدة: تاكسي للفندق

كلمات جديدة (New words)

لوين؟ ?where to

تفضّلي (to a woman) please go ahead

أخت[1] sister

طبعاً of course

بتحكي you speak

تعلّمتِ you learned

وَلا or

أكيد certainly

---

[1] أخت is also a friendly way of addressing a woman.

تعابير

أهلاً (وسهلاً) فيكِ welcome to you

أكثر مِن more than

أسئلة

١.   لوين إملي رايحة (going)؟ _____

٢.   من وين إملي؟ _____

٣.   وين تعلّمت عربي؟ _____

٤.   الجامعة كبيرة ولا (or) صغيرة؟ _____

٥.   كم طالب فيها؟ _____

النصّ الثاني-قراءة: أجرة الباصات

دينار	فلس	الى
المملكة الأردنيّة الهاشميّة		
وزارة الداخليّة		
أجرة الباصات من مطار علياء الدولي		
٤	—	عمان-وسط البلد
٥	٢٥٠	عمان-موقف الباصات الشمالي
٩	٥٠٠	السلط
١٥	٥٠٠	جرش
٢٥	—	إربد
١٠	٢٥٠	الزرقاء
١٠	٢٥٠	مأدبا
١٤	٥٠٠	الكرك
٢٨	—	معان
٤٠	—	العقبة

كلمات جديدة

أجرَة fare, rent

فِلس (دينار fils (there are 1000 fils in one

مَوقِف stop

الى=ل to

تعابير

مَطار علياء الدولي Alia' International Airport

وسط البلَد downtown

سؤال (Question)

كم أجرة الباص من مطار علياء الدولي إلى؟

جرش   عمّان-وسط البلد

العقبة   معان

الدرس الثالث

 قراءة: إملي وليمز

إملي وليمز طالبة أمريكية في جامعة تكساس في أوستن. سافرت للأردن الأسبوع الماضي. سافرت بالطائرة طبعاً.

طارت الطائرة من مطار "جي إف كي" في نيويورك الساعة ٨:٣٠ مساء يوم الثلاثاء ووصلت مطار عمّان الساعة ٤ بعد الظهر يوم الأربعاء.

عائلة إملي من مدينة إثاكا في ولاية نيويورك. أبوها اسمه هنري وهو أستاذ في جامعة كورنيل، وأمّها اسمها إليزابث وتعمل في بنك. عند إملي أخ واحد اسمه ماثيو وأخت واحدة اسمها ميشيل. تسكن ميشيل في مدينة نيويورك، ويسكن ماثيو في مدينة إثاكا.

كلمات جديدة

his name	اسمه	week	أسبوع
her name	اسمها	past, last	ماضي
she traveled	سافرت	airplane	طائرة=طيّارة
it, she flew	طارَت	of course	طبعاً
it, she arrived	وصلَت	airport	مَطار
she works	تَعمَل	evening	مساء
she lives	تسكُن	her father	أبوها
he lives	يسكُن	her mother	أمّها

تعابير

Emily has	عِند إملي
afternoon	بعد الظهر

أسئلة

1. Where is Emily from? _____
2. When did she travel to Jordan? _____
3. How did she travel there? _____
4. From which American airport did the plane take off? _____
5. When did Emily arrive in Amman? _____
6. What does Emily's father do? _____
7. Where does her mother work? _____
8. What is Emily's brother's name? _____
9. Who is Michelle? Where does she live? _____

تمرين رقم ١: أكمل الجُمل التاليّة عن إملي.

Complete the following facts about Emily by guessing the correct word.

١. إملي _____ في جامعة تكساس في مدينة أوستن.

٢. سافرت إملي للاردن _____ الماضي.

٣. سافرت إملي من _____ "جي إف كي" في نيويورك.

٤. عند إملي _____ واحد و _____ واحدة.

٥. _____ إملي من _____ إثاكا في _____ نيويورك.

الدرس الرابع

قواعد

1. Possession, revisited

As was briefly mentioned in Unit 1, possession in nouns is expressed by attaching a pronoun suffix to the noun:

his book	kitaab-uh	كتابه	كتاب+ـُـه
her book	kitaab-ha	كتابها	كتاب+ها
your (m.s.) book	kitaab-ak	كتابك	كتاب+َك
your (f.s.) book	kitaab-ik	كتابك	كتاب+ِك
my book	kitaab-i	كتابي	كتاب+ي

If the noun to which the pronoun suffix is attached ends in التاء المربوطة (ـة), as in the word غرفة "room", then a ت appears in the place of التاء المربوطة:

his room	ghurfa-t-uh	غرفته	غرفة+ـه
her room	ghurfa-t-ha	غرفتها	غرفة+ها
your (m.s.) room	ghurfa-t-ak	غرفتك	غرفة+ك
your (f.s.) room	ghurfa-t-ik	غرفتك	غرفة+ك
my room	ghurfa-t-i	غرفتي	غرفة+ي

تمرين رقم ١: (كتابي- في البيت)

Fill in the empty cells in the following table.[1] Notice the addition of و to أب and أخ and the كسرة ِ after the ك for the second feminine singular انتِ.

أمّ	أب	أخ	أخت	سيارة	اسم	بيت	
أمّه		أخوه		سيارته		بيتُه	هو-ـه his
	أبوها				اسمها		هي-ها her
أمّك	أبوك				اسمَك		انتَ-ـك your (m.s.)
		أخوك	أختِك	سيارتِك		بيتِك	انتِ-ـك your (f.s.)
		أخوي				بيتي	أنا-ي my

[1] m.s. = masculine singular, f.s. = feminine singular.

2. Possession with عند

The same set of suffixes used to express possession in nouns is also attached to the word عند to express possession in a way that parallels the use of the English verb *to have* in sentences like *I have a Japanese car* and *he has two sisters*.

he has	'ind-u	عنده
she has	'ind-ha	عندها
you, m.s., have	'ind-ak	عندَك
you, f.s., have	'ind-ik	عندِك
I have	'ind-i	عندي

تمرين رقم ٢: (كتابي – في البيت)

Fill in the empty cells in the following table without looking at the عند table above:

	هو
عندها	هي
	انتَ
	انتِ
	أَنا

3. The perfect tense (الفعل الماضي) – singular

Arabic verb tenses

Arabic verbs have two tenses: the perfect and the imperfect. The perfect corresponds roughly to the past tense in English and generally indicates completed action as in درس "he studied", and the imperfect corresponds to the present tense and indicates actions that have not been completed, as in أدرس "I study". The perfect tense will be introduced in this lesson.

Subject/person markers on the perfect verb

Different persons are expressed on the perfect verb by attaching different suffixes to it, except in the case of the third person masculine singular (the one corresponding to *he*), where no suffix is attached:

he studied	daras	دَرَس	–	(هو)
she studied	daras-at	دَرَسَت	‑َت	(هي)
you (m.s.) studied	daras-t	دَرَسْت	‑ْت	(انتَ)
you (f.s.) studied	daras-ti	دَرَسْت	‑ْتِ	(انتِ)
I studied	daras-t	دَرَسْت	‑ْت	(أَنا)

Note that the conjugations of انتَ and أَنا are identical.

From now on all verbs in the perfect will be cited in the vocabulary lists in their simplest form, i.e. the third person singular conjugation. So a verb like سافرت "I traveled" will be listed as سافر, which translates literally as "he traveled".

تمرين رقم ٣ (في البيت): املأ الفراغات

		he traveled سافر	
			هو
		سافرَت	هي
تعلَّمت			انتَ
	وصلتِ		انتِ
			أنا

تمرين رقم ٤: كتابة (في البيت)

هو   وصل لبيته.

هي   وصلت لبيتها.

انتَ   وصلْت ل ــــــــــ .

انتِ   ــــــــــــ .

أنا   ــــــــــــ .

تمرين رقم ٥: كتابة وحكي، في البيت وفي الصفّ.

تكوين جمل (create sentences about yourself):

اسمي ــــــــ ، عمري ــــــــ

اسم أخوي ــــــــ عمره ــــــــ

اسم أبوي ــــــــ ، عمره ــــــــ

اسم أمّي ــــــــ عمرها ــــــــ

تمرين رقم ٦: كتابة (في البيت) وحكي (في الصفّ)

Speak about yourself and your family. First write at home and then share orally in class. (Use عند).

عندي أخ واحد (أخوين، ثلاث إخوان)، وأخت واحدة (أختين، ثلاث أخوات)، اسم أخي/ أخوي ــــــــ ، واسم أختي ــــــــ .

4. Negation

In spoken Arabic, a distinction is made between negation of verbs and negation of non-verbal elements such as nouns, adjectives, adverbs, and prepositional phrases. The general rule in spoken Arabic is that verbs are negated with ما and non-verbal elements are negated with مش.

He didn't travel	ما سافر	He traveled	سافر
He doesn't speak	ما بيحكي	He speaks	بيحكي

But,

not a student	مش طالب	student	طالب
not big	مش كبير	big	كبير
not here	مش هون	here	هون
not from New York	مش من نيويورك	from New York	من نيويورك

5. The comparative

أكثر is the comparative form of كثير. It should be noted that the comparative and superlative in Arabic (forms equivalent to English *more* and *most*, respectively) use the same form of the adjective. So أكثر is translated as more or most, depending on the context. When used in the comparative sense the adjective is generally followed by the preposition من, which generally translates as *from*, but in this context it is translated as *than*.

تمرين رقم ٧ (في البيت): املأ الفراغات (fill in the empty cells)

Meaning	أكبَر مِن	كبير
smaller than		صغير
		قريب
	أبعد من	بعيد

Sociolinguistic corner

طائرة=طيّارة

In the introduction to this textbook, it was pointed out that two varieties of Arabic are used side by side, فُصحى, referred to in English as Modern Standard Arabic or MSA, and the colloquial. The colloquial used in this book is that spoken in the greater Syrian area (Syria, Lebanon, Jordan, and historical Palestine) and understood over most of the Arab-speaking world. It is called شامي (from بلاد الشام Greater Syria). The majority of words and grammatical structures are shared by the two varieties. Some words and structures are strictly فصحى, while others are strictly شامي. The following table shows some examples:

فصحى only	Colloquial	Shared
ماذا؟ what?	ايش؟ what?	نام he slept
ذهَب he went	راح he went	تعلّم he learned
		طالب student
		فندق hotel

Both طائرة and طيّارة are used in both varieties of Arabic. The difference is mainly that طائرة in شامي and طيّارة in فصحى is more likely to be used in شامي. The same thing can be said about إلى (فصحى) and ل (شامي), both meaning "to".

الدرس الخامس

كلمات الوحدة الجديدة (new words of the unit)

you (f.s.) learned تعلَّمتِ	her father أبوها
she works تَعمَل	fare, rent أُجرَة
(to a woman) please go ahead تفضّلي	sister, a friendly way of addressing a woman أُخت
university جامعة	week أسبوع
nationality جنسيّة	more than أكثر مِن
passport جَواز سَفَر	her mother أمّها
number رَقم	welcome to you أهلا (وسهلاً) فيكِ
visit زيارة	his name اسمه
he traveled سافر	her name اسمها
month (ج. شُهور) شَهر	to الى=ل
issue صُدور	you speak بتحكي
airplane طائرة=طيّارة	afternoon بعد الظُّهر
it, she flew طارَت	visa تأشيرة
of course طبعاً	date تاريخ
Emily has عِند إملي	she lives تسكُن

teacher أُستاذ=مُعلِّم	عُنوان address
مَكان place	فِعلاً indeed
profession مِهنة	فلس (دينار) fils (there are 1000 fils in one
stop مَوقِف	فُندُق hotel
هون here	لوين؟ where to?
وسط البَلَد downtown	ماضي past, last
it, she arrived وصلَت	مُدّة period, duration
or وَلا	مساء evening
birth ولادة	مَطار airport
he lives يسكُن	مطار علياء الدولي Alia' International Airport
it means يَعني	مع السلامة good-bye

تمرين رقم ١

Read the following passage, identify the possessive pronoun suffixes, then translate the noun and its suffix into English.

Example: اسمي "my name"

اسمي عبدالله. أنا من مدينة إربد في شمال الأردن. أنا طالب في جامعة اليرموك. عمري٢١ سنة. أنا ساكن مع أبي (أبوي) وأمّي وإخي (أخوي)[1] وأختي في بيت كبير في إربد. اسم أبي علي سمارة وعمره ٥٦ سنة، واسم أمي حليمة أبو اللبن وعمرها ٥١ سنة، واسم أخي فادي وعمره ٢٨ سنة، وعمر أختي ريم ١٨ سنة.

[1] In written Arabic (فصحى) the forms أبي "my father" and أخي "my brother" are used (without و), while in conversational Arabic أخوي and أبوي are more common.

Now rewrite the passage changing the first person (I) to the third person (he).

اسمه عبدالله. هو من مدينة إربد في ...

تمرين رقم ٢: حكي (في الصفّ)

Create a dialogue with your neighbor, take notes and then tell the class about him/her in the third person.

ايش اسمك؟
من وين انتَ؟
مدينة ... صغيرة/كبيرة؟
مدينة ... وين؟ جنوب، شمال ...

كم أخ وأخت عندك؟

ايش اسم أخوك؟ أختك؟

كم عمر أخوك، أختك؟

كيف الطقس في ... ؟

Summary of question words

when?	امتى؟
which (one), what?	أيّ؟
what?	ايش؟
how many, how much?	كمّ؟
how?	كيف؟
why?	ليش؟
who?	مين؟
where?	وين؟

تمرين رقم ٣: املأ الفراغات

الطائرة، جامعة، سافرَت، في، مطار، واحد، ولاية

إملي وليمز طالبة أمريكية في جامعة تكساس في أوستن. ــــــــــــ للأردن الأسبوع الماضي. سافرت بالطائرة طبعاً.

طارت ــــــــــــ من مطار "جي إف كي" في نيويورك الساعة ٨:٣٠ مساء يوم الثلاثاء ووصلت إلى ــــــــــــ عمّان الساعة ٤ بعد الظهر يوم الأربعاء.

عائلة إملي من مدينة إثاكا في ــــــــــــ نيويورك. أبوها اسمه هنري وهو أستاذ في ــــــــــــ كورنيل، وأمّها اسمها إليزابث وتعمل في بنك. عند إملي أخ ــــــــــــ اسمه ماثيو وأخت واحدة اسمها ميشيل. تسكن ميشيل ــــــــــــ مدينة نيويورك، ويسكن ماثيو في مدينة إثاكا.

تمرين رقم ٤: حكي (في الصفّ)

You are on your way to an Arab country. You meet an Arab on the plane! Introduce yourself and tell him/her about yourself, where you come from, what you do, your family, etc. (first and second person).

تمرين ٥: كلمات متقاطعة

	١	٢	٣	٤	٥	٦	٧	٨	٩	١٠
١										
٢										
٣										
٤										
٥										
٦										
٧										
٨										
٩										
١٠										

عمودي	أفقي
١. اسم ____ هنري واسم أمها إليزابث؛ طارت الطيّارة من ____ القاهرة الدولي الساعة ٧:٣٠.	١. في ال ____ سبعة أيّام؛ عكس (opposite) شرق
٣. عكس" قبل الظهر"	٣. عاصمة العراق
٥. انت بتحكي ____ كويّس؛ دولة عربيّة كبيرة	٥. عكس" غربي"
٧. عاصمة سوريا؛ ____ الزيارة؟ ٣ شهور.	٨. ____ جواز السفر، لو سمحت؟؛ من مصر.
٩. عكس" قبل"	١٠. فيه ٢٨ أو ٢٩ أو ٣٠ أو ٣١ يوم.
١٠. من اليمن	

الوحدة الرابعة: التاكسي والفندق

أهمّ الكلمات والتعابير الجديدة

صَندوق الموجودات	lost and found box	خِدمة	service
مَسافة	distance	حجز	to reserve
وصل	to arrive	لازِم	have to, must
رحلة	trip	بدَّك	you want
طويل	long	إذا	if
تَعبان	tired	مُمكِن	possible
مُوظَّف	employee	لو سَمحت، من فَضلك	if you please
أخذ	to take	كان معي	I had it (it was with me)
طلَب	to request, ask for	زَعلان	upset
فتّش (على)	to look for	آسِف	sorry
وَجَد	to find	ضيّعتيه	you lost it
حُدود	borders	إن شاء الله	God willing

تمرين رقم ١: وافق بين الكلمة والصورة

زَعلان، صَندوق الموجودات، طويل، تَعبان، مُوظَّفة

تمرين رقم ٢: املأ الفراغات

Choose the correct word or phrase from those in parentheses to complete each of the following sentences.

١. جواز السفر كان في ـ_____ (رحلة، صندوق الموجودات، خدمة).

٢. أنا ـ_____ (حجزت، سافرت، شربت) غرفة في الفندق قبل أسبوع.

٣. إملي ـ_____ (وصلت، فتّشت، وجدت) على جواز سفرها.

٤. ـ_____ (بدّك، آسف، زعلان) غرفة مع حمّام طبعاً؟

٥. ليش انتَ ـ_____ (لو سمحت، من فضلك، زعلان) اليوم؟

٦. مدينة إربد قريبة من ـ_____ (الرحلة، المسافة، الحُدود) السوريّة.

٧. لمّا وصلت البيت كنت ـ_____ (فتّش، تعبان، جبل) كثير.

٨. هو ـ_____ (أخذ، وصل، ضيّع) الشنطة في المطار.

الدرس الأول

النصّ الأوّل-مشاهدة: إملي في الفندق

كلمات جديدة

لازم	have to, must	اشربي!	drink!	خِدمة	service
طيّب	OK	بترجعي	you return	حَجز	to reserve
بدّك	you want	باشرب	I drink	بتعرفي	you know
إذا	if	أروح	I go	تعلّمتِ	you learned
مُمكِن	possible	قبل (قبل أسبوع)	before (a week ago)	أرجع	I go back
		بعدين	then	اقعدي!	sit down!

تعابير

لو سَمحت من فَضلك if you please

كان معي I had it (it was with me)

أسئلة

١. امتى إملي حجزت غرفة؟ ـــــــــــــــــــــــــــــــــ

٢. إملي بِدها (she wants) غرفة مع حمّام؟ ـــــــــــــــــــــــــــــــــ

٣. جواز السفر كان (was) مع إملي؟ ـــــــــــــــــــــــــــــــــ

٤. لوين رجعت (returned) إملي؟ ـــــــــــــــــــــــــــــــــ

٥. إملي بِدها تاكسي؟ ـــــــــــــــــــــــــــــــــ

النصّ الثاني–قراءة[1]: فنادق عمان

السعر في الليلة (بالدينار)	التصنيف	البُعد عن وسط عمّان بالكيلومتر	العنوان	اسم الفندق	
٥١	جيّد (٧٫٣ نقطة)	٣٫٧	شارع الملكة عالية، ص.ب. ٩٢٧٠٠٠	فندق ريجنسي بالاس	١
٥٤	جيّد جدّاً (٨٫٥ نقطة)	٤٫٧	الدوّار الخامس	فندق وأبراج شيراتون	٢
٥٠	جيّد جدّاً (٨٫٢ نقطة)	٣٫٧	شارع عبد الحميد شومان	فندق كمبينسكي	٣
٦٤	جيّد جدّاً (٨٫٢ نقطة)	٣٫٧	الشميساني، شارع عصام العجلوني	فندق ماريوت عمّان	٤
٦٩	جيّد جدّاً (٨٫٢ نقطة)	٣٫٢	الشميساني، شارع الملكة نور، ص.ب. ٩٥٠٦٢٩	فندق المريديان عمّان	٥

[1] A number with a decimal point like 3.7 can be read in two ways: ثلاثة فاصِلة سبعة (three, comma, seven) or ثلاثة وسبعة في العشرة (three and seven in ten).

	اسم الفندق	العنوان	البُعد عن وسط عمّان بالكيلومتر	التصنيف	السعر في الليلة (بالدينار)
٦	فندق كراون بلازا عمان	شارع الملك فيصل بن عبد العزيز، الدوار السادس	٥،٥	جيد (٧،٦ نقطة)	١٠٥
٧	فندق انتركونتننتال عمان	جبل عمان، شارع الملكة زين	١،٦	جيد جداً (٨،١ نقطة)	١٠٣
٨	فندق جراند حياة عمان	جبل عمان، شارع الحسين بن علي	١،٩	جيد جدّاً (٨،٣ نقطة)	١٠٦
٩	فندق هوليداي إن عمان	شارع المدينة المنوّرة	٧	جيد (٦،٨ نقطة)	١٢٨
١٠	فندق جراند بالاس جولدن توليب عمان	شارع الملكة علياء	٣،٧	جيد (٧،٤)	٥٦

كلمات جديدة

جِدّاً	very	سِعر	price, cost
جَبَل	mountain	لَيلة	night
تَصنيف	rating	جيِّد=كويِّس	good
		نُقطة	point

أسئلة

1. What do you think the two words عُنوان and بُعد mean?
2. What are the addresses of the following hotels: Kempinsky, Marriott, Crown Plaza, Holiday Inn?
3. How far are the following hotels from downtown Amman: Regency Palace, Meridian, Intercontinental, Grand Hyatt, Grand Palace-Golden Tulip?
4. How much does each of the following hotels cost per night: Regency Palace, Crown Plaza, Holiday Inn, Marriott?
5. Which hotel has the highest rating? Which has the lowest rating?

الدرس الثاني

النصّ الأوّل–مشاهدة: في التاكسي

كلمات جديدة

آسِف sorry	كَمان also
ضيّعتيه you lost it	سَوّيت I did
	زعلتِ you (f.s.) became upset

تعابير

صَندوق الموجودات lost and found box	إن شاء الله God willing

أسئلة

١. ليش إملي زعلانة؟ _____

٢. وين إملي ضيّعت (lost) جواز سفرها؟ _____

٣. وين مُمكن يكون (might be) جواز السفر؟ _____

النصّ الثاني–قراءة: المسافات بين المدن الأردنية

الحدود السورية	السلط	معان	الكرك	جرش	إربد	الحدود العراقية	العقبة	عمان	
									عمان
								٣٢٨	العقبة
							٦٤٥	٣٣١	الحدود العراقية
						٣٠٩	٤١٢	٨٩	إربد
					٣٨	٣١١	٣٧٤	٥١	جرش
				١٦٠	١٩٨	٤٣٤	٢٣٧	١١٨	الكرك
			١٤٤	٢٥٧	٢٩٥	٥٢٨	١١٧	٢١٢	معان
		٢٣٦	١٣٩	٥٠	٨٩	٣٥١	٣٥٣	٣٠	السلط
	٩٣	٢٩٨	٢٠٢	٤٣	٢٥	٣١٢	٤١٤	٩٤	الحدود السورية
٩٠	٤٤	٢٣٣	١٣٩	٥٩	٩٢	٣٠٨	٣٤٩	٢٣	الزرقاء

كلمات جديدة

مَسافة distance

حُدود borders

أسئلة

كم المسافة بالكيلومتر بين:

١.   عمّان وإربد؟ _____

٢.   عمّان وجَرَش؟ _____

٣.   مَعان والحدود العراقيّة؟ _____

٤.   العقبة والحدود السوريّة؟ _____

٥.   الكرك والسلط؟ _____

الدرس الثالث

قراءة: مُختارات من مذكّرات إملي (Selections from Emily's Diary)

وصلْت الى الأردن يوم الأربعاء ١/١٨. طارت الطائرة من مطار "جي إف كي" في نيويورك الساعة الثامنة والنصف مساء يوم الثلاثاء ١/١٧، ووصلَت الى مطار علياء الدولي في عمّان الساعة الرابعة بعد ظُهر يوم الأربعاء. كانت الرحلة طويلة، وكنت تعبانة كثيراً. أخذت سيّارة تاكسي من المطار الى الفندق. في الفندق طلب الموظّف جواز سفري. فتّشت على جواز سفري ولكن ما وجدته. ماذا حدث لجواز سفري؟ الله أعلم ...

تركت شنطتي في الفندق وأخذت سيّارة تاكسي الى المطار.

كلمات جديدة

حدَث to happen	مُوظّف employee	ثامِن 8th (الساعة الثامنة: 8 o'clock)
لكِن but	وصل to arrive	نِصْف=نُصّ half
ماذا؟=إيش؟ what?	أخذ to take	رابِع 4th
ترك to leave	طلَب to request, ask for	رِحلة trip
شنطة (ج. شنط) suitcase	فتّش (على) to look for	طويل long
	وَجَد to find	تَعبان tired

تعبير

الله أعلَم God knows

أسئلة

1. When did the plane arrive at Alia' International Airport? _____
2. How did Emily go from the airport to the hotel? _____
3. What was the problem at the hotel? _____
4. Why did Emily have to go back to the airport? _____

الدرس الرابع

قواعد

تمرين رقم ١: (في البيت): املأ الفراغات

	شنطة suitcase		
رحلتُه			هو–ـه/ه
			هي–ها
			انتَ–ـَك
		جواز سفرِك	انتِ–ـِك
	شنطتي		أنا–ـي/ي

عندي/معي

Like عند, the preposition مع is used to express possession. The main difference is that عند expresses possession in general, while مع expresses possessing or having something at the moment.

عندي ألف دولار.

معي ألف دولار.

تمرين رقم ٢: (كتابي في البيت)

Fill in the empty cells in the following table using مع

	هو
معها	هي
	انتَ
	انتِ
	أنا

Moving to the past with كان

كان (with its different conjugations) is used to "move" the time of an event or a situation to the past, as shown in the following examples:

كان عندي I had	عندي I have, own
كان معي I had (with me)	معي I have (with me)

تمرين رقم ٣: (كتابي في البيت)

		ضيّع he lost				ترَك
هو		ضيّع				
هي	حجرَت					
انتَ				وجدْت		
انتِ					طلبتِ	
أنا		أخذت				

The ordinal numbers ١–١٠

Ordinal numbers in Arabic behave as adjectives. When they follow the noun they modify they must agree with it in definiteness and gender, as in الساعة الثامنة "the 8th hour or 8 o'clock", where الثامنة modifies الساعة.

The following table shows the ordinal numbers 1st through 10th.

خامس fifth	رابع fourth	ثالث third	ثاني second	أوّل first
عاشِر tenth	تاسِع ninth	ثامِن eighth	سابِع seventh	سادِس sixth

With the exception of أوّل, the feminine form of the ordinal number is derived from the masculine form by the addition of التاء المربوطة.

Now fill in the empty cells in the following table.

خامِس	رابِع	ثالِث	ثاني	أوّل
				أولى

عاشِر	تاسِع	ثامِن	سابِع	سادِس
	تاسِعة			

الدرس الخامس

كلمات الوحدة الجديدة

بعدين then	باشرب I drink
تَعبان tired	أخذ to take
تعلَّمتِ you learned	أرجع I go back
جَبَل mountain	أروح I go
حجز to reserve	إذا if
حدَث to happen	إن شاء الله God willing
حُدود borders	اشربي! drink!
خِدمة service	اقعدي! sit down!
رِحلة trip	الله أعلَم God knows
سَوّيت I did	بترجعي you return
صَندوق الموجودات lost and found box	بتعرفي you know
ضيّعتيه you lost it	بدّك you want

لكن	but	طلَب	to request, ask for
لو سَمحت، من فَضلك	if you please	طويل	long
ماذا؟=إيش؟	what?	طيّب	OK
مَسافة	distance	عَدَد	number
مُمكن	possible	فتّش (على)	to look for
مُوظَّف	employee	قبل	before
نِصْف=نُصّ	half	كان معي	I had it (it was with me)
وَجَد	to find	كَمان	also
وصل	to arrive	لازِم	have to, must

تمارين

تمرين رقم ١

Identify the verbs in the perfect tense in the following passage and translate them, together with their subject markers, into English.

Example:

طارت   she (it) flew

إملي وليمز طالبة أمريكية من مدينة إثاكا في ولاية نيويورك. سافرت للأردن الأسبوع الماضي. هي سافرت بالطائرة طبعاً.

طارت الطائرة من مطار "جي إف كي" في نيويورك الساعة الثامنة مساء يوم الثلاثاء ووصلت مطار علياء الدولي في عمّان الساعة الرابعة بعد الظهر يوم الأربعاء.

تمرين رقم ٢: (في البيت)

Translate the following into Arabic.

1. I lost my passport.
2. The employee lost my passport.
3. He learned Arabic at al-Azhar (الأزهر) University.
4. She knew (عرفت) the teacher.
5. I did not know the teacher. (ما عرفت)
6. I did not find my suitcase. (ما وجدت)
7. He looked for the car at the airport.
8. You (f.) ordered a falafel sandwich (سندويشة فلافل) and I ordered pizza (بيتسا).
9. The student (m.) ordered coffee with milk and sugar (سُكّر).
10. Emily studied Arabic at the University of Texas.

تمرين رقم ٣: العكس (opposites)

Match each word in the first column with its opposite in the second column.

	أ	ب
١.	وجد	قصير
٢.	كثير	ما معه
٣.	معه	شويّة
٤.	كبير	بعد ما
٥.	قريب	مساء
٦.	طويل	ضيّع
٧.	قبل ما	بعيد
٨.	صباح	صغير

تمرين رقم ٤

Working with your partner, match each of the phrases in column أ with the appropriate response in column ب. For example, if your partner says صباح الخير, your response should be صباح النور.

I.

أ	ب
– صباح الخير	–غرفة مع حمّام لو سمحت.
– أي خِدمة؟	–صباح النور
–انت بتحكي عربي كويّس!	–في جامعة في امريكا.
–عندك جواز سفر؟	– شُكراً!
–وين تعلّمت العربي؟	– ٥٠ دينار بالليلة.
–كم أُجرة الغرفة لو سمحت؟	– طبعاً!

2.

ب	أ
– أهلاً فيك!	–معك شنطة؟
–ان شاء الله.	–في أي جامعة؟
–شنطتي....وين شنطتي؟ ضيّعت شنطتي!	–اهلاً وسهلاً في الفندق.
– في جامعة كورنيل في مدينة نيويورك.	– ليش انت زعلان؟ ان شاء الله الشنطة في المطار.

تمرين رقم ٥: احكي (في الصفّ)

Create a dialogue with your neighbor on one of the following. (Make your dialogue interesting and funny.)

A. One of you is a taxi driver and the other a passenger. The passenger tells the taxi driver where to go, they converse about family, the weather, where the passenger is from, etc., then they negotiate the price.

B. Checking into a hotel. One is the guest and the other the hotel clerk. The guest tells the clerk that he/she has a reservation for a day or two days, etc. Ask what the room number is, how much it costs, how far is the downtown area, restaurants, etc.

الوحدة الخامسة: جواز السفر

أهمّ الكلمات والتعابير الجديدة

صورَة picture	جِنسيّة citizenship
الحمد لله thank God	اقعُدي! !Sit down
كُل واحد everyone	غير معروف not known, unknown
ذهَبت=رُحت I went	خلّيني أشوف let me see
شُرطي policeman	مكتوب written
قُلت I said	شنطة يَد handbag
سألني he asked me	كامل full
إذا if	وَسَط middle
مُشكِلة problem	فتّش (على) to look (for)
لكِن but	سَفارَة embassy

صاحِب (ج. أصحاب) friend	هناك (there (is
وجدت I found	فكّر he thought
رجعت I returned	نِهاية end
تعبان tired	أَعطاني he gave me
بعد الظهر afternoon	دَعاني he invited me

تمارين

تمرين رقم ١: وافق بين الكلمة والصورة

سفارة، شرطي، شنطة يد، صورة، فتّش على، مكتوب، نهاية، صاحب، اقعد، أعطاني

تمرين رقم ٢: املأ الفراغات

١. ـــــــــــــــ (أعطيت، قعدت، فتشت) سائق التاكسي ١٠ دنانير.

٢. ـــــــــــــــ (فكّر، فتّش، نام) انّه الاسم الوسط هو اسم الأب.

٣. ـــــــــــــــ (سألني، دعاني، أعطاني) عن اسم أمّي واسم جدّي واسم عائلتي.

٤. ـــــــــــــــ (قلت له، فتّشت عليه، سألته) اسم أمي في جواز السفر.

٥. ـــــــــــــــ (كل واحد، كل يوم، عندما) في أمريكا عنده اسم أوّل واسم وسط.

٦. فتشت على جواز سفري، ـــــــــــــــ (لكن، نعم، ثاني) ما وجدته.

الدرس الأوّل

النصّ الأوّل–مُشاهَدة: ضيعت جواز سفري

كلمات جديدة

استريحي	Rest, relax!	نَعَم	yes
اقعُدي!	Sit down!	أوّل	first
		جِنسيّة	citizenship

تعابير

خلّيني أشوف	let me see	ما باذكُر	I don't remember
		غير معروف	not known, unknown

أسئلة

١.   امتى إملي ضيّعت جواز سفرها؟

٢.   ايش اسم أبو إملي؟

٣.   إملي بتتذكر (remembers) رقم جواز سفرها؟

النصّ الثاني–قراءة: صندوق الموجودات

مطار علياء الدولي

صندوق الموجودات

١.   شنطة كبيرة لونها أسود، باسم "السيد أحمد سَلمان".
العنوان: السالميّة، الكويت. مكتوب عليها "ملابس للأولاد".

٢.   شنطة يد صغيرة لونها بنّي.

٣.   جواز سفر أمريكي باسم "إملي هوب وليمز".

٤.   جاكيت رجّالي لونه بنّي.

٥.   تلفون موبايل "موتورولا"، لونه أحمر.

٦.   كتاب بعنوان "جمهورية أفلاطون" باسم سليم عبدالله الشافعي.

٧.   ساعة يد "أوميغا" رجّاليّة.

كلمات جديدة

رِجّالي for men	عليها on it	شنطة suitcase
جُمهوريّة republic	مَلابِس clothes	لون color
		مكتوب written

تعبير

شنطة يَد handbag

أسئلة

١. أكمل الجدول التالي:

1. Fill in the empty cells in the following table based on the passage above. Ignore those marked with x's.

name (of owner) الاسم	color لون	thing, object الشيء
أحمد سلمان		شنطة كبيرة
xxx		شنطة يد صغيرة
إملي هوب وليمز	xxx	
xxx	أحمر	
	xxx	جمهورية أفلاطون

2. What do you think the phrase جمهورية أفلاطون means?

الدرس الثاني

مشاهدة: اسمِك الكامل لو سمحتِ!

كلمات جديدة

قُلتِ you said	كامل full
وَسَط middle	بَسّ but

استنّى!	Wait!	فتِّش عليه!	Look for it!
سَفارَة	embassy	أكيد	certainly
صورَة	picture	طَيّب	OK

تعابير

الحمد لله   thank God

كُل واحد   everyone

أسئلة

١.   أيش اسم إملي الكامل؟

٢.   أيش اسم أبو إملي؟

٣.   أيش المشكلة (problem)؟

٤.   ليش الشرطي (policeman) كان بدّه (wanted) يحكي مع السفارة الأمريكيّة؟

٥.   أيش قال (said) الشرطي (policeman) لإملي لمّا (when) قالت "ليش تحكي مع السفارة؟"

الدرس الثالث

(((• قراءة: مذكّرات إملى

في المطار ذهبت الى شرطي وقلت له إنّني ضيّعت جواز سفري. سألني عن اسمي واسم أبي واسم جدّي واسم أمّي واسم عائلتي، ثمّ قال: "إذا الأردني ضيّع جواز سفره، هذه مشكلة صغيرة، ولكن إذا الأمريكي ضيّع جواز سفره، هذه مشكلة كبيرة."

جلست، وفتّش الشرطي في صندوق الموجودات. كان جواز السفر في الصندوق، ولكن كانت هناك مشكلة: فكّر الشرطي أنّ الاسم الوسط اسم أبي.

ولكن في النهاية أعطاني جواز السفر، وقال: "انت بتحكي عربي كوّيس." ثمّ دعاني لأشرب الشاي معه ومع أصحابه.

فرحتُ كثيراً عندما وجدت جواز سفري في المطار. رجعت الى الفندق ونمت. نمت حتى الساعة الثانية بعد الظهر. كنت تعبانة كثيراً.

كلمات جديدة

he thought فكّر		I went ذهَبت=رُحت	
that أنّ		policeman شُرطي	
end نهاية		I said قُلت	
he gave me أعطاني		to him لَهُ	
he invited me دَعاني		that I إنّني	
with مع		he asked me سألني	
friend (ج. أصحاب) صاحِب		about عن	
I became happy, was happy فرحتُ		grandfather جدّ=أب الأب، أب الأمّ	
a lot, very كثيراً		then, and then ثمّ=بَعدين	
when عندَما=لمّا		if إذا	
I found وجدت		problem مُشكلة	
I returned رجعت		but لكن	
I slept نمت		I sat down جلَسْت	
until حتّى		he looked for (على) فتّش	
tired تعبان		there (is) هناك	

تعابير

afternoon بعد الظهر		second hour, two o'clock الساعة الثانية	

أسئلة

1. What is a big problem, according to the policeman?
2. Where was the passport?
3. What was the problem with the name?
4. What did the policeman invite Emily to do?
5. Until what time did Emily sleep when she went back to the hotel?

الدرس الرابع

قواعد

١. الإضافة (the construct)

In Unit 1, you were introduced to one of the most basic grammatical structures in Arabic called إضافة (the construct). The examples given were:

كتاب الطالب the student's book

عاصمة مصر the capital of Egypt, Egypt's capital

Structurally, إضافة is closely related to possession. For example, the two important points mentioned about إضافة (the pronunciation of التاء المربوطة as ت and the absence of the definite article on the first term) also apply in the case of noun + possessive pronoun combinations as in كتابه (his book), and عاصمتها (its/her capital, from the word عاصمة) but not الكتابه*.

تمرين رقم ١: املأ الفراغات

her passport	جواز سفرها	Muna's passport	جواز سفر مُنى
		Ahmad's passport	جواز سفر أحمد
			اسم الطالب
			اسم الطالبة
	عائلتها		عائلة إملي
its (her) color		the color of the bag	لون الشنطة
			لون الجاكيت
his friends			أصحاب الشرطي

تمرين رقم ٢

Each of the nouns and particles marked with an asterisk has a possessive pronoun. Below the passage write down the noun that each pronoun refers to. The first one is given as an example.

في المطار ذهبت الى شرطي وقلت له* إنّني ضيّعت جواز سفري. سألني عن اسمي واسم أبي واسم جدّي واسم أمّي واسم عائلتي، ثمّ قال: "إذا الأردني ضيّع جواز سفره*، هذه مشكلة صغيرة، ولكن إذا الأمريكي ضيّع جواز سفره*، هذه مشكلة كبيرة."

ولكن في النهاية أعطاني جواز السفر، وقال: "انت بتحكي عربي كوّيس." ثمّ دعاني لأشرب الشاي معه* ومع أصحابه*.

له—شُرطي

2. More on negation

There are certain systematic grammatical differences between فصحى and شامي. Those differences will be pointed out as they appear. One of these differences lies in the system of negation. For negating non-verbal elements, شامي uses مش while فصحى uses غير (and ليس which will be introduced later).

	فصحى	شامي
Not known	غير معروف	مِش معروف

3. Verb types: sound and hollow

Arabic words are divided into three categories: *verbs*, *nouns*, and *particles*. Particles are words or parts of words like prepositions, conjunctions, the definite article, question words, and other "function" elements.

Verbs and nouns form the major categories, which include the great majority of words in the language. All verbs and nouns derive from roots of three- or, less commonly, four-letter roots. Four-letter roots will be excluded here because of their rare occurrence in this book.

Arabic verbs that are based on three-letter roots behave in distinct ways depending on their structure. Two common verb types are *sound* and *hollow*.

Sound verbs have three consonants in the three consonant positions, no doubling of any two consonants, and no ا, و, or ى in any of these positions. Verbs like كتب "he wrote", عرف "he knew", and سمع "he heard" are sound verbs.

Hollow verbs have ا in the second root slot in the perfect tense of the verb: كان "he was", راح "he went", نام "he slept", قال "he said".

Whereas persons or subjects are indicated by simply attaching a suffix to a sound verb, certain adjustments are made to hollow verbs when the same suffixes are attached, as shown in the following table. Note in particular that the hollow verb retains the ا in the third person conjugation (هو، هي) but loses it in the second and first conjugations (انتَ، انتِ، أنا).

	Hollow		Sound	
(هو)	كتب	katab	كان	kaan
(هي)	كتبَتْ	katabat	كانت	kaanat
(انتَ)	كتبْتْ	katabt	كُنتْ	kunt
(انتِ)	كتبتِ	katabti	كُنتِ	kunti
(أنا)	كتبْتْ	katabt	كُنتْ	kunt

Notes

1. As was mentioned earlier, the perfect conjugations of انتَ and أنا are identical.
2. In the Arabic grammar tradition, the conjugation of verbs proceeds from the third person to the second and first persons.
3. The third person singular masculine form, the هو (he) conjugation is the simplest.

تمرين رقم ٣ (كتابي في البيت): املأ الفراغات.

Fill in the empty cells in the table by using the correct form of the verb. Some cells have already been filled in.

هو	أخذ	قال		سافر	نام		
هي						كانَت	وجدَت
انتَ				سافرْت			
انتِ	أخذتِ				نمتِ		
أنا			وصلت				

4. Pronouns attached to prepositions

The pronoun suffixes that are used to indicate possession (عندي، كتابها) are also attached to prepositions to express the equivalent of English constructions consisting of a preposition and an object pronoun such as *on it, in them, to you*, etc.

(شامي) إل to	(فصحى) لـ to	على on	مَع with	مِن from		
ilu إلُه	lahu لَه	'aleeh عليه	ma'u معُه	minnu منّه	he/him	هو
ilha إلها	laha لَها	'aleeha عليها	ma'ha معها	minha منها	she/her	هي
ilak إلَك	lak لَك	'aleek عليك	ma'ak معَك	minnak منّك	you (m.s.)/ your	انتَ
ilik إلِك	laki لَكِ	'aleeki عليكِ	ma'ik معِك	minnik منّك	you (f.s.)/ your	انتِ
ili إلي	lii لي	'alayy عَلَيّ	ma'i معي	minni منّي	I/my	أنا

5. Object pronouns

The same set of pronoun suffixes are attached to verbs to indicate the objects of these verbs. The English equivalents are words like *them, her, me* in sentences like *I saw them, He visited her, My son called me*, etc.

Notes

1. The object pronoun follows the subject marker. So think of the verb with the object pronoun as being constructed in two steps:
   a. construct the verb with its subject marker,
   b. attach the object pronoun.

2. The object pronoun for me is ني not just ي, as in the possessive.
3. When the object pronoun is preceded by a long vowel as in the word أعطى "he gave", the second person singular feminine and masculine are distinguished by a كسرة after the ك of the pronoun.

you lost انتَ ضيّعت	he gave هو أعطى	
ضيّعته	أعطاه	هو
ضيّعتها	أعطاها	هي
x	أعطاك	انتَ
x	أعطاكِ	انتِ
ضيّعتني	أعطاني	أنا

Note that when an object pronoun is attached to the verb أعطى the ألف مقصورة is changed to regular ألف. أعطا: ألف مقصورة is a word-final phenomenon.

تمرين رقم ٤: املأ الفراغات (Fill in the empty cells)

.١

	شنطته	هو
جواز سفرها		هي
		انتَ
		انتِ
		أنا

.٢

		فكّر	هو
	طلبَت		هي
			انتَ
you (f.s.) understood فهمتِ			انتِ
			أنا

.٣

I found أنا وجدت	he asked هو سأل	
	سأله	هو
وجدتها		هي
		انتَ
وجدتِك		انتِ
x	سألني	أنا

الدرس الخامس

كلمات الوحدة الجديدة

ضيّعتيه	you lost it	أعطاني	he gave me
طَيّب	OK	أكيد	certainly
عليها	on it	أوّل	first
عن	about	إذا	if
عندَما=لمّا	when	إنّني	that I
غير معروف	not known, unknown	استنّى!	Wait!
فتِّش عليه	look for it	اقعُدي!	Sit down!
فرِحت	I became happy, was happy	الحمد لله	thank God
فكّر	he thought	الساعة الثانية	second hour, two o'clock
قُلت	I said	ثاني	second
قُلت	you said	ثمّ=بَعدين	then, and then
كامِل	full	جدّ=أب الأب، أب الأمّ	grandfather
كُل واحد	everyone	جلَست	I sat down
لكِن	but	جُمهوريّة	republic
لَهُ	to him	جِنسيّة	citizenship
لون	color	خلّيني أشوف	let me see
ما باذكُر	I don't remember	دَعاني	he invited me
مُشكلة	problem	ذهَبت	I went
مكتوب	written	رِجّالي	for men
مَلابِس	clothes	سألني	he asked me
نَعَم	yes	سَفارة	embassy
نِمت	I slept	شُرطي	policeman
نِهاية	end	شنطة	suitcase
وَ	and	شنطة يَد	handbag
وَسَط	middle	صاحِب (ج. أصحاب)	friend
		صورة	picture

تمرين رقم ١

Matching: write the word or phrase underneath the corresponding picture.

كتاب، شرطي، صورة، صندوق، شنطة يد، جواز سفر، ساعة، سائق تاكسي،
ملابس، اصحاب، سفارة

تمرين رقم ٢

Multiple choice: circle the correct verb and translate each sentence into English:

١. أنا (ضيّعت/سافرت/جلست) جواز سفري في المطار.

٢. شرطي المطار (قعد/تركني/سألني) عن اسمي ورقم جواز سفري واسم ابي وامي وجنسيتي.

٣. إملي (حكت/تركت/فكّرت) شنطتها في الفندق ورجعت للمطار.

٤. إملي (فتّشت/ضيّعت/وجدت) جواز سفرها في صندوق الموجودات.

٥. إملي ما (فتشت/ذكرت/ذهبت) رقم جواز السفر.

تمرين رقم ٣

A. Possession: fill in the empty cells.

مشكلة	جنسية	مفتاح	جواز سفر	شنطة	
	nationality				
					هو
			جواز سفرها		هي
					انتَ
		مفتاحكِ			انتِ
					انا

B. The perfect tense: fill in the empty cells.

ضيّع	سأل	فهم	ترك	جلس	
				to sit	
					هو
	سألت				هي
					انتَ
		فهمتِ			انتِ
			تركت		انا

C. Verbs with object pronouns: translate the following sentences into Arabic using the appropriate verbs in A above.

1. I lost her
2. She asked her
3. You (m.s.) understood him
4. I left you in the airport
5. You (f.s.) lost me

تمرين رقم ٤: كتابة

Writing: re-write the following sentences changing the underlined words in the first person (I) to the third person (he/she).

١. تركت <u>شنطتي</u> في الفندق.

٢. <u>أبي</u> (أبوي) اسمه هنري <u>وامي</u> اسمها اليزبث <u>واختي</u> اسمها ميشيل.

٣. <u>سيارتي</u> في <u>بيتي</u>.

٤. ضيّعت جواز <u>سفري</u> في المطعم.

٥. كان <u>حظي</u> (my luck) كويّس <u>لأني</u> وجدت جواز <u>سفري</u> في صندوق الموجودات.

٦. <u>طلبت</u> تاكسي من المطار للفندق.

تمرين شفهي رقم ٥

Working in pairs, act out one of the following situations that Emily has been in (each dialogue should be no more than a few minutes):

1. Emily loses her passport (.... كان معي/وين راح جواز سفري؟)
2. Emily is confused about the naming system in Jordan (.... هون في الاردن ما فيه اسم وسط)
3. Emily is thankful to find her passport (.... الحمد لله وجدت جواز سفري/كان في صندوق الموجودات)
4. Emily takes a taxi from the airport back to the hotel (.... تاكسي، تاكسي! لوين؟ لفندق الاندلس)
5. Emily is finally at the hotel and is very tired (.... ايش رقم غرفتي لو سمحت)
6. Tell the story of Emily (in the third person) focusing on what you know about her so far, her family, her experience with the passport and how names are listed in Jordan, etc.

الوحدة السادسة: الأكل في المطعم

أهمّ الكلمات والتعابير الجديدة

رزّ	rice	في رأَيك	in your opinion
سَريع	fast	كُلّ شيء	everything
سَلَطة	salad	أكلة	dish, food
شيء حلو	something sweet	اعطيني	give me
طريق	road	بَيض	eggs
طلَب–يطلُب	to order	تاخُذي	you take
عشاء	dinner	حَلَويّات	sweets, dessert
غالي	expensive	خَروف	lamb
غَداء	lunch	خصوصاً	specially
فُطور	breakfast	خُضار	vegetables
لازِم	must, should, it is necessary	رَخيص	cheap

dishes (things eaten) مَأكولات	مُمتاز excellent
evening مَساء	مُمكِن maybe, perhaps
drinks مشروبات	مَوْجود found, available
baked, grilled مشوي	يَسار left
restaurant (مَطعَم (ج. مَطاعِم	يَمين right

تمرين رقم ١

Copy each word in row ب into the space provided under its opposite in row أ:

أسود	بعد	رخيص	يسار	شرق	شمال	قريب	أ
غالي	جنوب	قبل	بعيد	يمين	أبيض	غرب	ب

تمرين رقم ٢: املأ الفراغات

١.   مطعم الشعب _____ (عشاء، أقرب، غالي) من مطعم السلام.

٢.   مطعم السلام _____ (فطور، أرخص، طريق) من مطعم الشعب.

٣.   _____ (كل شيء، عشاء، غالي) كويّس في مطعم القدس.

٤.   الكنافة في مطعم القدس _____ (لازم، ممتازة، مأكولات)

٥.   أكلت _____ (مشروبات، لحم دجاج مشوي، طريق) في مطعم ريم البوادي.

٦.   _____ (أقرب، رخيص، أعطيني) دجاج مع خضار لو سمحت.

٧.   أكلت _____ (أحسن، في رأيك، الغداء) الساعة ٣ بعد الظهر.

الدرس الأوّل

النصّ الأوّل–مشاهدة: فيه مطعم قريب؟

كلمات جديدة

أَقْرب	closer	بِتروح	you go
رَخيص	cheap	روحي!	Go!
أيّ؟	which?	دُغري	straight
أرخَص	cheaper	يَمين	right
مُمكِن	maybe, perhaps	يَسار	left
وَلّا	or	مُمتاز	excellent
كيلو	kilometer	بَسّ	only

تعبير

زيّ بَعَض   like one another, similar

أسئلة

١.   أيّ مطعم أقرب، مطعم السلام أو مطعم الشعب؟ ــــــــــــــــــــــــــــــ

٢.   كيف الأكل في مطعم السلام؟ ــــــــــــــــــــــــــــــ

٣.   أي مطعم أرخص مطعم السلام أو مطعم الشعب؟ ــــــــــــــــــــــــــــــ

٤.   حسب (according to) إملي، مطعم السلام قريب أو بعيد؟ ــــــــــــــــــــــــــــــ

٥.   مطعم السلام على اليسار أو على اليمين؟ ــــــــــــــــــــــــــــــ

٦.   كم شارع إملي بتتعرف في عمّان؟ ــــــــــــــــــــــــــــــ

النصّ الثاني-قراءة: مطاعم عمّان

المطاعم العربية	رقم الهاتف	الموقع
أبو أحمد	٤٦٤١٨٧٩	الدوار الثالث
البستان	٥٦٦١٥٥٥	طريق الجامعة الاردنية
البيادر	٤١٢٧٥٥٦	طريق المطار
الكلحة	٥٨٦٤٢٤٢	الشميساني
القدس	٤٦٣٠١٦٨	شارع الملك حسين
الديوان	٤٦١٨١٨١	فندق الشرق الأوسط
المنسف	٥٦٠٧٦٠٧	فندق الماريوت
الزوادة	٥٥٣٢٤١٣	الفحيص
عطا علي	٥٦٦٨٦٨٢	الشميساني
دار أوتيل	٥٦٠٧١٩٣	الشميساني
فيصل القاضي	٥٦٠٥٨٨١	جبل الحسين
جبري	٥٦٨٨١١١	شارع الجاردنز
كان زمان	٤١٢٨٣٩٣	طريق المطار
قرية النخيل		طريق المطار
ريم البوادي	٥٥١٥٤١٩	دوار الواحة
تراس عكاظ	٤٦٤١٣٦١	فندق الاردن
الفردوس	٧١١١١٣	مرج الحمام
فخر الدين	٤٦٥٢٣٩٩	الدوار الثالث
تنورين	٥٥١٥٩٨٧	سوق أم اذينة
ميس الريم	٥٥٣٦٩٩٠	أم اذينة
طواحين الهواء	٥٣٤٦٠٦٠	شارع الجاردنز
الوجبات السريعة		
بوسطن فرايد تشكن	٥٨٦٣٩٥٥	شارع المدينة المنورة
دجاج كنتاكي	٥٦٧١٦٠٨	الشميساني
ماكدونالدز	٥٨٦٥٢٧٩	الصويفية
صب واي	٥٨٥٦١٦٥	شارع مكة
بلو فيج	٥٩٢٨٨٠٠	عبدون

المطاعم الهندية	رقم الهاتف	الموقع
كشمير-الأرجيلة	٤٦٥٩٥٢٠	جبل عمان
المطعم الهندي	٥٨١٩٨٢٩	الدوار الثامن
المطاعم الإيطالية		
ألفريدو	٥٨٢١٧٠٥	شارع مكة
لا كوسينا	٥٩٣٣٣٥٥	عبدون
ماما ميا	٥٦٨٢١٢٢	الشميساني
روميرو	٤٦٤٤٢٢٧	الدوار الثالث
كازاريشو	٥٩٣٤٧٧٣	عبدون
جرابا	٤٦٣٨٢١٢	الدوار الثالث
المطاعم الفرنسية		
لاتراس	٥٦٠١٦٧٥	الشميساني
لاميزون فيرت	٥٦٨٥٧٤٦	الشميساني
المطاعم الاسبانية		
بونيتا	٤٦١٥٠٦١	الدوار الثالث

المطاعم الصينية	رقم الهاتف	الموقع
تشن	٥٥١٨٢١٤	الدوار الأول
حدائق سيتشوان	٥٥٣١١٧٤	الدوار الثالث
الصين	٤٦٣٨٩٦٨	الشميساني

كلمات جديدة

هِندي	Indian	مَطعَم (ج. مَطاعِم)	restaurant
صيني	Chinese	هاتِف=تلفون	
سَريع	fast	مَوقِع	location
		طريق	road

أسئلة

1. How many Chinese restaurants are in the list? What are they?
2. How many fast-food restaurants?
3. What are the phone numbers of the following restaurants: Al-Quds, Jabri, Reem al-Bawadi, Mays al-Reem, Tawaheen al-Hawa, the Indian Restaurant, Jraba, and Bonita?
4. Where are the following restaurants located: Al-Bustan, al-Kalha, Al-Mansaf, Ata Ali, Kan Zaman, Tannourin, Kentucky Fried Chicken, Kashmeer-Argeela, Alfredo, La Maison Verte, Setchuan Gardens?

الدرس الثاني

النصّ الأوّل–مشاهدة: في مطعم السلام

كلمات جديدة

مشوي	baked, grilled	شيء	thing, something
خُضار	vegetables	مَوْجود	found, available
رُزّ	rice	اعطيني	give me
كنافة، هريسة، بقلاوة	names of dessert	طلَب–يطلُب	to order
		أكلة	dish, food

تعابير

كُلّ شيء everything

في رأيك in your opinion

شيء حلو something sweet

يسلموا ايديك thank you (literally, may God bless your hands)

تِكرَم عينك you are welcome

أسئلة

١. إيش إملي شربت في المطعم؟ _____

٢. فيه دجاج مع خضار في المطعم؟ _____

٣. إيش إملي طلبت تاكل؟ _____

٤. فيه بيرة في المطعم؟ _____

٥. أيّ شيء حلو أكلت إملي؟ _____

النصّ الثاني: قراءة

	دينار	فلس	
مطعم السلام مَأكولات عربية وغربية مفتوح كل يوم من الساعة الثامنة في الصباح الى العاشرة في المساء			
الفطور	١	٢٠٠	حمص
	١	٢٠٠	فول
	–	٩٠٠	سندويشة فلافل
	٣	٢٠٠	بيض (عدد ٢)
الغداء/العشاء	٣	٥٠٠	خضار باللحمة
	٢	٧٥٠	دجاج (ربع دجاجة)
	٣	٧٥٠	شيش كباب (خروف)
	٣	–	سمك
	–	٣٠٠	رُز
	١	٢٠٠	سلطة خضار
المشروبات	١		شاي، قهوة عربيّة
	١	٢٥٠	قهوة أمريكيّة (مع حليب)
	١	٢٥٠	عصير فواكه (برتقال، تفاح)
	١		بيبسي، ميراندا، سفن أب
الحلويات	–	٩٠٠	بقلاوة
	١	–	كنافة
	–	٧٥٠	هريسة

كلمات جديدة

eggs بَيض		dishes (things eaten) مأكولات	
lunch غَداء		open مفتوح	
quarter رُبع		morning صَباح	
lamb خَروف		breakfast فُطور	
salad سَلَطة		evening مَساء	
drinks مشروبات		fils (1/1000 of a dinar) فِلس	
sweets, dessert حَلَوِيّات		dinar (Jordanian currency) (ج. دنانير) دينار	
		fava beans فول	

أسئلة

1. What are the hours of al-Salam Restaurant? _____

2. How much does each of the following cost at al-Salam Restaurant? Hummus, shish kebab, vegetable salad, *baklawa*? _____

3. What drinks are found at al-Salam Restaurant? _____

الدرس الثالث

مشاهدة: إذا بدك أكل عربي كويس

كلمات جديدة

more expensive أغلى		not yet لِسه	
you ride تركبي		better, the best أحسَن	
service car سَرفيس		specially خصوصاً	
therefore, then إذاً		grilled مَشوي	
		expensive غالي	

تعبير

على كيفِك as you wish

أسئلة

١. أيش أحسن أكلات في مطعم القدس؟ _____

٢. كيف الكنافة في مطعم القدس؟ _____

٣. أيّ مطعم أغلى ريم البوادي أو القدس؟ _____

٤. وين إملي رايحة تاكل؟ ليش (why)؟ _____

الدرس الرابع

قواعد

1. Wanting with بدّ

The word بدّ is used in combination with a pronoun suffix (the same set of suffixes that are used to indicate possession) to express the equivalent of the English verb *to want*:

he wants	bidd-uh	بدّه
she wants	bidd-ha	بدها
you (m.s.) want	bidd-ak	بدَّك
you (f.s.) want	bidd-ik	بدِّك
I want	bidd-i	بدّي

2. The imperfect

As was mentioned previously, Arabic verbs have two tenses: the perfect and the imperfect. The conjugation of the perfect verb was introduced in Unit 4. In this unit the conjugation of the imperfect verb, which generally refers to actions that have not been completed, will be introduced.

As was pointed out in the discussion of the perfect, the doer of the action of the verb is expressed by attaching a suffix except in the case of the third masculine singular: سافر (he traveled), such as سافرَت (she traveled) and سافرْت (I traveled).

Subject markers are expressed in the imperfect verb by attaching a prefix or, in some cases, both a prefix and a suffix, to the verb:

he knows	ya-'rif	يعرف	يَـَ	هو
she knows	ta-'rif	تعرف	تَـَ	هي
you (m.s.) know	ta-'rif	تعرف	تَـَ	انتَ
you (f.s.) know	ta-'rif-i	تعرفي	تَـَي	انتِ
I know	'a-'rif	أعرف	أـَ	أنا

Note that the conjugations for هي and انتَ are identical.

The prefix *b-* is attached to the imperfect verb in شامي when such a verb is not preceded by another verb:

Do you know a good restaurant?	بتعرف مطعم كويّس؟
He eats at home.	بياكل في البيت.

Note also that in place of the English infinitive Arabic uses fully conjugated verb forms (without ب):

You want to eat. (You want you eat.)	بدّك تاكل.
He wants to travel. (He wants he travels.)	بدّه يسافر.

In verbs described in Unit 5 as hollow, an و, less commonly ي, appears in place of the ا of the perfect. The following table shows the conjugation of the hollow verb كان in the perfect and imperfect:

Imperfect	Perfect	
يكون	كان	هو
تكون	كانَت	هي
تكون	كُنت	انتَ
تكوني	كُنتِ	انتِ
أكون	كُنت	أنا

In addition to *sound* verbs like كتب and عرف and *hollow* verbs like كان and راح, Arabic has a third type called *lame* verbs. These verbs generally have ي as their third root letter, which alternates with ى (ألف مقصورة) depending on the subject/person marker attached. The following table shows the conjugation of the lame verb حكى "He spoke".

Imperfect	Perfect	
يحكي	حكى	هو
تحكي	حكَت	هي
تحكي	حكيت	انتَ
تحكي	حكيتِ	انتِ
أحكي	حكيت	أنا

تمرين رقم ١: (مكتوب)

املأ الفراغات

كتَب-يكتُب		سافر/يسافر		مشى/يمشي		أكل/ياكل		
				يمشي			أكل	هو
					مشَت	تاكل		هي
							أكلت	انتَ
تكتُبي			سافرتِ	تمشي		تاكلي		انتِ
	كتبت	أسافر						أنا

3. The comparative and superlative

The comparative and superlative forms of adjectives have the same structure. The comparative/superlative forms on the left are derived from the adjectives on the right:

bigger, the biggest أكبر	big كبير
father, the farthest أبعد	far بعيد
cheaper, the cheapest أرخص	cheap, inexpensive رخيص
colder, the coldest أبرد	cold بارد
cleaner أنظف	clean نظيف
tastier أطيَب	tasty طيّب

The comparative is generally followed by the preposition مِن, and the superlative directly by the noun. Compare:

Al-Salam Restaurant is cleaner than al-Sha'b Restaurant.	مطعم السلام أنظف من مطعم الشعب.
Food in al-Quds Restaurant is the tastiest in Amman.	الأكل في مطعم القدس أطيب أكل في عمّان.

Note that the comparative/superlative form does not change as a function of gender (masculine/feminine) or number (singular/plural).

This restaurant is the cheapest (restaurant).	هذا المطعم أرخص مطعَم.
My car is cheaper than Ahmad's car.	سيّارتي أرخص من سيّارة أحمد.
Korean cars are the cheapest cars.	السيّارات الكوريّة أرخص سيّارات.

تمرين رقم ٢: (المقارنة)

أ. املأ الفراغات

Fill in the cells giving the comperative for each adjective and give its meaning in English

	أبرد	بارِد
		قريب
tastier		
	أحسن	كويّس
	أبعد	
cheaper		
bigger		
	أغلى	
cleaner		
		صغير

ب. ترجم إلى العربيّة

1. My house is closer than your house.
2. His house is the closest (house).
3. The University of Texas has more than 50 thousand students.
4. The city of Chicago is bigger than Boston but smaller than New York City.
5. The trip from Chicago is longer than the trip from New York City.

4. كل شيء، كُلّ الأكل

The word كُلّ can mean both "every", "each" as well as "all" or "the whole of". In general, when it is followed by an indefinite noun, it is translated as "every, each", but when it is followed by a definite noun, it is translated as "all, the whole of".

Now translate the following phrases into English:

	كُلّ واحد عنده اسم أوّل واسم وسط
	كُلّ شيء موجود
	كل الأكل كويّس

5. لا والله

Arabic speakers use the word الله "God" in many expressions where an English translation with "God" would be inappropriate or unidiomatic. In some cases, it is simply a filler and should be left out of the translation.

Idiomatic translation	Literal translation	التعبير
I don't really know	By God I don't know.	والله ما باعرف
I hope so, maybe.	If God wills.	إن شاء الله
Trust me.	God is your witness.	الله وكيلَك

الدرس الخامس

كلمات الوحدة الجديدة

سَرفيس service car		أحسَن better, the best	
سَلَطة salad		أرخَص cheaper	
شيء thing, something		أطيَب tastier, the tastiest	
شيء حلو something sweet		أغلى more expensive	
صَباح morning		أقْرب closer	
صيني Chinese		أكلة dish, food	
طريق road		أيّ؟ which?	
طلَب-يطلُب to order		اعطيني give me	
على كيفِك as you wish		التي=اللي which, that	
غالي expensive		بتروح you go	
غَداء lunch		بَسّ only	
غير other than		بَعض some	
فُطور breakfast		بَيض eggs	
فِلس fils (1/1000 of a dinar)		تاخُذي you take	
فول fava beans		تكرم عينك thank you	
في رأيك in your opinion		حَلويّات sweets, dessert	
كُل شيء everything		خَروف lamb	
كنافة، هريسة، بقلاوة names of desserts		خصوصاً specially	
كيلو kilo		خُضار vegetables	
لازم must, should, it is necessary that		دُغري straight	
مأكولات dishes (things eaten)		دينار dinar (Jordanian currency)	
مَساء evening		رُبع quarter	
مشروبات drinks		رَخيص cheap	
مشوي baked, grilled		رزّ rice	
مَطعَم (ج. مَطاعِم) restaurant		روحي! Go!	
مفتوح open		زيّ بعَض like one another, similar	

excellent	مُمتاز	Indian	هِندي
maybe, perhaps	مُمكِن	or	وَلّا
found, available	مَوْجود	left	يَسار
location	مَوقِع	right	يَمين
هاتِف=تلفون			

أغنية (اسمع واحفظ)

(كلمات: منذر يونس، غناء: جواد إياد قبها)

'al-huwwaara l-huwwaara	عالهوّارة الهوارة
Dan rented a car	دان استأجر سيّارة
Traveled in it to the airport	سافر فيها للمطار
And flew in the first plane.	وطار بأوّل طيّارة
Dan traveled to Beirut,	سافر دان لبيروت
To speak Arabic and eat mulberries.	يحكي عربي وياكل توت.
Dan traveled to Syria,	سافر دان لسوريّة
To speak Arabic and drink water,	يحكي عربي ويشرب ميّة.
Dan traveled to Palestine,	سافر دان لفلسطين
To speak Arabic and eat figs.	يحكي عربي وياكل تين.
Dan traveled to Khartoum,	سافر دان للخرطوم
to speak Arabic and eat garlic.	يحكي عربي وياكل ثوم.
Dan traveled to Iraq,	سافر دان للعراق
to speak Arabic in the markets.	يحكي عربي في الأسواق.
Dan traveled to Tangier and Fez,	سافر دان طنجة وفاس
to speak Arabic with the people.	يحكي عربي مع الناس.

Dan traveled to Istanbul,	سافر دان لاسطنبول
to speak Turkish and eat fava beans.	يحكي تركي ويأكل فول.
Dan traveled to Versailles,	سافر دان لفرساي
to speak French and drink tea.	يحكي فرنسي ويشرب شاي.

تمرين رقم ١

In your notebook, write each of the food items under its correct category. Which item can technically be under two categories?!

كنافة، هريسة، بطاطا، خروف، سمك، دجاج، لحم بقر، برتقال، حليب، موز، تفاح، بندورة، بقلاوة، شاي، قهوة، بيبسي، فول، سفن اب، ميراندا، عصير، عصير ليمون، كابتشينو

مشروبات	خُضار	حلويات	لحم	فواكه

تمرين رقم ٢

Write each of the following food items under the appropriate meal type.

بيض، كورن فليكس مع حليب، سلطة، سمك، دجاج مع خُضار، همبورجر، بان كيك، رُزّ، خبز، سندويشة جبن

غداء	فطور

تمرين رقم ٣

Write down the opposite of the word in the space provided.

	أبعد		رخيص
	مساء		كبير
	يمين		بعيد

تمرين رقم ٤

Connect the letters to form words and translate each one into English.

		م أ ك و ل ا ت
baked, grilled		م ش و ي
		ف ل ا ف ل
		ب ي ض
		م ش ر و ب ا ت
		خ ص و ص ا ً
		ح ل ي ب
		ا ل أ ر د ن
		ا ل م ا ض ي
		م م ت ا ز

تمرين رقم ٥

Word search: Translate each of the following words into English, then find it in the table below. Some letters are used more than once.

	دقيقة		اقرب
	او		اي
	ركب		سُكر
	مشروبات		مع
	لا		موجود
	رجع		يمين
	بيت		بندورة
			فول

ف	د	و	ج	و	م	ر	ا	س	ي	ا
و	ق	ر	ك	ف	م	ز	م	ك	م	ق
ل	ي	ك	د	ب	ع	ع	ج	ر	ي	ر
ا	ق	ب	ك	ي	ة	ر	و	د	ن	ب
و	ة	ا	ل	ت	ا	ب	و	ر	ش	م

تمرين رقم ٦: شفهي (في الصفّ)

A. You and your classmate want to go to a restaurant to eat. You cannot agree on a restaurant. Negotiate with each other and tell your partner why your choice is better.
Example: It is cleaner, cheaper, closer, good food, not crowded, they have the best _____, etc.

B. In the restaurant. One or two people go to an Arab/Middle East restaurant and order food, drinks, and dessert.

الوحدة السابعة: السكن

أهمّ الكلمات والتعابير الجديدة

طاولة	table	إعلان	announcement, notice
فُرن	oven	إيجار (للإيجار)	rent (for rent)
كاسة (ج. كاسات)	cup	اشتَرى-يشتَري	to buy
كُرسي (ج. كَراسي)	chair	انتقل-ينتقل	to move
كلّم-يكلّم=حكى-يحكي مع	to speak with, call	ثلاّجة	refrigerator
كَهرَباء	electricity	جَريدة	newspaper
مَصعَد	elevator	حَديث	modern
مَفروش	furnished	رئيسي	main
منطَقة (ج. مناطق)	area	ركِب-يركَب	to ride
مَوقِع	location	سَرير	bed
نظّف-ينظّف	to clean	سوق	market
هُناك=فيه	there is	شُقّة فُندُقيّة	hotel apartment
		صَحن (ج. صُحون)	dish

تمارين تحضيرية

تمرين رقم ١: جمع/مفرد: أكمل الجدول

يوم	صحن	شهر	مِنطقة	كُرسي	أسبوع	شقّة
						apartment
	صُحون					شُقَق

تمرين رقم ٢: املأ الفراغات

١. فدوى _____ (حتى، نظّفت، غطّت) الغرفة قبل ما إملي انتقلت للشقّة.

٢. في الشقّة _____ (طاولة، كهرباء، فُرن) كبيرة و٦ كراسي.

٣. الشقّة في _____ (وقت، جريدة، منطقة) ممتازة في بيروت.

٤. ذهبت الى _____ (الكامل، السوق، الشقّة) واشتريت سرير وطاولة وكراسي.

٥. فدوى _____ (فكّرت، اشتريت، لاقيت) إملي عربيّة لأنّها بتحكي عربي ممتاز.

٦. _____ (كلّمت، ركبت، لاقيت) الباص من البيت للجامعة، الباص أخذ حوالي ربع ساعة.

الدرس الأوّل

النصّ الأوّل–مشاهدة: وين رايحة تسكني يا إملي؟

كلمات جديدة

كيفِك=كيف حالِك

مُريح	comfortable	تَمام	great, perfect
صَحّ	true, correct	سأل–يسأل	to ask
لاقى–يلاقي=وجَد–يوجَد	to find	قَعَد–يقعُد	to stay
جَريدة	newspaper	فكّر–يفكّر	to think
هَي	here is	فِكرة	idea
إعلان	announcement, notice	مَفروش	furnished

تعابير

طول الوَقت the whole time

شَقّة فُندُقيّة hotel apartment

لا شكراً على واجب you are welcome, not a problem

أسئلة

١. إيش المشكلة في السكن مع العائلة؟ ـــــــــــــــــــــــ

٢. إيش المشكلة في الشقق الفندقيّة؟ ـــــــــــــــــــــــ

٣. في رأي الموظفة، وين لازم تسكن إملي؟ ـــــــــــــــــــــ

٤. إيش كان في الجريدة؟ ـــــــــــــــــــــــ

النصّ الثاني-قراءة: للإيجار

١.

> للإيجار
>
> شقق "الأندلُسية" في عمان الغربية
>
> شقق مفروشة، موقع ممتاز في عمان الغربية.
>
> شبابيك "دبل جلاس".
>
> انتركوم وكاميرات حِراسة ٢٤ ساعة في اليوم.
>
> مطبخ كامل مع ثلاجة، فرن غاز ايطالي حديث آخر موديل.
>
> غرفة أكل كبيرة، غرفة نوم، غرفة جلوس مع تلفزيون بلازما ٢٣ انش، حمّام جاكوزي
>
> مصعد ايطالي وكراج سيارة
>
> تلفون: ٦٧٩٩-٨٠

٢.

> للإيجار
>
> شُقَق في منطقة الجبيهة-عمان
>
> للطلاب: شقق صغيرة وشقق كبيرة وشقق استوديو
>
> شقة مفروشة للإيجار: اسبوعي ٣٥٠ دينار، شهري ١٤٠٠ دينار : سنوي ٨٠٠٠
>
> دينار غرفتين نوم، حمامين، غرفة جلوس
>
> تلفون: ٨٩٣٥-٧٥

كلمات جديدة

فُرن oven		إيجار (للإيجار) rent (for rent)	
حَديث modern		مَوقِع location	
آخِر latest, most recent		حِراسة security/guard	
مَصعَد elevator		كامِل full, complete	
مِنطَقة area		ثلّاجة refrigerator	

أسئلة

1. There are several English words in the two ads. Draw a circle around each of them.
2. What is the weekly, monthly, and yearly rent of the furnished apartment in the *Jubeiha* area?

الدرس الثاني

مشاهدة: فيه غرفة للإيجار؟

كلمات جديدة

سَرير bed	رَئيسي main
جَديد new	وحدِك by yourself
كَهرَباء electricity	ثاني other, second
باستنّاك (استنّى-يستنّى) I wait for you	ثلّاجة refrigerator
سُؤال question	فُرن oven
أخير last	كُرسي (ج. كَراسي) chair
اسأَل! Ask!	طاوِلة table
مِثل like	لازِم must, have to
تخصُّص specialization	اشتَرى-يشتَري to buy

تعابير

أيّ وَقت any time
عَن جَدّ؟ seriously?

أسئلة

١.   كيف الغرفة اللي (which) سألت عنها إملي؟ _____

٢.   هي بعيدة عن الجامعة؟ _____

٣.   من إيش هي قريبة كمان؟ _____

٤.   مين ساكن في الشقّة؟ _____

٥.   إيش فيه أثاث (furniture) في الشقّة؟ _____

٦.   إيش ما فيها؟ _____

٧.   كم أجرة الشقّة في الشهر؟ _____

٨.   أي السؤال الأخير اللي سألته إملي؟ _____

٩.   رايح يكون فيه (is there going to be) مشكلة؟ ليش أو ليش لأ؟ _____

الدرس الثالث

قراءة: مذكّرات إملي

أسكن الآن في فندق الأندلس، لكن أريد أن اسكن في شقة. الفندق نظيف وقريب من الجامعة، لكن الفنادق غالية طبعاً، وانا طالبة فقيرة! أريد أن أسكن مع طالبات عربيّات حتى أتكلّم العربيّة كل الوقت.

أريد شقّة قريبة من الجامعة. لا أريد أن أشتري سيّارة. يمكن طبعاً أن أركب الباص، الباص رخيص وهناك باص كلّ خمس أو عشر دقائق، لكن أحبّ المشي، خصوصاً لأنّ الطقس هنا ممتاز في هذه الأيّام.

قرأت إعلاناً في الجريدة عن غرفة للإيجار في شقّة. كلّمت طالبة اسمها فدوى وسألتها عن الغرفة، فقالت إنّها تسكن في شقّة مع طالبة أخرى وهناك غرفة للايجار. ذهبت إلى الشقّة والتقيت بفدوى وصاحبتها رانية، ورأيت الغرفة. قالت فدوى إنّها آسفة لأنّ الملابس والكُتب والصحون وكاسات الشاي في كلّ مكان. وقالت إنّها سَوفَ تنظّف الشقّة قبل أن أنتقل اليها.

أنا الآن لا أعرف ماذا أعمل. هل أسكن مع فدوى وصاحبتها؟ أخاف أن تبقى الملابس والكتب والصحون وكاسات الشاي في كلّ مكان. ولكن ...

كلمات جديدة

رأى-يرى=شاف-يشوف to see	الآن=هلّأ now
مَلابس clothes	أراد-يُريد (أن) to want (to)
صحن (ج. صُحون) dish	فَقير poor
كاسة (ج. كاسات) cup	حَتّى in order to
سَوفَ will	تكلّم-يتكلّم=حكى-يحكي to speak with, call
نظّف-ينظّف to clean	يُمكِن it is possible that
قبل أن=قبل ما before	ركِب-يركَب to ride
انتقل-ينتقل to move	هُناك=فيه there is
ماذا؟=إيش؟ what?	مَشي walking
هَل whether (also used to ask yes/no questions)	خُصوصاً especially
خاف-يخاف to be afraid	أخرى=ثانية another
بقي-يبقى to remain	التقى-يلتقي to meet

أسئلة

1. Why does Emily want to live in an apartment?
2. Why does she want to live with Arab students?
3. Why does Emily want an apartment close to the university?
4. Who are Fadwa and Ranya?
5. Why was Fadwa sorry?
6. What is Fadwa going to do with the clothes, dishes, and tea cups?
7. Do you think that Emily should move to the apartment? Why? Why not?

تمرين: أكمل الجُمل التاليّة

Comprehension Exercise: complete the following sentences based on the reading about Emily's Diary.

١. تسكن إملى _____ (هلّأ) في فندق الاندلس.

٢. إملي _____ _____ تسكن في شقة مع طالبات عربيّات.

٣. الفندق _____ وقريب من الجامعة، لكن _____ غالي كثير.

٤. إملي _____ شقة قريبة من الجامعة لأنها لا _____ _____ تشتري سيّارة.

٥. قرأت إملي إعلاناً في _____ عن غرفة للايجار في شقّة.

٦. تسكن فدوى مع صاحبتها _____.

٧. كانت الملابس و_____ و_____ وكاسات _____ في كُلّ مكان.

٨. قالت فدوى انها _____ وسوف تنظّف _____ قبل أن تنتقل اليها إملي.

٩. إملي تريد أن تسكن مع طالبات عربيّات _____ تتكلّم العربيّة طول _____.

١٠. إملي تحب _____ خصوصاً لأنّ _____ في عمّان مُمتاز.

الدرس الرابع

قواعد

١. راح - يروح - رايِح

Whereas رُحت (I went), and أروح (I go) are verbs, the related word رايِح is not. It is in fact a noun, "a goer", although the English translation may render it as verbal: "going". It is grammatically treated like a noun or an adjective and not a verb. That is why in a sentence like: إيش رايحة تدرسي؟ "What are you going to study?", رايحة ends in تاء مربوطة and does not have the prefix and suffix characteristic of the imperfect form of the verb. The following table compares the different forms of رايح as a noun with those of another noun مسافِر "traveler".

	pl. f.	pl. m.	sing. f.	sing. m.
traveler	مُسافِرات	مسافِرين	مسافِرة	مُسافِر
going (a goer)	رايحات	رايحين	رايحة	رايِح

The verb following رايح (or its derivatives) is in the imperfect tense and is fully conjugated for person. It also carries future meaning such as "going to study".

هو	رايح يدرس
هي	رايحة تدرس
انتَ	رايح تدرس
انتِ	رايحة تدرسي
أنا	رايح أدرس

2. The imperative الأمر

The imperative form of the verb in Levantine Arabic is derived from the imperfect form following two steps:

1. drop the imperfect prefix,
2. insert a vowel if the resulting form begins with a two-consonant sequence.

Imperative form		Removal of imperfect prefix		Imperfect form	
قول	اكتُب	قول	كتُب	تقول	تكتُب
quul	iktubu	quul	ktub	taquul	taktub
Say!	Write!			you (m.s.) say	you (m.s.) write

Three exceptional verbs

Although the two verbs أخذ, "he took", and أكل, "he ate", generally behave like sound verbs in the perfect and imperfect conjugations, their imperative forms do not follow the rules above. On the other hand, the imperative form of the verb "to come" is not based on the verb أجا–ييجي, which is used to express the idea of coming in the perfect and the imperfect, but is derived from a different source altogether. All three imperative forms should be learned as exceptions.

Imperative	Perfect-imperfect
خُذ، خُذي	أخذ–ياخُذ
كُل، كُلي	أكل–ياكُل
تَعال–تَعالي	أجا–ييجي

تمرين

Fill in the empty cells in the following table

انتِ			انتَ		
Imperative	Imperfect	Perfect	Imperative	Imperfect	Perfect
اقعدي	تقعدي	قعدتِ	اقعد	تقعد	قعدت
شوفي	تشوفي	شفتِ	شوف	تشوف	شُفت
ادرسي					
					رُحت
				تحكي	
اشرَبي					

3. Agreement in noun-adjective phrases

Adjectives generally agree with the nouns they modify in gender, number, and definiteness:

An Arab male student	طالب عربي
An Arab female student	طالبة عربيّة
Arab female students	طالبات عربيّات

If the modified noun has a non-human plural reference, then it is treated as a singular feminine noun for purposes of agreement:

(The) hotels are expensive.	الفنادق غالية
Inexpensive modern apartments	شقق رخيصة حديثة
These days (هذه = this, feminine)	هذه الأيّام

4. The case system in فصحى

Nouns and adjectives فصحى may have different endings according to their function in the sentence. The rules of case and mood assignment are numerous and can be quite intimidating to the beginning learner. Fortunately for you as an Arabic student, spoken Arabic does not have a case system. The relevance of the system increases as your writing skills develop because writing in Arabic is done mainly in فصحى. For now, all you need to remember is that إعلان and إعلاناً are two forms of the same word, with no difference whatsoever in meaning. When you start writing term papers in Arabic, you will need to know to write إعلاناً if the word is the object of a verb and إعلان if it is the subject.

You may have noticed that a number of Arabic adverbs end in اً, such as شكراً، عفواً، طبعاً، خصوصاً, etc. While اً may have been a case marker at some point, you should think of these words as having one form only, with اً.

Sociolinguistic corner

1. While in شامي, the stem بدّ (with an attached pronominal suffix) is used to indicate "wanting", فصحى uses the verb أراد–يُريد.

	فصحى	شامي
هو	أراد–يُريد	بدّه
هي	أرادَت–تُريد	بدها
انتَ	أرَدت–تُريد	بدّك
انتِ	أردتِ–تريدي(ن)	بدِّك
أنا	أردْت–أريد	بدّي

أراد is followed by the particle أن translated as "to" when a verb follows:

أريد أن أسكن I want to live

أن also follows the word يُمكِن (or مُمكِن) "it is possible that, perhaps". Compare:

	شامي	فصحى
I want to live	بدّي أسكن	أريد أن أسكن
It is possible (for me) to ride	يمكن أركب	يمكن أن أركب

When a noun follows يريد–أراد and يمكن, no أن is used, as in أريد شقّة قريبة من الجامعة.

2. هل is a فصحى particle that initiates questions which require a yes/no answer. The equivalent in شامي has no such particle but uses a rising intonation.

	شامي	فصحى
Do I live with Fadwa and her friend?	أسكن مع فدوى وصاحبتها؟	هل أسكن مع فدوى وصاحبتها؟

3. سوفَ
Note that سوفَ is the فصحى equivalent of رايح "going to" in شامي, as you read in Emily's Diary: سوفَ تنظّف الشقّة "she will clean the apartment".

4. لا أعرف/ما باعرف
It was pointed out in the discussion of negation in Unit 3 that in شامي verbs are negated by ما and non-verbal elements by مش. The rules of negation in فصحى are more complicated than those of شامي, with distinctions made in the former among verbs referring to the past, present, or future. فصحى rules of negation will be discussed in more detail in Unit 15, but for now it will help you to know that verbs in the imperfect (present) are negated by لا, as in لا أعرف "I don't know".

الدرس الخامس

كلمات الوحدة الجديدة

إيجار rent (للإيجار for rent)	آخِر latest, most recent
اسأَل! Ask!	أخرى=ثانية another
اشتَرى-يشتَري to buy	أخير last
الآن=هلأ now	أيّ وَقت any time
التقى-يلتقي to meet	إعلان announcement, notice

to think	فكّر–يفكّر	to move	انتقل–ينتقِل
idea	فِكرة	I wait for you	باستنّاك (استنّى–يستنّى)
before	قبل أن=قبل ما	to remain	بقي–يبقى
to stay	قَعَد–يقعُد	specialization	تخصُّص
cup	كاسة (ج. كاسات)	تكلّم–يتكلّم=حكى–يحكي	
full, complete	كامِل	to speak with, call	
book	كِتاب (ج. كُتُب)	great, perfect	تَمام
chair	كُرسي (ج. كَراسي)	other, second	ثاني
electricity	كَهرَباء	refrigerator	ثلاّجة
كيفك=كيف حالك		new	جَديد
you are welcome, not a problem	لا شكراً على واجب	newspaper	جَريدة
		in order to	حَتّى
must, have to	لازم	modern	حَديث
to find	لاقى–يلاقي=وجَد–يوجَد	security/guard	حِراسة
what?	ماذا؟=إيش؟	to be afraid	خاف–يخاف
like	مثل	especially	خُصوصاً
comfortable	مُريح	to see	رأى–يرى=شاف–يشوف
walking	مَشي	main	رئيسي
elevator	مَصعَد	to ride	ركِب–يركَب
furnished	مَفروش	to ask	سأل–يسأل
clothes	مَلابِس	question	سُؤال
area	مِنطَقة	bed	سَرير
location	مَوقِع	hotel apartment	شُقَة فُندُقيّة
to clean	نظّف–ينظّف	true, correct	صَحّ
whether (also used to ask yes/no questions)	هَل	dish	صحن (ج. صُحون)
there is	هُناك=فيه	table	طاولة
here is	هَي	the whole time	طول الوَقت
by yourself	وحدك	seriously?	عَن جَدّ؟
it is possible that	يُمكِن	oven	فُرن
		poor	فَقير

أغنية: اسمع وأكمل الفراغات

(كلمات: منذر يونس، غِناء: جواد إياد قبها)

Small house	بيت ـــــــــــــــ،
Big door	باب ـــــــــــــــ،
Hot kitchen	ـــــــــــــــ حامي،
A lot of people:	ناس كثير:
My father and my mother	أبوي و ـــــــــــــــ،
My maternal uncle and paternal uncle	خالي وعمّي،
My brother and my sister	ـــــــــــــــ وأختي،
My grandfather and my grandmother	سيدي وستّي،
A lot of people,	ناس ـــــــــــــــ،
A lot of food,	ـــــــــــــــ كثير،
Coffee and tea,	قهوة و ـــــــــــــــ،
...	...
Where is the juice?	وين ـــــــــــــــ؟

كلمات متقاطعة (مكتوب في البيت)

١٠	٩	٨	٧	٦	٥	٤	٣	٢	١	
										١
										٢
										٣
										٤
										٥
										٦
										٧
										٨
										٩
										١٠

عمودي	أفقي
١. مُفرد (singular) مناطق؛ في الشقّة المفروشة	١. جمع "مطعم"؛ عكس "غني"
٣. عكس "آخِر"؛ في الشقّة المفروشة، فيها أشياء باردة	٣. يدرس في المدرسة أو الجامعة
٥. من "أربعة"	٤. موجود في الشقّة المفروشة
٧. جمع "فلس"؛ من فُصول (seasons) السنة	٥. من "اثنين"
٩. من اليمن	٧. عكس "أوّل"؛ عكس "غالي"
١٠. في الشقّة المفروشة، نأكل فيها	٩. بين (between) خمسة وسبعة.
	١٠. عاصمة الأردن

احكي واكتب (حضّر في البيت واحكي في الصف)

Prepare at home, speak in class, and then write it up (around 50 words) and turn it in.

1. Describe your house/apartment/room to your partner. Let him/her know where it is, the furniture/appliances it has, how many students live there, the monthly/yearly rent, whether the internet/water/electricity are included in the rent, etc.

2. Create a dialogue with your classmate. It could be more than two people. One side has a room in a house or apartment to rent, and the other is looking for a room. Ask/answer questions about the rent, the furniture, the location, etc. Make an appointment to see the apartment. Negotiate the rent.

الوحدة الثامنة: التسوّق

أهمّ الكلمات والتعابير الجديدة

مَشغول busy	watermelon بطّيخ
قرّر-يقرّر to decide	balcony بَلكونة
مُريح comfortable	market سوق
سِعر (ج. أسعار) price	food طَعام=أكل
شُغل work	to meet لاقى-يلاقي
بكثير by a lot, very	pricing (system) تسعيرة
طَيِّب tasty	total مجموع
أقلّ مِن less than	local بَلَدي
نوم sleeping	to forget نسي-ينسى

تمرين رقم ١: وافق بين الكلمة والصورة

بطيخ   بلكونة   سوق   طعام   لاقى-يلاقي

تمرين رقم ٢: املأ الفراغات

١.   هذا التفاح _____. (تسعيرة، مجموع، بلدي)

٢.   اليوم أنا _____. (نوم، نسي، مشغول)

٣.   إملي _____ أن تسكن مع فدوى لأنّها كانت تعبانة من الفندق. (قرّرت، لاقَت، نسيت)

٤.   هذا الكرسي _____. لمّا قعدت عليه نمت. (مشغول، مُريح، مجموع)

٥.   _____ (الشغل، الطعام، النوم) في الأردن _____ (طيّب، شراء، أرخص) من الطعام في أمريكا _____. (بكثير، على شان، سِعر)

النصّ الأوّل-مشاهدة: إملي بدها تشتري سرير

كلمات جديدة

أسهل easier		مَشغول busy	
رجع-يرجَع to return		فاضي available, not busy	
منيح=كويس		شيء (ج. أشياء) thing, item	
اغراض items, things (for house, etc.)		مول mall	
		أسرع faster	

تعابير

ليش لأ؟ Why not?

إيش رأيِك؟ What is your opinion?

أسئلة

١.   أيش إملي بدّها تشتري؟   _____

٢.   لأيّ ساعة فدوى مشغولة؟   _____

٣.   من وين ممكن يشتروا (they buy) سرير؟   _____

٤.   كيف رايحين يروحوا (they go) حتى يشتروا سرير؟ ليش؟   _____

النصّ الثاني–مشاهدة: إملي تتسوّق للمطبخ؟

كلمات جديدة

يمين right		مُريح comfortable
نسي–ينسى to forget		أرض floor
شاف–يشوف to see		نوم sleeping
غير another, other		سوق market
مَلحمة butcher shop		لاقى–يلاقي to meet

تعابير

بكثير by a lot

بعد الظهر afternoon

مثل مبارح like yesterday

أسئلة

١.   امتى رايحين يروحوا للسوق؟   _____

٢.   أيش رايحة إملي تشتري؟   _____

٣.   أيش نسيت فدوى؟   _____

النصّ الثالث–مشاهدة: إملي في الملحمة

كلمات جديدة

تسعيرة (system) pricing

حُكومة government

بَلَدي local

زَعّل–يزعّل to make someone upset

حَدا one, anyone

حضرتِك formal way of saying "you" to a woman

تعبير

ميّة في الميّة ١٠٠%

على شان هيك for this reason

أسئلة

١. حسب اللّحّام (according to the butcher)، ليش اللحم في ملحمة "الإخلاص" أغلى؟

_____

٢. كم كيلو لحم إملي اشترت؟

_____

الدرس الثاني

مشاهدة: إملي في سوق الخضار

كلمات جديدة

قَدّيش؟=كَم؟ how much, how many?

فضّل–يفضّل to prefer

قِرش piastre, 10 fils

ساعد–يساعد to help

جرّب–يجرّب to try something out

كيس bag

بطّيخ watermelon

مجموع total

تعابير

من فضلك=لو سمحت

على شانِك for you

بصراحة frankly

اثنين كيلو two kilograms

حاضر another way of saying "yes" or "right away"

على عِيوني I will be happy to ... (literally on my eyes)

شكراً جزيلا thank you very much

يسلموا ايديك thank you (literally may God bless your hand)

أسئلة

١. كم نوع (kind, type) موز فيه؟ _____

٢. بكم الموز الصومالي؟ _____

٣. كم نوع تفّاح فيه؟ _____

٤. إيش أحسن تفّاح حسب بيّاع (seller) الخضار؟ _____

٥. إيش اشترت إملي؟ _____

٦. إملي اشترت بطيخ أو لأ؟ _____

٧. كم المجموع؟ _____

الدرس الثالث

(((قراءة: مذكّرات إملي

قرّرت أن أسكن مع فَدوى وصاحبتها. الشقّة ليست نظيفة كثيراً، فالكتب والملابس والكاسات والصحون في كلّ مكان. ولكن هكذا كانت شقّتي عندما كنت في الولايات المتّحدة.

الشقّة كبيرة: فيها ثلاث غرف نوم وغرفة جلوس وحمام ومطبخ صغير، وفيها أيضاً بلكونة صغيرة. وهي رخيصة ومفروشة وقريبة من الجامعة.

ذهبَت فدوى معي أوّل أمس الى "مكّة مول" واشترينا سريراً. اليوم ذهبت الى سوق الخضار واشتريت فواكه وخضار وحليب وعصير وخبز.

أسعار الخضار والفواكه في السوق وأسعار الأكل في المطاعم أرخص من أمريكا بكثير. كيلو البندورة مثلاً بأقلّ من دينار، يعني أقلّ من دولار ونصف. رخيص جدّاً، وطيّب جدّاً أيضاً. الفواكه والخضار هنا أطيب بكثير من الفواكه والخضار في أمريكا.

كلمات جديدة

طَعام=أكل food	قرّر–يقرّر to decide
مثلاً for example	ليسَ، ليسَت=مِش not
بكثير by a lot, very	هكذا=هيك thus, this way
يعني it means, in other words	عندَما=لَمّا when
نصف=نُصّ half	أيضاً=كَمان also
طَيِّب tasty	بَلكونة balcony
	سِعر (ج. أسعار) price

تعابير

أوّل أمس=أوّل مبارح the day before yesterday

أقلّ مِن less than

أسئلة

1. How was Emily's apartment in America?
2. What does Fadwa's apartment have?
3. Why did Emily and Fadwa go to Makka Mall?
4. Compare the food in Jordan with the food in America.

تمرين

The following words, all taken from Emily's Diary above, end in the "accusative" case marker ا. All of them are adverbs except one. Identify the one word that is not an adverb and indicate its function in the sentence (subject, object of a verb, or object of a preposition): كثيراً، أيضاً، سريراً، مثلاً، جدّاً.

الدرس الرابع

قواعد

٦. ليس

As was mentioned earlier, while شامي uses مِش, فصحى negates non-verbal elements with ليس or غير. The latter is conjugated for person as a hollow verb in the perfect:

هو ليسَ، هي ليسَت، انتَ لستَ، انتِ لستِ، أنا لستُ

ف .2

ف is a conjunction similar in many respects to و "and". The main difference is that ف has an additional meaning of "so", "since", or "because", depending on the context. A good English rendering of ف in writing is the semi-colon (;).

Now translate the following sentence into English:

الشقّة ليست نظيفة كثيراً، فالكتب والملابس والكاسات والصحون في كلّ مكان.

اثنين كيلو .3

You learned in Unit 1 that Arabic has dual numbers. So the equivalent of English "two houses" is بيتين. You also learned that with the numbers 3–10, the plural form of the noun is used: ثلاث بيوت. There are a few nouns, mainly associated with foreign currencies (dollar, Euro, pound (guinea)) and weights and measures (meter, kilometer, gram, kilogram) that violate this rule. Examples are:

اثنين كيلو، ثلاثة كيلو، أربعة دولار، ستة يورو، ١٠ جنيه

4. Subject-person markers: the plural

So far, you've been introduced to the five singular pronouns (هو، هي، انتَ، انت، أنا) and the five corresponding verb conjugations. Spoken Arabic has another three pronouns referring to the plural. The following table includes all eight in their separate forms and as they appear on the verb درس in its perfect and imperfect forms.

Imperfect/Present		Perfect/Present		Pronoun
yadrus	يدرُس	daras	درَس	هو he
tadrus	تدرُس	darasat	درسَت	هي she
yadrusuu	يدرسوا	darasuu	درسوا	هُمّ they
tadrus	تدرُس	darast	درست	انتَ you (m.s.)
tadrusii	تدرسي	darasti	درستِ	انت you (f.s.)
tadrusuu	تدرسوا	darastu	درستوا	انتو you (pl.)
'adrus	أدرُس	darast	درست	أنا I
nadrus	نَدرُس	darasna	درسنا	احنا we

Note that the ا at the end of the plural forms درستوا/تدرسوا and درسوا/يدرسوا is silent; it is written but not pronounced.

تمرين رقم ١ مكتوب (في البيت)

	كتَب-يكتُب		تعلّم-يتعلّم		اشترى-يشتري	
هو						يشتري
هي		تكتُب				
هم	كتبوا			تعلّموا		
انتَ						
انتِ	كتبتِ				تتعلّمي	
انتو	تكتبوا		تعلّمتوا			
أنا			تعلّمت			
احنا	نكتُب					

تمرين رقم ٢

Conjugate each verb given in parentheses in the perfect (past) plural tense.

١. املي وفدوى _____ (اشترى) سرير من المول.

إملي وفدوى اشتروا سرير من المول.

٢. الاستاذ والطلاب _____ (ذهب) الى المطعم.

٣. الطلاب _____ (درس) العربية في جامعة كورنيل.

٤. انا و صاحبي _____ (قرر) ان نسكن في شقة قريبة من الجامعة.

٥. انتو _____ (أكل) في مطعم "صحراء"؟

٦. لأ، احنا _____ (أكل) في مطعم "علاء الدين"!

٧. الأولاد _____ (كان) في غرفة الجلوس.

٨. املي وفدوى _____ (أخذ) التاكسي من الفندق للسوق.

٩. انتو _____ (كتب) كتاب؟!

١٠. املي والشرطي _____ (فتّش) على جواز السفر.

5. Roots and families

It was mentioned in Unit 5 that most Arabic verbs and nouns are derived from three or four-letter roots. Four-letter roots will be excluded from grammar discussions in this book because of their rare occurrence.

Roots are the basic elements of meaning, and words derived from the same root represent extensions or modifications of the basic meaning of that root. For example, the root ك.ت.ب /ktb/ has the basic meaning of "writing". The following list includes some of the words derived from this root and their meanings:

to correspond	كاتَب	he wrote	كتَب
writer	كاتِب	it was written	انْكَتَب
writing	كِتابة	something written, a letter	مَكتوب
booklet	كُتَيِّب	book	كِتاب
office	مَكتَب	correspondence	مُكاتَبة
old Qur'anic school	كُتّاب	library, bookshop	مَكتَبة

تمرين رقم ٣ (في البيت)

The following words are derived from 10 roots. Group together the words that derive from the same root and give its general meaning. Follow the example given.

أجرة، للإيجار   أ.ج.ر   rent

أجرةً، أرخص، أسكن، أقرب، أنظف، الجمعة، المجموع، المشروبات، تخصّصنا، تسكني، تشربي، تقريباً، تنظّف، جامعة، خصوصاً، رخيص، قريب، شُغل، لحمة، للإيجار، للشرب، مشغولة، ملحمة، نظيف.

6. The إضافة, the adjective phrase, and the equational sentence

The إضافة construction is described as consisting of two nouns with a special relationship, like غرفة جلوس، عاصمة سوريا, etc. It is important to distinguish this construction from noun-adjective phrases and certain noun-noun and noun-adjective combinations that function as full sentences. The following examples illustrate the difference between these three types of structure:

إضافة		عاصمة الدولة	the country's capital, the capital of the country
Noun-adjective phrase	definite	المدينة الكبيرة	the big city
	indefinite	مدينة كبيرة	a big city
Complete (equational) sentence		المدينة كبيرة	The city is big.

تمرين رقم ٤ (كتابي، في البيت)

a. For each of the following, give an English translation, then indicate whether it is an إضافة construction, a noun-phrase combination or an equational sentence.

b. Give a different example of each of the structures in the space provided.

Your example	إضافة	The government's pricing (system)	تسعيرة الحكومة
			ملحمة ثانية
			ملحمة "الإخلاص"
			التسعيرة الحكومية
			موز بلدي
			تفّاح أمريكي
			الموز الصومالي
			الشقّة نظيفة
			الولايات المتّحدة
			غرفة نوم
			مطبخ صغير
			بلكونة صغيرة
			الشقّة مفروشة
			سوق الخضار
			أسعار الطعام

٧. أقلّ مِن

Note that أقلّ (مِن) is the comparative form of قليل "few, little". It looks different from other comparative forms because it is derived from a "doubled" root in which the second and third consonants are identical. In certain words derived from that root such as أقلّ, the two lams form a "geminate" or "doubled" consonant; in others, such as قليل, the two lams are separated by a vowel such as ي in this case.

Sociolinguistic corner

Some of the words written in Emily's Diary are found in فصحى, and have equivalents in شامي:

فصحى	شامي
ليس، ليست	مش
هكذا	هيك
عندما	لمّا
أيضاً	كمان
ذهبت	رُحت
أمس	مبارح
جدّاً	كثير
هُنا	هون

الدرس الخامس

كلمات الوحدة الجديدة

easier أسهل

closer أقرب

less than أقلّ مِن

أوّل أمس=أوّل مبارح

the day before yesterday

also أيضاً=كَمان

What is your opinion? إيش رأيك؟

two kilograms اثنين كيلو

items, things (for house, etc.) اغراض

watermelon بطّيخ

afternoon بعد الظهر

by a lot, very بكثير

local بَلَدي

balcony بَلكونة

pricing (system) تسعيرة

to try something out جرّب-يجرّب

another way of saying "yes" حاضر

or "right away"

one, anyone حَدا=حَدّ

formal way of حضرتك

saying "you" to a woman

government حُكومة

to return رجع-يرجَع

to make someone upset زعّل-يزعّل

price (ج. أسعار) سِعر

market سوق

why not? ليش لأ؟		to see شاف-يشوف	
like yesterday مثل مبارح		work شُغل	
for example مثلاً		thank you very much شكراً جزيلاً	
total مجموع		thing, item شيء (ج. أشياء)	
comfortable مُريح		food طَعام=أكل	
busy مَشغول		tasty طَيِّب	
من فضلك=لو سمحت		for this reason على شان هيك	
منيح=كويس		for you على شانِك	
mall مول		I will be happy to ... على عيوني	
100% ميّة في الميّة		(literally on my eyes)	
to forget نسي-ينسى		when عندَما=لمّا	
half نِصف=نُصّ		another, other غير	
sleeping نوم		available, not busy فاضي	
thus, this way هكَذا=هيك		how much, how many? قَدّيش؟=كَم؟	
yislamu ideyk يسلموا ايديك		to decide قرّر-يقرِّر	
thank you (literally may			
God bless your hand)		bag كيس	
it means, in other words يعني		to meet لاقى-يلاقي	
right يمين		not ليسَ، ليسَت=مِش	

تمرين رقم ١: جذور وعائلات

Give the root for each of the following words and then group them in families. Follow the example.

أسعار، أقلّ، يشتغل، طعام، مجموع، سِعر، سريع، شُغل، مطعم، تسعيرة، الجامعة، بسُرعة، مشغول، نوم، الجمعة، قليل، ينام، اجتماعي، أسرع.

مثال (example)

سريع، بسُرعة، أسرع   س.ر.ع   fast, speed

تمرين رقم ٢

Form sentences using the comparative. Follow the example.

هذه الشقّة/شقتك/رخيص
هذه الشقّة أرخص من شقتك.

١. اللغة الفرنسيّة/اللغة العربيّة/سهل

٢. الأكل العربي/الأكل الفرنسي/طيّب

٣. سعر البندورة في السوق/سعر التفّاح/قليل

٤. سيارة الكورڤت/سيارة الفيراري/سريع

تمرين رقم ٣

Emily wants to travel with her friend Dan! Include Emily in Dan's adventures and conjugate each verb accordingly!
Examples:

دان استأجر سيّارة ← دان واملي استأجروا سيّارة

يحكي عربي وياكل توت ← يحكوا عربي وياكلوا توت.

'al-huwwaara l-huwwaara	عالهوّارة الهوارة
Dan rented a car	دان استأجر سيّارة
Traveled in it to the airport	سافر فيها للمطار
And flew in the first plane.	وطار بأوّل طيّارة
Dan traveled to Beirut,	سافر دان لبيروت
To speak Arabic and eat mulberries.	يحكي عربي وياكل توت.
Dan traveled to Syria,	سافر دان لسوريّة
To speak Arabic and drink water,	يحكي عربي ويشرب ميّة.
Dan traveled to Palestine,	سافر دان لفلسطين
To speak Arabic and eat figs.	يحكي عربي وياكل تين.
Dan traveled to Khartoum,	سافر دان للخرطوم
To speak Arabic and eat garlic.	يحكي عربي وياكل ثوم.
Dan traveled to Iraq,	سافر دان للعراق
To speak Arabic in the markets.	يحكي عربي في الأسواق.

Dan traveled to Tangier and Fez,	سافر دان طنجة وفاس
To speak Arabic with the people.	يحكي عربي مع الناس.
Dan traveled to Istanbul,	سافر دان لاسطنبول
To speak Turkish and eat fava beans.	يحكي تركي وياكل فول.
Dan traveled to Versailles,	سافر دان لفرساي
To speak French and drink tea.	يحكي فرنسي ويشرب شاي.

تمرين رقم ٤: احكي واكتب

1. Create a dialogue with your classmate in which one of you is a salesperson and the other a customer in an Arab fruit and vegetable market. Ask about and negotiate prices, pay or receive payment. Make it funny and interesting.

2. Plan a trip to go shopping with your roommate. Discuss transportation to and from where you will be shopping, what time, what you will be buying, etc.

3. Describe an interesting or strange shopping experience that happened to you or to someone you know, first by telling the other students in the class and then in writing (about 50 words).

الوحدة التاسعة: في دكّان الملابس

أهمّ الكلمات والتعابير الجديدة

أصفر	yellow	لون (ج. ألوان)	color
أحمر	red	اِختلف-يختلف	to differ
أخضر	green	مَحَلّ (ج. محلات)=دُكّان	shop
بُني	brown	مصنوع	made
بُرتقالي	orange	حلو	pretty (sweet)
رمادي	gray	مُفضّل	favorite
لبِس-يلبَس	to wear	شاهد-يشاهد=تفرّج-يتفرّج	to watch
ما أجمَل!	how beautiful!	منطِقة (ج. مَناطِق)	area
مش بطّال	not bad	أزرق	blue
مُلوّن	colored	أسود	black
تجاريّ	commercial	أبيض	white

تمرين رقم ١: املأ الفراغات

Fill in the blanks by using words from the list above. Make sure you use the correct form of the word (with or without the definite article for nouns and adjectives, the correct tense for verbs, etc.). The first one is given as an example.

١. في رأيي، ـــــــــــــ الأزرق أجمل من ـــــــــــــ الأحمر.

في رأيي، اللون الأزرق أجمل من اللون الأحمر.

٢. مكّة مول في عمّان لا ـــــــــــــ عن مولات أمريكا وأوروبا.

٣. هناك ـــــــــــــ في وسط البلد.

٤. كثير من الملابس في الأردن ـــــــــــــ في الصين.

٥. اللون الأزرق هو لوني ـــــــــــــ

٦. ـــــــــــــ محمد الفيلم الجديد في السينما.

٧. الأسعار في ـــــــــــــ عمّان الغربيّة أغلى من الأسعار في ـــــــــــــ عمّان الأخرى (other).

٨. يقع البحر ـــــــــــــ شمال تركيّا.

٩. يقع البحر ـــــــــــــ في غرب السعودية.

١٠. يقع البحر ـــــــــــــ المتوسط شمال مصر.

١١. القميص ـــــــــــــ باللونين، الأصفر والبرتقالي.

الدرس الأول

النصّ الأوّل–مشاهدة: إملي تشتري ملابس

كلمات جديدة

مَحَلّ=دُكّان shop	شورت (ج. شورتات) shorts
بَعض some	بَلاش without, no need for
مِنطَقة (ج. مَناطِق) area	إذَن therefore, in that case

تعبير

ما حَدّ، ما حَدا no one

أسئلة

١. ليش وسط البلد كويّس لشراء (for buying) الملابس، حسب فدوى؟

٢. إيش إملي بدها تشتري؟

٣. مين بيلبس شورتات في الأردن؟

النصّ الثاني-مشاهدة: ما أحلى هالكوفيّة!

كلمات جديدة

لبس-يلبَس to wear		شو=ايش what	
بَرْد cold	كوفيّة=حَطّة headdress	
	حِلو pretty (sweet)	

تعبير

ما أجمَل! how beautiful!

أسئلة

١. ليش، في رأيك، فدوى ما فهمت معنى "كوفيّة"؟

٢. مين بيلبس الحطّة (الكوفيّة) في الأردن، حسب فدوى؟

٣. في رأيك، إملي رايحة تشتري حطّة؟

الدرس الثاني

مشاهدة: إملي في دكّان الملابس

كلمات جديدة

غامق dark		أزرق blue	
to raise the price, to make something more expensive غلّى-يغلّي		أحلى nicer-looking, prettier	
سعر (ج. أسعار) price		مُفضّل favorite	
كفّى-يكفّي to be enough		تماماً totally	
خَلاص that's it, finished		فاتِح light	

we have معانا=مَعنا		enough	كافي
time وَقت		socks	جُرابات
to look, watch تفرّج-يتفرّج		to put	حَطّ-يحُطّ
foreigner أجنبي (ج. أجانِب)		bag	كيس
coffee shop, café مَقهى		hookah	أرجيلة

تعابير

على راحِتكم whatever you (pl.) are comfortable with

عَشانِك=على شانِك for you, for your sake

حَرام عليك! !it's not right, it's too much

تكرم عينك you're most welcome, whatever pleases you

ملابس داخليّة underwear

بلا دراسة بلا بطّيخ (nonsense (literally: no study no watermelon

أسئلة

١. إيش لون إملي المفضّل؟

٢. إيش لون فدوى المفضّل؟

٣. إيش لونك المفضّل؟

٤. كم دينار دفعت (paid) إملي للقميص؟

٥. ليش صاحب المحلّ (the shop owner) رفع السعر، في رأي فدوى؟

٦. لوين فدوى بدها تروح بعد محلّ الملابس؟ ليش؟

٧. ليش فدوى قالت "بلا دراسة بلا بطّيخ"؟

الدرس الثالث

قراءة: مذكّرات إملي

يوم الجمعة الماضي ذهبت أنا وفَدوى الى وسط عمّان واشتريت بعض الملابس: قميص وبنطلون وكوفيّة لونها أحمر وأبيض. (في الأردن اسم الكوفيّة "حطّة"). الكوفيّة أو الحطّة مصنوعة في الصين. كلّ شيء هنا، كما في أمريكا، مصنوع في الصين.

أمس ذهبت أنا وفدوى الى "مكة مول" في عمان الغربية. مكّة مول نظيف وفيه محلّات تجاريّة كثيرة.

في مكّة مول شربنا قهوة أمريكيّة وأرجيلة، ثمّ شاهدنا فلم "امريكا". يحكي الفلم قصّة سيّدة فلسطينية هاجرت هي وابنها "فادي" الى امريكا. في رأيي الفلم ممتاز، وخصوصاً لأنّ لغته العربيّة سهلة.

مكّة مول لا يختلف عن مولات أمريكا وأوروبا، والسينما التي فيه لا تختلف عن السينما في أمريكا وأوروبا أيضاً. قلت في نفسي، جئت الى الأردن حتى أرى وأسمع وأعيش الثقافة العربيّة، والثقافة العربيّة ليست في مكّة مول ولكن في مناطق عمّان القديمة.

كلمات جديدة

هاجر-يُهاجِر	to emigrate	بعض	some
لُغة	language	مصنوع	made
سَهل	easy	الصين	China
الّتي	which, that (f.)	كما	as
اختلف-يختلف	to differ	أمس=مبارح	
نفس (نفسي myself)	self	تجاريّ	commercial
جاء-يجيء (جئت I came)	to come	أرجيلة	hookah
رأى-يرى	to see	شاهد-يشاهِد=تفرّج-يتفرّج	to watch
سمع-يسمع	to hear	حكى-يحكي	to tell, narrate
عاش-يعيش	to live	قصّة	story
ثقافة	culture	سيّدة	lady

أسئلة

1. What did Emily buy last Friday?
2. What color was the *hatta* that Emily bought?
3. Where is it made?
4. How did Emily describe Makka Mall?
5. What did Emily and Fadwa do at Makka Mall?
6. What is the story of the movie *Amreeka* about?
7. Why does Emily think it's an excellent movie?
8. What was Emily's conclusion about Makka Mall and the old areas of Amman?

تمرين ١: املأ الفراغات Fill in the blanks from memory

١. يوم _____ الماضي ذهبت إملي وفدوى الى وسط عمّان واشتروا بعض _____ .

٢. الكوفيّة أو الحطّة لونها _____ و _____ .

٣. كلّ شيء في الأردن، كما في أمريكا، _____ في الصين.

٤.   مكّة مول نظيف وفيه محلّات _____ كثيرة.

٥.   السينما في مكّة مول لا _____ عن السينما في أمريكا وأوروبا حسب إملي.

تمرين رقم ٢

Read the passage again and identify five of each of the following categories:

صِفة – adjective	اسم – noun	فعل – verb

الدرس الرابع

قواعد

تمرين رقم ١ (مكتوب-في البيت)

	شاهَد-يُشاهِد to watch					
	imperfect	perfect	imperfect	perfect	imperfect	perfect
هو						
هي					تشرَب	
هم						
انتَ						
انتِ						
انتو			ترجعوا			
أنا						
احنا						

1. Plural possessive pronouns

Just as there are eight subject markers for the verb, there are eight pronouns that are attached to nouns and particles to indicate possession and other functions, five singular and three plural. The following table shows these pronouns as they are suffixed to a noun, and to the particles عند، مع, and بدّ.

بدُّه	مَعُه	عندُه	كتابُه	ـهُ	هو
بدّها	مَعها	عندها	كتابها	ـها	هي
بدّهُم	مَعهُم	عندهُم	كتابهُم	ـهُم	هم
بدَّك	مَعَك	عندَك	كتابَك	ـَك	انتَ
بدِّك	مَعِك	عندِك	كتابِك	ـِك	انتِ
بدّكُم	مَعكُم	عندكُم	كتابكُم	ـكُم	انتو
بدّي	مَعي	عندي	كتابي	ـي	أنا
بدّنا	مَعنا	عندنا	كتابنا	ـنا	احنا

تمرين رقم ٢

a. For each of the following, give an English translation, then indicate whether it is an إضافة construction, an adjective-noun phrase or an equational sentence. Follow the examples:

Adjective-noun phrase	A Palestinian lady	سيّدة فلسطينية
Equational sentence		مكّة مول نظيف
		محلّات تجاريّة كثيرة
		قهوة أمريكية
	the story of a woman	قصّة سيّدة
		الثقافة العربيّة
		المُدُن الأردنيّة

b. Give another example from the reading passage of each of the above structures and translate it into English.

2. لغته السهلة

Note the definite article on the word السهلة. The adjective is definite because it modifies a definite noun which is made definite by attaching the possessive suffix to it. The phrase is translated as: Its easy language.

تمرين رقم ٣: ترجم الى الإنجليزية

محلّات تجاريّة كثيرة _____

مناطق عمّان القديمة _____

المناطق القديمة في المدن الأردنيّة الأخرى _____

Sociolinguistic corner

1. While in English you say "Emily, Robert, and I", in Arabic you say "I, Emily, and Robert", the speaker being listed first. That is why Emily says: أمس ذهبت أنا وفدوى الى مكة مول.

2. Some شامي and فصحى correspondences (complete the table).

	شامي	فصحى
I went	رُحت	ذهبت
	اللي	التي
then, and then	بَعدين	ثُمَّ
	تفرّجنا	شاهَدنا
	ما بيختلف	لا يختلف
	كمان	
I see		أرى
	مِش	ليسَت

الدرس الخامس

كلمات الوحدة الجديدة

شاهد-يشاهِد=تفرّج-يتفرّج to watch	أجنَبي (ج. أجانِب) foreigner
عاش-يعيش to live	أحلى nicer-looking, prettier
عَشانك=على شانك for you, for your sake	أرجيلة hookah
على راحِتكم as you like, whatever you (pl.) are comfortable with	أزرق blue
	أمس=مبارح
غامِق dark	إذَن therefore, in that case
غلّى-يغلّي to raise the price, to make something more expensive	اختلف-يختلف to differ
	الصين China
فاتح light	بَرْد cold
قصّة story	بَعض some
كافي enough	بلا دراسة بلا بطّيخ nonsense (literally: no study no watermelon)
كفّى-يكفّي to be enough	
كما as	بَلاش without, no need for
كوفيّة=حَطّة headdress	تجاريّ commercial
كيس bag	تكرم عينك you're most welcome, whatever pleases you
لبس-يلبَس to wear	
لُغة language	تماماً totally
ما أجمَل! how beautiful!	ثقافة culture
ما حَدّ، ما حَدا no one	جاء-يجيء (جئت I came) to come
مَحَلّ=دُكّان shop	جْرابات socks
مصنوع made	حَرام عليك! it's not right, it's too much!
معانا=مَعنا we have	حَطّ-يحُطّ to put
مُفضّل favorite	حكى-يحكي to tell, narrate
ملابس داخليّة underwear	حلو pretty (sweet)
منطِقة (ج. مَناطق) area	خَلاص that's it, finished
نفس self (نفسي myself)	رأى-يرى to see
هاجر-يُهاجِر to emigrate	سعر (ج. أسعار) price
وَقت time	سمع-يسمع to hear
يالله let's	سَهل easy
	سيّدة lady

تمرين رقم ١: قراءة وكتابة (وافق بين الكلمة والصورة. اكتب الكلمة تحت الصورة المناسبة.)

قميص، بنطلون، كُندرة، شورت، ملابس داخليّة، ملابس، جاكيت، فُستان

تمرين رقم ٢: أكمل الجدول (الجمع والمعنى بالإنجليزيّة)

منطقة	أجنبي	تمرين	كيس	سوق	سعر
			bag		
			أكياس		

تمرين رقم ٣: أكمل الجدول (العكس)

فاتح	كبير	قليل	سهل
			صَعب

تمرين رقم ٤

Rearrange the letters in each of the following words, write them down, and translate them into English. Six of the nine words have the same "structure". How would you describe this structure?

١. ض ب ي أ

٢. ف أ ر ص

٣. أ ض ر خ

٤. ر أ م ح

٥. أ د و س

٦. ت ب ق ر ل ا ي

٧. ي ب نّ

٨. ا د ر م ي

٩. ر أ ز ق

تمرين رقم ٥: احكي عن شخص في الصف

Describe someone in the classroom based on the type and color of their clothing and have the rest of the class guess who it is.

تمرين رقم ٦: احكي (في الصفّ) واكتب (في البيت)

Prepare at home, speak in class, then write a composition of about 50 words to turn in: description of a trip in which you shopped and bought some clothes.

يوم _____ الماضي ذهبت أنا و _____ و _____ الى المول/السوق/نيويورك واشتريت ...

الوحدة العاشرة: الدراسة

أهمّ الكلمات والتعابير الجديدة

subject, course مادّة		to be founded تأسّس
sciences, branches of knowledge علوم		center مَركَز (ج. مَراكِز)
study دراسة (ج. دراسات)		oldest, most ancient أقدم
for the first time لأوّل مرّة		century قَرن
Ph.D., doctorate دكتوراه		to fail (an exam) رسب-يرسب
the Islamic Religion الدين الإسلامي		to pass (an exam), succeed نجح-ينجح
was built بُني		to obtain (على) حصل-يحصل
commerce, trade, business تجارة		Bachelor's بكالوريوس
law school كُلّية حُقوق		test امتحان
medical school كُلّية طبّ		specialization, major تخصُّص
education, instruction تعليم		mosque جامع=مَسجِد
cost تكلِفة (ج. تكاليف)		private خاصّ

مِنحة	scholarship	كلّف–يُكلّف	to cost
نتيجة (ج. نتائج)	result	حكومي	public, governmental
يُعتَبَر	is considered	دخل–يدخل	to enter
		علامة (ج. علامات)	grade

تمرين رقم ١: املأ الفراغات

١. جامعة "الأزهر" في القاهرة _____ (تأسّس، مركز، أقدم) جامعة في العالم.

٢. درس في الكلّيّة و _____ (رسب، نجح، حصل على) شهادة البكالوريوس.

٣. _____ (إمتحان، تخصّص، تأسّست) جامعة هارڤارد في _____ (جامع، سنة، خاص) ١٦٣٦.

٤. الجامع "الأزهر" _____ (مادّة، علوم، مركز) مُهمّ للدراسات العربيّة والإسلاميّة.

٥. سُمح للبنات الدراسة في الجامع "الأزهر" _____ (تعليم، تكليف، لأوّل مرّة) في الستينات من القرن العشرين.

الدرس الأوّل

النصّ الأوّل–مشاهدة: دراسة إملي ▶

كلمات جديدة

دكتوراه	Ph.D., doctorate	أَدَب	literature
سمع–يسمع	to hear	تاريخ	history
تخصّص	specialization, major	مادّة (ج. موادّ)	subject, course
قبل ما=قبل	before	أخذ–ياخذ	to take
		بكالوريوس	Bachelor's

أسئلة

١. إيش رايحة إملّي تدرس؟ _____

٢. كم مادّة رايحة تاخذ؟ _____

٣. وين درست إملي البكالوريوس؟ _____

٤. إيش بتدرس في تكساس؟ _____

٥. إيش تخصّص إملي هلأ؟ _____

النصّ الثاني-مشاهدة: الجامعات الأمريكية والجامعات الأردنيّة

كلمات جديدة

education, instruction تعليم	private خاصّ	كُلّيّة (ج. كُلّيّات) college
opposite عَكس	like, such as زَيّ=مِثل	مُمكن possibly, perhaps
to cost كلّف-يكلف	دِراسة (ج. دراسات) study	public, governmental حكومي

تعبير

ما سمعت إلا .. I did not hear (anything) except, I only heard

أسئلة

١. كم جامعة في أمريكا حسب إملي؟ _____

٢. كم جامعة في الأردن حسب فدوى؟ _____

٣. كم بتكلف الجامعات الأمريكيّة الخاصة؟ الحكوميّة؟ _____

٤. كيف التعليم في الجامعات الحكوميّة في الأردن؟ ليش؟ _____

تمرين رقم ١: الجمع

ما هو جمع كُلّ من الكلمات التالية؟

Complete the crossword puzzle by providing the plural of the following words:

٦. ألْف	٥. طالب	٤. مدرسة	٣. دراسة	٢. جامعة	١. مادة

الدرس الثاني

قراءة: جامعات عربية قديمة

من أهمّ وأقدم مراكز التعليم في العالم العربي ثلاث جامعات هي: جامعة "الأزهر" في القاهرة وجامعة "الزيتونة" في مدينة تونس عاصمة تونس وجامعة "القرويين" في مدينة فاس في المغرب. كانت كلّ مِن هذه الجامعات مدرسة في جامع، يدرس فيها الطلّاب علوم الدين الإسلامي واللغة العربية.

جامع وجامعة الزيتونة

بُني جامع الزيتونة في القرن الثامن الميلادي، وأصبح من أهمّ مراكز التعليم في تونس.

جامع وجامعة القرويّين

تأسّس جامع القرويّين في سنة ٨٥٩ م. وكان عدد طلّابه في القرن الرابع عشر أكثر من ثمانية آلاف طالب. بعد استقلال المغرب في سنة ١٩٥٦ تأسّست كلّيّة حُقوق وسُمح للبنات بالدراسة لأوّل مرّة.

جامع وجامعة الأزهر

تأسّس الجامع الأزهر حوالي سنة ٩٧٠ م. ويُعتَبَر أهمّ مركز للدراسات العربيّة والإسلاميّة في العالم. في الستينات من القرن العشرين تأسّست في جامعة الأزهر كلّيّة طبّ وكلّيّة هندسة. وسُمح للبنات بالدراسة فيها في سنة ١٩٦٢.

كلمات جديدة

تعليم	education	أهمّ	more, most important
تأسّس	to be founded	أقدم	more, most ancient
استقلال	independence	مَركَز (ج. مَراكِز)	center
سُمِح	was permitted	جامع=مَسجد	mosque
بِنْت (ج. بَنات)	girl	عِلم (ج. علوم)	science, branch of knowledge
دِراسة	study	بُنِي	was built
إسلامي	Islamic	قَرن	century
يُعتَبَر	is considered	ميلادي	A.D.
		أصبح-يُصبِح=صار-يصير	to become

تعابير

كُلّيّة حُقوق	law school	كُلّ مِن	each of
لأوّل مرّة	for the first time	الدين الإسلامي	the Islamic religion
		اللغة العربيّة	the Arabic language

تمرين رقم ١: أكمل الجدول التالي

سنة التأسيس	الموقع	اسم الجامع/الجامعة
		جامع الزيتونة
٨٥٩ ميلادي (م.)		
	القاهرة	

أسئلة

1. What was the initial focus of all three universities??
2. What was the population of al-Qarawiyyiin University in the 14th century?
3. When was a School of Medicine founded at al-Azhar Mosque/University?
4. When were girls allowed into al-Azhar and al-Qarawiyyiin?
5. Complete the following table about your college/university:

خاصة/حكوميّة	عدد الطُلاب (تقريباً)	سنة التأسيس	الموقع	اسم الجامعة

الدرس الثالث

((•)) **قراءة: مذكّرات إملي**

توجيهي. امتحان التوجيهي. أسئلة التوجيهي. نتائج التوجيهي. كلّ الناس يتكلّمون عن امتحان التوجيهي.

يقول الناس هنا إنّ امتحان التوجيهي مُهمّ جدّاً.

الطلاب الذين يحصلون على علامات عالية يدرسون الطبّ والهندسة واللغة الإنجليزيّة وعلوم الكمبيوتر. والطلاب الذين لا يحصلون على علامات عالية يدرسون التاريخ واللغة العربيّة والتجارة. والطلاب الذين يرسبون (لا ينجحون) في الامتحان لا يدخلون الجامعة.

ريم أخت فدوى الصغيرة سوفَ تأخذ امتحان التوجيهي في شهر حُزيران، وهي خائفة، لأنّ الامتحان صعب. سألتها ماذا تريد أن تفعل إذا نجحت في الامتحان، فقالت إنّها تريد السفر الى أمريكا للدراسة في جامعة أمريكيّة، وسألتني عن الجامعات الأمريكيّة وتكاليف الدراسة وكيف تحصل على منحة. كثير من الطلاب الأردنيّين سألوني نفس السؤال: كيف يحصلون على منحة للدراسة في جامعة أمريكيّة؟

كلمات جديدة

تِجارة	commerce, trade, business	امتحان	test
رسب-يرسب	to fail (an exam)	نتيجة (ج. نتائج)	result
نجح-ينجح	to pass (an exam), succeed	تكلّم-يتكلّم=حكى-يحكي	
دخل-يدخل	to enter	هُنا	here
خائف	afraid	إنّ	that
صعب	difficult	جدّاً=كثير	very
أن	to	الذين	who
تكلِفة (ج. تكاليف)	cost	حصل-يحصل (على)	to obtain
نفس	same	علامة (ج. علامات)	grade
مِنحة	scholarship	عالي	high

أسئلة

1. What is everyone talking about? _____
2. What can the student who passes the Tawjihi exam do? _____
3. What can students with high grades in the Tawjihi exam study? _____
4. What do those with low grades study? _____
5. Why is Reem worried? _____
6. What does Reem want to do if she passes the Tawjihi exam? _____
7. What is the question that many Jordanians ask? _____

ترجم/ي الى الإنجليزية

سألتها ماذا تريد أن تفعل إذا نجحت في الامتحان، فقالت إنّها تريد السفر الى أمريكا للدراسة في جامعة أمريكيّة، وسألتني عن الجامعات الأمريكيّة.

كثير من الطلاب الأردنيّين سألوني نفس السؤال.

Note that سألوني consists of سألوا+ني. The ا is a word-final phenomenon and is dropped when attached to an object pronoun.

الدرس الرابع

قواعد

١. مِن أهمّ/أهمّ مِن

Note that مِن أهمّ translates as "among the most important, or one of the most important", while أهمّ مِن translates as "more important than". This is true of occurrences of the preposition مِن before or after comparative adjectives. Compare the following:

| Amman is bigger than Irbid. | عمّان أكبر من إربد. |
| Irbid is among the biggest cities in Jordan. | إربد من أكبر المُدُن الأردنيّة. |

Remember that when the comparative/superlative form of the adjective is followed by the noun directly, it has the superlative meaning:

| Amman is the largest city in Jordan. | عمّان أكبر مدينة في الأردن. |

تمرين رقم ١

Translate the following sentences into English.

١.   جامع الزيتونة من أهمّ مراكز التعليم في تونس.

٢.   الجامع الأزهر أهمّ مركز للدراسات العربيّة والإسلاميّة في العالم.

٣.   في جامعة تكساس أكثر من خمسين ألف طالب.

٤.   مطعم السلام أقرب من مطعم الشعب.

٥.   الأكل في مطعم القدس مِن أحسن الأكل في عمّان.

٦.   مطعم ريم البوادي أغلى من مطعم القدس.

٧.   كنافة مطعم القدس أطيب كنافة في عمّان.

تمرين رقم ٢

Now translate the following three sentences into Arabic.

1.   Al-Sha'b Restaurant is cheaper than al-Salam Restaurant. _____

2.   Riim al-Bawadi Restaurant is one of the most expensive restaurants in Amman.

_____

3.   Al-Quds Restaurant is the best restaurant in Amman.

_____

2. The different uses of ما

You have seen ما used in negation. It negates verbs in both فصحى and شامي as well as certain non-verbal elements functioning as verbs indicating existence possession, and wanting.

ما negating verbs:

ما وجدته. I did not find it.

ما نامَت. She did not sleep.

ما negating non-verbal elements functioning as verbs:

ما فيه شمس اليوم There is no sun today.

ما عندي سيّارة. I don't have a car.

ما معي فلوس. I don't have money.

ما بدّي سندويشة فلافل. I don't want a falafel sandwich.

ما is also used in a completely different way: after prepositions like مثل قبل, بعد, and followed by a verb, it has no meaning of its own. So بعد ما translates as "after", the same as بعد, and قبل ما translates as "before".

تمرين رقم ٣

Translate the following into English.

وين درستِ قبل ما جيتِ للأردن؟ ــــــــــــــــــــــــــ

أنا ما درست عربي قبل ما جيت للأردن. ــــــــــــــــــــــــــ

3. Verb-subject (dis)agreement

Arabic sentences may start with the verb or the subject. In فصحى, a verb that precedes the subject remains in the singular even when the subject is in the plural.

يقول الناس هنا إنّ امتحان التوجيهي مهمّ جدّاً.

يدرس فيها الطلّاب علوم الدين الإسلامي واللغة العربية.

If the subject-verb order is used, then the verb agrees in number with its subject:

الناس هنا يقولون إنّ امتحان التوجيهي مهمّ جدّاً.

الطلّاب يدرسون فيها علوم الدين الإسلامي واللغة العربية.

4. Relative pronouns

The word *who* in the sentence *The student who was first in the class received a prize* is called a relative pronoun. Other English relative pronouns include *which*, *that*, *whose*, and *whom*. The equivalent of all of these pronouns in شامي is اللي. In فصحى, distinctions are made between masculine and feminine and between singular, dual, and plural relative pronouns. Only the three فصحى relative pronouns commonly used are introduced in this book. These are الذي, التي, and الذين.

Who, that, which (masculine, singular)	الذي
Who, that, which (feminine, singular)	التي
Who, that, which (masculine, plural)	الذين

Now translate the following sentences into English:

١. السينما التي فيه لا تختلف عن السينما في أمريكا وأوروبا أيضاً.

٢. الطلاب الذين يحصلون على علامات عالية يدرسون الطبّ والهندسة واللغة الإنجليزيّة وعلوم الكمبيوتر.

٣. والطلاب الذين يرسبون (لا ينجحون) في الامتحان لا يدخلون الجامعة.

Sociolinguistic corner

The passive in فصحى

In فُصحى passive meaning can be expressed in verbs by changing the vowel pattern. Such passive formation does not exist in شامي. (The passive in both فصحى and شامي will be discussed in more detail later. For now remember that the verbs يُعتَبَر, بُنِي, and سُمِح are the passive counterparts of سَمَح, بَنى, and اعتَبر.)

It was built.	buniy	بُنِي	He built.	banaa	بَنى
It was allowed.	sumiH	سُمِح	He allowed.	samaH	سَمَح
It is considered.	yu'tabar	يُعتَبَر	He considered.	i'tabar	اعتَبَر

يدرسوا/يدرسون

فصحى has a system of moods for imperfect verbs whereby such verbs have different endings depending on whether they are or are not preceded by certain particles. The mood system will be discussed in more detail later. For now, all you need to know is that يدرسوا and يدرسون have the same meaning: "they study" or "they are studying". The verbs يتكلّمون، يحصلون، يدرسون، يرسبون، ينجحون، يدخلون found in مذكّرات إملي above have the following equivalents in شامي: يتكلّموا، يحصلوا، يدرسوا، يرسبوا، ينجحوا، يدخلوا.
Some فصحى/شامي differences:

شامي	فصحى
صار	أصبح
بيحكوا، بيتكلّموا	يتكلّمون
اللي	الذين
كثير	جِدّاً
ما بينجحوا	لا ينجحون
رايحة تاخُذ	سوف تأخذ
ايش	ماذا
بدها	تريد أن
بتعمل	تفعل

الدرس الخامس

كلمات الوحدة الجديدة

public, governmental حكومي		to take أخذ-ياخذ	
afraid خائف		literature أدَب	
private خاصّ		to become أصبح-يُصبح=صار-يصير	
to enter دخل-يدخل		more, most ancient أقدم	
study (ج. دراسات) دراسة		to أن	
Ph.D., doctorate دكتوراه		more, most important أهمّ	
like, such as ذي=مثل		Islamic إسلامي	
to fail (an exam) رسب-يرسب		that إنّ	
was permitted سُمح		independence استقلال	
to hear سمع-يسمع		who, that, which (feminine, singular) التي	
difficult صعب		the Islamic Religion الدين الإسلامي	
high عالي		who, that, which (masculine, singular) الذي	
opposite عكس		who, that, which (masculine, plural) الذين	
grade (ج. علامات) علامة		the Arabic language اللغة العربيّة	
science, branch of knowledge (ج. علوم) عِلم		test امتحان	
before قبل ما=قبل		Bachelor's بكالوريوس	
century قَرن		girl (ج. بَنات) بِنْت	
each of كُلّ مِن		was built بُني	
to cost كلّف-يكلّف		history تاريخ	
college (ج. كُليّات) كُليّة		to be founded تأسّس	
law school كُليّة حُقوق		commerce, trade, business تجارة	
for the first time لأوّل مرّة		specialization, major تخصُّص	
I did not hear (anything) except, I only heard ما سمعت إلا..		education تعليم	
subject, course (ج. موادّ) مادّة		cost (ج. تكاليف) تكلفة	
center (ج. مَراكِز) مَركَز		تكلّم-يتكلّم=حكى-يحكي	
possibly, perhaps مُمكن		mosque جامع=مَسجد	
		very جدّاً=كثير	
		to obtain حصل-يحصل (على)	

مِنحة scholarship

ميلادي A.D.

نتيجة (ج. نتائج) result

نجح–ينجح to pass (an exam), succeed

نفس same

هُنا here

يُعتَبَر is considered

))) أغنية: عندي درس

(كلمات: منذر يونس، غِناء: جواد إياد قبها)

I have a class at 11	عندي درس الساعة ١١
He has a class at 12	عنده درس الساعة ١٢
If he is not really tired	إذا هو فعلاً مش تعبان
Let's go to the store	يالله نطلع للدكّان.
If he is still not busy	إذا هو لسّه مش مشغول
We walk immediately after that	بعده نمشي على طول
Forget about the noise and the students	ننسى الدوشة والطلاّب،
Drink tea and eat fava beans	نشرب شاي وناكل فول.

تمرين رقم ١: المفرد والجمع

أكمل الجدول

نتيجة	مركز	تكلفة	عِلم	بنت	مادّة	المفرد
					subject	المعنى بالإنجليزية
					موادّ	الجمع

تمرين رقم ٢: قراءة وكتابة

Connect the letters to make words and then write the meanings of these words. Follow the example.

Specialization, major	تخصّص	ت خ ص ص	١.
		د ر ا س ة	٢.
		ك ل ّ ف	٣.
		ح ك و م ي	٤.
		ت ع ل ي م	٥.
		ت أ س ّ س	٦.
		ع ا ل َ م	٧.
		ع ل ا م ة	٨.
		م ن ح ة	٩.
		ا م ت ح ا ن	١٠.

تمرين رقم ٣: العكس

Copy each word in column ب next to its opposite in column أ.

ب		أ
رسب		خاصّة
مُنخفض		قديم
خاص		كبير
رخيص		صعب
قصير		نجح
عامّة		عالي
وجد		ضيّع
حديث (جديد)		حكومي
صغير		غالي
سَهل		طويل

تمرين رقم ٤: كلمات متقاطعة

	١	٢	٣	٤	٥	٦	٧	٨	٩	١٠
١										
٢										
٣										
٤										
٥										
٦										
٧										
٨										
٩										
١٠										

عمودي	أفقي
١. عكس "شرق"؛ دولة عربيّة صغيرة في غرب آسيا	١. عكس رخيص؛ عكس جديد أو حديث
٣. عاصمة بريطانيا؛ دولة عربية جنوب المملكة العربيّة السعوديّة	٣. عاصمة العراق؛ عكس "رسب"
٥. عكس قديم	٦. عندما؛ عكس "أقلّ"
٦. اسم حرف (letter) عربي	٧. دولة عربيّة صغيرة في غرب آسيا
٧. الشهر الرابع	٨. مئة سنة
٩. عكس قديم؛ شاف	٩. عكس "عالي"

مناقشة وكتابة

Choose one of the following topics:

1. Create a dialogue with another student in which you discuss your reasons for choosing the school you are attending. Then write it up in about 50 words.
2. Study the history of your university or college (or any other university you like), prepare a short outline and present it to the class. Then write it up in about 50 words.

الوحدة رقم ١١: المهن

أهمّ الكلمات الجديدة

مُحاسِب	accountant	استعمل–يستعمِل	to use
مُدير	director, manager	اشتغل–يشتغِل	to work
مُساعِد	assistant	المدرسة الثانوية	secondary (high) school
مُستشفى	hospital	تمريض	nursing
مع بعض	together	ربّة بيت	housewife
مُمرّضة	nurse	صاحب (ج. أصحاب)	friend, boyfriend
مُناسب	suitable	طبيب (ج. أطِبّاء)	doctor, physician
		كلّيّة الحقوق	law school

تمرين رقم ١: إملاء الفراغات

١.   اسمي "مايكل" لكن _____ "مايك" أكثر من "مايكل".

٢.   انا طبيب و _____ في _____ قريب من الجامعة.

٣.   درست _____ في الجامعة، وأنا الآن ممرّض.

٤.   ابي _____ في بنك.

٥.   هذه الشقّة _____ لأنّها رخيصة وقريبة من الجامعة.

٦.   ربة البيت هي _____ البيت!

تمرين رقم ٢: ترتيب حروف وتكوين كلمات وترجمة. أكمل/ي الفراغات.

المعنى	الكلمة	
nurse	ممرّض	١. م ض م ر
_____	_____	٢. ب ي ب ط
_____	_____	٣. ة م س ح ا ب
_____	_____	٤. ي د م ر
_____	_____	٥. ع د م س ا

الدرس الأوّل

النصّ الأوّل–مشاهدة: عائلة إملي

كلمات جديدة

صار-يصير=أصبح-يُصبِح to become	لِسّه still
هاي=هذه	مُساعد assistant
قصّة story	مُدير director, manager
قعد-يقعد to sit	كثار (كثير .pl of) many, a lot

تعابير

together مع بعض	law school كلّيّة الحقوق
housewife ربّة بيت	secondary (high) school المدرسة الثانوية

أسئلة

١.   مين أكبر، إملي ولّا أخوها؟ _____

٢.   إيش بيعملوا أخو وأخت إملي؟ _____

٣.   إيش بتعمل أم إملي؟ _____

النصّ الثاني–مشاهدة: عائلة فدوى

كلمات جديدة

nursing تمريض	هَيّ=هذا
nurse ممرضة	doctor, physician (طبيب (ج. أطبّاء
good, sweet حلو	other, second ثاني
accountant مُحاسب	trade, business تجارة
the tastiest, best أزكى	teacher مُعلّم

أسئلة

١.   إيش بيعملوا أبو وأم فدوى؟

٢.   اعمل جدول بأسامي إخوان وأخوات فدوى وعمل كلّ واحد فيهم.

(Make a table of Fadwa's brothers and sisters and their professions.)

تمرين (شفهي (oral) في الصفّ): استعمل الكلمات او العبارات التالية في جُمل او حوارات (dialogues).

أكبر ولّا أصغر، المدرسة الثانوية، أبوك وأمّك (أبوي وأمّي)، مُساعد مُدير، عندي (أربع إخوان)، مع بَعض، ربّة بيت، قصّة طويلة، صار مهندس (طبيب، محاسب، الخ.)، اللغة العربيّة، امتِحان التوجيهي

الدرس الثاني

مشاهدة: انتِ مخطوبة ولا لأ؟

كلمات جديدة

خُطوبة	engagement	كاسة	glass, cup
زَواج	marriage	جاب-يجيب	to bring
صحيح	correct, true	مات-يموت	to die
صاحب (ج. أصحاب)	friend, boyfriend	هالاسم=هذا الإسم	
شابّ (ج. شباب)	young man, youth	لاقى-يلاقي=وجد-يوجد	to find
سمَح-يسمَح	to allow	مُناسب	suitable
عادي	normal, OK, fine	أبداً	at all, never
		مخطوب	engaged

تعابير

يسلموا إيديك! Thank you (lit. bless your hands)!

صحّة وهنا! Bon appetit!

أسئلة

١. مين جاب ميّة لإملي؟ _____

٢. كم عمر أخ وأخت إملي؟ _____

٣. ليش فكّرت أم فادي اسم مات مش مناسب؟ _____

٤. ايش الأسئلة الغريبة (strange) اللي سألتها أم فادي؟ _____

تمرين رقم ١ (شفهي في الصفّ): استعمل الكلمات او العبارات التالية في جُمل او حوارات قصيرة.

بتحبّ (تشرب)، (عائلة كبيرة) ولا (صغيرة)، أحسن من، صحيح انّ....، أكثر الناس

تمرين رقم ٢ (شفهي في الصفّ)

Working in pairs, act out the role of Emily and Umm Fadi. Be sure to use as many strange questions as possible!

الدرس الثالث

قراءة: مذكّرات إملي

عائلة فدوى كبيرة. أكثر العائلات الأردنيّة كبيرة. عند فدوى ثلاث أخوات وأربعة إخوان. أبو فدوى "أبو فادي" (لأنّ اسم ابنه الأكبر فادي) عنده مطعم في إربد. و "أم فادي" ربّة بيت.

كان أبو فادي يُريد أن يصبح أولاده وبناته أطبّاء ومهندسين، ولكن واحداً فقط (مُهنّد) صار طبيباً وواحداً (أحمد) صار مهندساً.

فادي مساعد مدير في فندق في عمّان، وأيمن مُعلّم لغة عربيّة في دولة الإمارات العربيّة المتّحدة.

أخت فدوى الكبيرة اسمها مُنى، وهي الآن ممرّضة في مستشفى في إربد، ورشا تعمل محاسِبة في بنك. أصغر بنت في العائلة هي ريم، عمرها ١٨ سنة وهي طالبة في المدرسة الثانويّة.

سألتني أمّ فادي أسئلة كثيرة. بعض هذه الأسئلة كانت غريبة. سألتني إذا كنت مخطوبة أم لا، وهل عندي صاحب في أمريكا.

قرّرت أن لا أقول إنّ اسم أخي مات. كلّما قلت مات يفكّر الناس أنّ أخي مات! ثمّ أقول لهم اسمه مات يعني ماثيو.

لن أستعمل مات أبداً.

كلمات جديدة

أم=أو or (used in direct and indirect questions)		أخ (ج. إخوة، إخوان) brother	
قرّر-يقرر to decide		الأكبر the oldest	
كلّما whenever		أراد-يُريد=بدّه to want	
ثُمَّ then		اصبح=يصبح to become	
لَن will not		فقط=بَسّ only	
		غريب strange	

أسئلة

١. كم أخ وأخت عند فدوى؟ _____

٢. ماذا كان أبو فدوى يريد أن يصبح أولاده وبناته؟ _____

٣. ماذا تعمل مُنى؟ _____

٤. مَن الأصغر في العائلة؟ كم عمره/ها؟ ماذا يعمل/تعمل؟ _____

٥. ما هي الأسئلة الغريبة التي سألتها أم فادي؟ _____

٦. ماذا قرّرت إملي أن تعمل؟ لماذا؟ _____

1. How many brothers and sisters does Fadwa have?
2. What did Abu Fadi want his sons and daughters to become?
3. What does Muna do?
4. Who is the youngest in the family? How old is he/she? What does he/she do?
5. What were the strange questions which Umm Fadi asked?
6. What did Emily decide to do? Why?

تمرين رقم ١: اكمل الجُمل في القائمة أ باستعمال الكلمات/التعابير المُناسبة في القائمة ب، كما في المثال.

Complete each of the phrases in Column أ by using the appropriate word or phrase from Column ب, as in the example.

ب	أ
مطعم في إربد.	١. عائلة فدوى وأكثر العائلات الأردنيّة ____
مساعد مدير في فندق في عمّان.	٢. ام فادي تعمل في البيت يعني ____
كبيرة.	٣. "أبو فادي" عنده ____
هي ربة بيت.	٤. فادي أكبر ولد في العائلة وهو ____
محاسبة في بنك.	٥. أيمن مُعلّم لغة ____
المدرسة الثانويّة.	٦. مُنى درست التمريض في الجامعة وهي الآن ____
عربيّة.	٧. رشا درست التجارة وهي ____
ممرّضة في مستشفى.	٨. ريم اصغر واحده في العائلة وهي طالبة في ____
إذا هي مخطوبة.	٩. قررت إملي ان تقول اسم أخوها ماثيو لأن ____
حسب أم فادي هذا الإسم ليس مُناسب.	١٠. سألت أم فادي إملي ____

مِثال

١. عائلة فدوى وأكثر العائلات الأردنيّة كبيرة.

الدرس الرابع

قواعد

١. ما قُلتِ لي=ما قُلتيلي

Note that when the subject marker تِ (you, f.s.) is followed by a suffix, the كسرة in it is lengthened to ي, as in the following:

you saw him	شُفتيه	you saw	شفتِ
you wrote it, f.	كتبتيها	you wrote	كتبتِ
you said to me	قلتيلي	you said	قلتِ

2. Plural formation

You learned in Unit 1 that an Arabic noun can be singular, dual, or plural:

طالبة	طالبتين	طالبات

The rule of the dual is straightforward and regular: you simply attach the suffix ين to the noun. If the noun has تاء مربوطة it is changed to regular ت, as seen in طالبة/طالبتين.

Plural formation is not as straightforward as dual formation. A noun is made plural in one of two ways:

a. By adding a suffix. This is called sound plural.
b. By an internal vowel change. This is called broken plural.

Sound plurals

Sound plurals are also of two types: masculine and feminine.

a. Masculine sound plurals are formed from nouns of masculine gender by adding the suffix ين (iin) to the noun. Most nouns pluralized in this way refer to humans. Many are derived from other words.

أردُنيّين	Jordanian	أردني
مهندسين	engineer	مهندس

b. Feminine sound plurals, more common than masculine sound plurals, are formed from nouns of feminine gender, generally ending in التاء المربوطة by adding the suffix ات to the noun and dropping التاء المربوطة:

أردنيّات	Jordanian (f.)	أردنيّة
مهندسات	engineer (f.)	مهندسة
جامعات	university	جامعة
علامات	grade	علامة

Many masculine nouns are pluralized as sound feminine plurals.

مطارات	airport	مطار
امتحانات	test	امتحان

Broken plurals

These plurals are formed by changing the vowels of the word; the consonants are usually not affected. Think of the English words *goose-geese, foot-feet, woman-women*.

The use of the terms *sound* and *broken* to refer to plurals might be misleading, since it might suggest that sound plurals involve the majority of nouns. In fact this is not the case. Broken plurals in Arabic are at least as common as sound plurals and involve the most common types of nouns.

Broken plurals follow patterns, some of which are more widespread than others. Some of the more common types are represented by the following words:

الجمع	المُفرد	الجَمع	المُفرد
مطاعم	restaurant مطعَم	مكاتب	office مكتَب
مراكِز	center مركَز	مطابِخ	kitchen مَطبَخ
بُيوت	house بيت	شُهور	month شَهر
دكاكين	shop دكّان	أسابيع	week أسبوع
مُدن	city مدينة	كُتُب	book كِتاب
كُتّاب	writer كاتِب	طُلّاب	student طالِب
أيّام	day يوم	أولاد	boy وَلَد
أخبار	news item خَبَر	أفلام	film فِلْم

At this stage it is easiest for you simply to memorize the plural forms. In time and as you continue building your vocabulary, you will develop intuitions for the correct broken plural patterns.

3. Separate and attached pronouns

Arabic distinguishes two sets of pronouns that can be inflected for number (singular-plural), gender (masculine-feminine), and person (first, second, third).

The first set consists of personal pronouns, which are not attached to other words. These include:

هو، هي، هم، انتَ، انتِ، انتو (انتم)، أنا، احنا (نحن)

.شامي in احنا and انتو equivalents of فصحى are the نحن and أنتم

These pronouns are often omitted when they have the same reference as subject markers in verbs. So in a phrase like هو يدرس, the prefix ي of يدرس is sufficient to identify the subject of the verb and هو can be omitted.

The second set consists of pronouns that are alway attached to a noun, a verb, preposition, or another particle such as إنّ، لكن، لأن، عند، بدّ, etc. These pronouns cannot be omitted. They include:

ه، ها، هم، كَ، كِ، كُم، (ن)ي، نا

When attached to nouns, pronouns convey the meaning of possession (his, her, etc.), and when attached to verbs, they function as object pronouns (him, her.). Note that when ي is suffixed to a verb, an ن precedes it: علّمني (he taught me).

Examples:

Possessive pronouns

هذا كتابي. هذه سيارتنا. جامعتهم كبيرة.

Object pronoun

أبي علّمني الكتابة والقراءة.

Preposition + pronoun

ركب معي في السيارة

تمرين رقم ١

Read the following paragraph and answer the questions in Arabic using a pronoun to replace the underlined noun or nouns. The answer for the first question is given as an example.

اسمي نهى. أخي أيمن طالب في الجامعة. في جامعة أيمن خمس كليات كبيرة: كلية الطب، وكلية الهندسة، وكلية الحقوق، وكلية الآداب واللغات، وكلية التجارة. أخي الأكبر اسمه عمر. هو مدير في شركة محاسبة كبيرة. في شركته ٥٠٪ من الموظفين من الهند أو باكستان. أختي سعاد تزوّجت الشهر الماضي. زوجها برناردو أيطالي، ولأبيه وأمّه بيت في روما، فانتقلت سعاد مع زوجها إلى أيطاليا. أخي الصغير اسمه فؤاد وهو طالب في المدرسة الثانوية. المدرسة قريبة، تبعد عن البيت حوالي عشرين متر.

أسئلة

١. كم أخ وأخت عند <u>نهى</u>؟
<u>عندها</u> ثلاث إخوان وأخت واحدة.

٢. كم كلية في جامعة <u>أيمن</u>؟

_____

٣. كم في المئة (الميّة) من <u>الموظفين</u> غير عرب؟

_____

٤. أين بيت أب وأم <u>برناردو</u>؟

_____

٥. كم متراً تبعد مدرسة فؤاد عن <u>البيت</u>؟

_____

Sociolinguistic corner

١. جاء-يجيء/أجا-ييجي

The verb أجا "he came"–ييجي "he comes", is one of the least regular verbs in Arabic. The best way to learn it at this point is simply to try to memorize its different conjugations. The following table shows its conjugation in both شامي and فصحى. (Note that نحن and انتم in فصحى are the equivalents of انتو and احنا in شامي, respectively.)

	فصحى		شامي	
	Imperfect	Perfect	Imperfect	Perfect
هو	يجيء	جاء	ييجي	أجا
هي	تجيء	جاءت	تيجي	أجَت
هم	يجيئون/يجيؤوا	جاءوا	ييجوا	أجوا
انتَ	تجيء	جئتَ	تيجي	جيت
انتِ	تجيئين/تجيئي	جئتِ	تيجي	جيتِ
انتو/أنتُم	تجيئون	جئتُم	تيجوا	جيتوا
أنا	أجيء	جئتُ	آجي	جيت
احنا/نحنُ	نجيء	جئنا	نيجي	جينا

2. The two verbs حصَل-يحصُل (على) and أراد-يُريد are used mainly in فصحى. The following table shows their conjugations in the perfect and imperfect.

First, fill in the empty cells, then compare this table with that of the conjugation table of verbs in شامي in Unit 8 and highlight the differences between the two.

حصَل-يحصُل (على)		أراد-يُريد		
Imperfect	Perfect	Imperfect	Perfect	
			أراد	هو
تحصُل	حصلَت		أرادَت	هي
		يُريدون		هم
			أرَدْت	انتَ
		تُريدين		انتِ
تحصلون	حصلتُم	تُريدون	أردتم	أنتُم
			أردتُ	أنا
				نحنُ

الدرس الخامس

كلمات الوحدة

the oldest الأكبر	at all/never أبداً
secondary (high) school المدرسة الثانوية	brother (ج. إخوة، إخوان) أخ
trade/business تجارة	to want أراد-يُريد=بدّه
nursing تمريض	the tastiest, best أزكى
other, second ثاني	or (used in direct and أم=أو
then ثمّ	indirect questions)
to bring جاب-يجيب	to use استعمل-يستعمِل
good, sweet حلو	to work اشتغل-يشتغل
engagement خُطوبة	to become اصبح=يصبح

law school كلّيّة الحقوق	housewife ربّة بيت
to find لاقى-يلاقي=وجد-يوجد	marriage زَواج
still لسّه	to allow سمَح-يسمَح
will not لن	young man, youth (شباب .شابّ (ج
to die مات-يموت	friend, boyfriend (أصحاب .صاحب (ج
accountant مُحاسب	to become صار-يصير=أصبح-يُصبِح
engaged مخطوب	correct, true صحيح
director, manager مُدير	doctor, physician (أطِبّاء .طبيب (ج
assistant مُساعد	normal, OK, fine عادي
hospital مُستشفى	strange غريب
together مع بعض	only فقط=بَسّ
teacher مُعلّم	to decide قرّر-يقرر
nurse مُمرّضة	story قصّة
suitable مُناسب	to sit قعد-يقعد
هالاسم=هذا الإسم	glass, cup كاسة
هاي=هذه	many, a lot (pl. of كثير) كثار
here is=هَيّ	whenever كلّما

تمرين رقم ١

Read مذكّرات إملي again, and match the names of the people in Column أ with the professions in Column ب:

ب	أ
مهندس	أبو فادي
ممرّضة	أحمد
معلّم	أم فادي
مساعد مدير	أيمن
محاسبة	رشا
عنده مطعم	ريم
طبيب	فادي
طالبة	مُنى
ربّة بيت	مهنّد

تمرين رقم ٢

Complete each sentence by filling in the blanks with any appropriate word for the work-place of each occupation

مثال: ابي مدير وهو يعمل في <u>مكتب</u>.

١.   امي طبّاخة وتعمل في _____

٢.   اخي عمره ١٧ سنة وهو طالب في _____

٣.   المهندس يعمل في _____

٤.   المحاسب _____

٥.   ربة البيت تعمل في _____

٦.   الطبيبة تعمل في _____

٧.   المُمرّض يعمل في _____

٨.   الاستاذ يعمل في _____

٩.   رجل الأعمال (businessman) يعمل في _____

١٠. جميلة سكرتيرة وتعمل في _____

تمرين رقم ٣: كلمات مُتقاطعة

Crossword puzzle

	١	٢	٣	٤	٥	٦	٧	٨	٩	١٠
١										
٢										
٣										
٤										
٥										
٦										
٧										
٨										
٩										
١٠										

(عمودي) Down	(أفقي) Across
١. يعمل في مطبخ مطعم؛ فادي ـــــــ مدير	١. يعمل في مستشفى؛ يعمل في بنك
٣. المسؤول (person in charge) في بنك أو مدرسة أو مكتب	٣. جذر (root) "نسيت"
٤. نسكن فيه	٥. تعمل في جامعة او كُلّية
٦. درس هندسة في الجامعة	٦. ندرسها في المدرسة أو الجامعة
٧. تدرسه الممرضة في الجامعة	٨. تعمل في البيت
٨. ابي استاذ وـــــــ محاسبة في بنك	٩. بيتي بعيد ـــــــ الجامعة؛ أخو الأب
٩. حرف جرّ	١٠. اسم اخت فدوى الصغيرة؛ حرف جرّ
١٠. يدرسه الطبيب في الجامعة (معكوسة backwards)؛ تعمل في مستشفى (معكوسة)	(preposition)

تمرين رقم ٤: حضّر واحكي واكتب

Prepare a short description of one of the professions below, present it in class, then write it up as a composition of about 50 words at home. You can make up a name for the person or persons in the picture, discuss his/her age, profession, place of work, etc. Be creative.

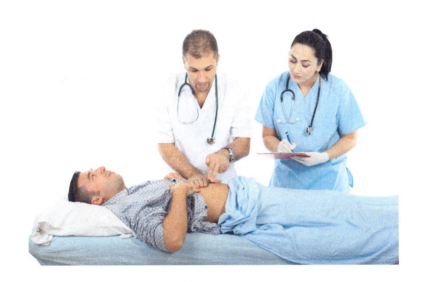

أهمّ كلمات الوحدة الجديدة

طلَب-يطلُب to request, ask for	ارتاح-يرتاح to rest
طلِع-يطلَع to come out	تَعبان tired, unwell
في الفِراش in bed	حَساسيّة allergy
لا سَمَح الله! God forbid!	خاف-يخاف to be afraid
مُخيف frightening	راس head
مرِض-يمرَض to become sick	زاكي delicious
مَريض sick	سبَب cause, reason
مَسكين poor, unfortunate	سَلامتك! I hope you are OK!
وَجَع pain	شعَر-يشعُر to feel
يَجب أن=لازم must, should	شكله He looks like (his appearance)

تمرين رقم ١

١. املي كانت تعبانة و _____ (ارتاحت، طلعت، خافت) في بيت فدوى.

٢. شاهدت فيلماً _____ (مسكين، مُخيفاً، راس) في السينما.

٣. في المُستشفى _____ (سألني، شعرت، ارتحت) الطبيب بعض الأسئلة.

٤. _____ (اشعر، يجب أن، أطلب) أدرس حتى انجح في الإمتحان!

٥. _____ (طلع، مرض، طلب) محمد تاكسي من الفندق الى المطار.

٦. بعض الناس في أمريكا عندهم _____ (وجع، حساسيّة، سبب) للحليب واللبن.

٧. لم أدرس (ما درست) كثيراً لانني كنت مريضاً وكنت _____ (في الفراش، مسكين، شكلي) طول الوقت.

٨. إنتَ مريض، _____؟ (لا سمح الله، إن شاء، الحمد لله)!

٩. عندي إمتحان فـ _____ (مريض، يجب، طلب) أن أدرُس.

١٠. الأكل في مطعم الجامعة _____ (زاكي، وجع، تعبان) جدّاً.

الدرس الأوّل

النصّ الأوّل–مشاهدة: المنسف

كلمات جديدة

ما حدا=ما حد	no one, nobody	زاكي	delicious
اشي=شيء	something	رُزّ	rice
بَقَر	cow(s)	لبَن	yogurt
خَنزير	pork, pig	بهارات	spices
		خَروف	lamb

تعابير

صحّتين وعافية Bon appetit (lit. may you have good health)

ما حد بيوكل/بياكُل nobody eats

هذه أوّل مرّة this is the first time

أسئلة

١.   ايش في المنسف؟ _____

٢.   املي أكلت منسف قبل هذه المرة؟ _____

٣.   ايش نوع (kind, type) اللحم اللي بياكلوه الناس بالأردن؟ _____

٤.   ايش نوع اللحم اللي بياكلوه أكثر الناس بأمريكا، حسب املي؟ _____

النصّ الثاني–مشاهدة: شاي أو قهوة؟

كلمات جديدة

جاب–يجيب to bring		مَرّة time (مرّة ثانية another time)	
سُكّر sugar		يا=او	
		بِدون without	

تعابير

هلأ شربنا شاي we've just had tea

يسلموا ايديك! May God bless your hands!

صحة وهناء! Bon appetit!

أسئلة

١.   إيش إملي طلبت تشرب؟ _____

٢.   كيف بدّها القهوة؟ _____

٣.   أم فادي بدها تشرب شيء؟ _____

تمرين شفهي (في مجموعات)

تكوين جمل أو حوارات قصيرة جديدة تحتوي على التعابير التالية: هذه أوّل مرّة (باكل منسف)، ما فيه حد/حدا (بياكل لحم خنزير بالأردن)، هلّأ (شربنا شاي)، ب(سكّر) ولّا/أو بدون (سكّر)، يسلموا أيديك، صحّة وعافية

الدرس الثاني

النصّ الأوّل–مشاهدة: فيه وجع في راسي وبطني

كلمات جديدة

راس	head	نَعَم	yes
بَطن	belly, stomach	طلَب–يطلُب	to request, ask for
هَيّ	here is	مَريض	sick
جار	neighbor	وَجَع	pain

تعابير

مالِك؟	what is wrong (with you)?	سَلامتك!	I hope you are OK!
موجود عنّا	available (to us)	موجوعة شي؟	are you in pain?

أسئلة

١. ليش إملي بدها تاكسي؟ _____

٢. وين فيه وجَع؟ _____

٣. مين أبو عبدالله؟ _____

النصّ الثاني–مشاهدة: كلّنا أكلنا منسف وما مرضنا!

كلمات جديدة

استنّى–يستنّى	to wait	مَسكين	poor, unfortunate
طلِع–يطلَع	to come out	تَعبان	tired, unwell
أعطى–يعطي	to give	مرِض–يمرَض	to become sick
دواء	medicine	معقول	possible/thinkable
ارتاح–يرتاح	to rest	حَساسيّة	allergy
صار–يصير	to happen	أكيد	certainly

تعابير

بسيطة simple matter	ما كلّنا=كُلّنا all of us
شَكله He looks like (his appearance)	ما حدّش=ولا واحد not one
هالمرّة this time	لا سمح الله God forbid

اسئلة

١. ليش إملي مريضة حسب فدوى، أم فادي، وأبو عبدالله؟ ـــــــــــــــــــــــــــــــــــــ

٢. ايش لازم إملي تعمل حتى ترجع مثل ما كانت؟ ـــــــــــــــــــــــــــــــــــــ

تمرين رقم ١ شفهي (في مجموعات)

تكوين جمل أو حوارات قصيرة تحتوي على التعابير التالية: سلامتَك/سلامتِك، شكراً (الله يسلّمك)، خمس دقايق (بيكون هون)، شكله (تعبان، زعلان ...)، أكيد (عندها برد) لا تعب ولا برد، هذا من لحمة الخروف، ليش ما نستنّى شويّة (ونشوف ايش بيقول الطبيب)

الدرس الثالث

قراءة: مذكّرات إملي

أكتب مذكّراتي الآن في بيت فدوى. ركبنا الباص إلى إربد بعد ظُهر أمس. كانت رحلة الباص مُخيفة: كان السائق يتكلّم مع رجل جالس في المقدّمة. أحياناً كان يرفع يده عن عجلة القيادة، وأحياناً أخرى كان يتكلّم على الموبايل ... والباص يمشي بسرعة كبيرة.

أخذنا تاكسي من محطّة باصات إربد إلى بيت فدوى. وصلنا البيت الساعة الثانية بعد الظهر. ومنذ وصولي وحتى الآن مرضت (أنا الآن مريضة في الفراش) وأنا آكل وأشرب: عصير، شاي، قهوة، فواكه، منسف، شاي مرّة ثانية ...

كان الغداء اليوم "منسف". كان المنسف طيّب جدّاً، ممكن أطيب أكلة أكلتها في حياتي.

بعد الغداء شربنا الشاي والعصير والقهوة وأكلنا الفواكه.

حوالي الساعة الرابعة بعد الظهر شعرت بوجع في رأسي وبطني، وكنت أريد أن أذهب الى المستشفى، ولكن فدوى قالت إنّ جارهم أبو عبدالله طبيب.

الدرس الرابع

قواعد

1. More on moving to the past with كان

The verb كان and its derivatives are used to refer to states of the past, as the English equivalents was/were do:

He was tired. كان تعبان.	I was in the hospital. كنت في المستشفى.

You've seen instances where كان is used in combination with words like عند and مع to "move" the reference of these words to the past:

I had كان عندي	I have عندي

كان is also used with other particles, adverbs, and verbs to express past actions or states:

I wanted كنت بدّي		I want بدّي	
it was necessary, ought to كان لازم		it is necessary that, must لازم	
I thought, I used to think كنت أفكّر		I think بافكّر	
I wanted كنت أريد		I want أريد	

تمرين رقم ١: ترجم الى الإنجليزية

١. كانت رحلة الباص مخيفة. كان السائق يتكلّم مع رجل جالس في المقدّمة.

٢. كنت أريد أن أذهب الى المستشفى.

تمرين رقم ٢: كان Now write at least 2 sentences using

تمرين رقم ٣

Change the following sentences to the past, using كان. The first one is given as an example.

مسكينة، هي مريضة.

مسكينة، (هي) كانت مريضة.

١.   الرحلة مخيفة.

٢.   يريد أن يرتاح قبل الأمتحان.

٣.   أنا وأخي وأختي نركب الباص صباح كل يوم.

٤.   يأكلون المنسف كل يوم جمعة.

٥.   المشكلة بسيطة.

2. Roots and verb stems

Arabic words are divided into three main categories: *verbs*, *nouns*, and *particles*. Particles are words or parts of words like prepositions, conjunctions, the definite article, question words, and other "function" elements. Verbs and nouns are the main categories, which include the great majority of words in the language. All verbs and nouns derive from three or, less commonly, four-letter roots. The latter will be excluded because of their rare occurrence in this book.

Three-consonant roots are divided into the following five types:

1. *Sound roots* have three consonants in the three consonant positions, no doubling of any two consonants, and no ا, و, or ى in any of the three root positions.

to write	ك.ت.ب
to hear	س.م.ع
to know	ع.ر.ف

2. *Assimilated roots* have و in the first root slot:

to find	و.ج.د
to arrive	و.ص.ل

3. *Hollow roots* have و or ي in the second root slot, which is often realized as ا in the perfect tense of the verb:

He was/will be	كان/يكون	ك.و.ن
He said/says	قال/يقول	ق.و.ل
He flew/flies	طار/يطير	ط.ي.ر

4. *Lame roots* typically have ي (less commonly و in the third root slot) which is realized as ألف مقصورة-ى, (pronounced exactly like ا) in the perfect form of the verb. Examples of lame roots are

He walked/walks	مشى–يمشي	م.ش.ي
He invited/invites	دعا–يدعو	د.ع.و
He spoke/speaks	حكى–يحكي	ح.ك.ي

5. *Doubled roots* have the same consonant in second and third positions:

| He passed/passes | مرّ–يمرّ | م.ر.ر |
| He liked/likes | حبّ–يحِبّ | ح.ب.ب |

Words are built from roots following regular patterns. There are verbal patterns (for verbs) and nominal patterns (for nouns and adjectives). One of the most common nominal patterns is the one that the following adjectives belong to:

نظيف، رخيص، قريب، بعيد، صغير، كبير.

Nominal patterns will be discussed in detail later.

There are 12 verbal patterns or forms, called أوزان (singular وزن) that are commonly used in modern Arabic. One important step in recognizing the form of a specific verb is to identify its stem, which refers to the verb in its simplest form: *the third person masculine singular in the past tense*, the equivalent of *he -ed* in English, as in درس "he studied", دَرَّس "he taught", تزوّج "he got married", اشتغل "he worked", etc.

تمرين رقم ٤

With reference to the above discussion, fill in the empty cells in the following table. All the verbs in the table are taken from the reading passage in lesson 3.

Root Type	Root	Stem	Translation	Verb
sound	ك.ت.ب	كتب	I write	أكتب
				ركبنا
	ك.و.ن		She was	كانت
	و.ص.ل			وصلنا
				شعرت
				قال
				وسألني
	ر.ي.ح	استراح		أستريح
				أفكّر
			and I return	وأرجع

Note that in roots like س.ء.ل, the middle letter is همزة, which is a consonant. Such roots are considered sound.

Sociolinguistic corner

شامي	فُصحى
مبارح	أمس
مِن	مُنذ
هلأ	الآن
كُنت بدّي	كُنت أريد
أروح	أذهب
أجا	جاء
لازم	يَجب أن
بُكرة	غداً

الدرس الخامس

كلمات الوحدة

أحياناً sometimes

استراح–يستريح to rest

اشي=شيء something

الآن=هلّاً now

بِدون without

بسرعة with speed

بَطن belly, stomach

بقَر cow(s)

بهارات spices

جاب–يجيب to bring

جار neighbor

جالِس sitting

خَروف lamb

خَنزير pork, pig

راس head

رَجُل man

رحلة trip

رُزّ rice

رفع–يرفَع to raise

زاكي delicious

سائِق driver

سُكّر sugar

سَلامتك! I hope you are OK!

شَعَر–يشعُر to feel

معدتي stomach   صحة وهناء! Bon appetit!

مُقدِّمة front part   صحّتين وعافية Bon appetit (lit. may you have good health)

مُنذُ since

موجود عنّا available (to us)   طلَب-يطلُب to request, ask for

موجوعة شي؟ are you hurt?   عَجلة القِيادة steering wheel

نَعَم yes   فراش bed

هذه أوّل مرّة the first time   لبَن yogurt

هَيّ=هون   ما حد بيوكل (بياكُل) nobody eats

وَجَع pain   ما حدا=ما حد not one/nobody

وصول arrival   مالِك؟ what is wrong?

يا=او   محطة bus stop

يَجب أن=لازم must, should   مُخيف frightening

يَدَه his hand   مَرّة time (مرّة ثانية another time)

يسلموا ايديك! May God bless your hands!   مَريض sick

أغنية: قال الطبيب

(كلمات: منذر يونس، غِناء: آدم محمد قبها)

The doctor said,	قال الطبيب
Drink milk,	اشرب حليب
And eat fruit,	وكُل فواكه
And eat grain,	وكل حبوب
And oranges	وبرتقال
From the north	من الشمال
And eat vegetables,	وكل خضار
From the south.	من الجنوب.

تمرين رقم ١

Study the cumulative vocabulary list in this lesson and create three groups (مجموعات) of words, the first group containing words (or expressions) related to health, the second containing words and expressions related to food, and the third words and expressions related to body parts. If a word has more than one occurrence, list it only once.

تمرين رقم ٢: خمّن الكلمة (نشاط جماعي)

Group activity (guess the word): one student describes a word, gives an example, or draws an object and the other students guess it. For example,

يعيش في البحر (أو في الميّة): سمك.

١. رُزّ   ٢. لبن   ٣. بِهارات   ٤. خروف   ٥. بقر   ٦. خنزير   ٧. دجاج

٨. سمك   ٩. قهوة   ١٠. شاي   ١١. سُكر   ١٢. حليب   ١٣. عصير

تمرين رقم ٣: حضّر في البيت، ناقش في الصفّ، واكتب في البيت.

Prepare at home, discuss in class, and then write up a composition of about 50 words about the following topic:

You ate something and got sick. How did you get sick, how did you feel, what did you do to feel better … ? Make sure you use the words introduced in this unit.

الوحدة رقم ١٣: المواصلات

أهمّ الكلمات الجديدة

أمين safe	طريق road
استنّى-يستنّى (to wait (for	عدّاد counter, meter
تَدخين smoking	فرق difference
دائماً always	لافتة sign
دخّن-يدخّن to smoke	مَمنوع prohibited, not allowed
دفَع-يدفع to pay	مُواصَلات عامّة public transportation
راكِب (ج. رُكّاب) passenger	نزل-ينزِل to descend, come down
سائق driver	نوع (ج. أنواع) type, kind
صاحِب owner	وقّف-يوقِّف to stop (someone)

تمرين رقم ١: (املأ الفراغات)

١. قال _____ (طريق، سائق، موظّف) التاكسي لإملي "انتِ بتحكي عربي كويّس".

٢. محمّد _____ (صاحب، تدخين، دائماً) مشغول في المدرسة والعائلة والعمل.

٣. المواصلات _____ (ممنوع، الموظّف، العامّة) في الأردن رخيصة جدّاً.

٤. _____ (دفع، لافتة، التدخين) ممنوع في الباصات لكن كثير من الناس يدخّنون.

٥. الأكل في هذا المطعم غالي جدّاً، الأسبوع الماضي _____ (عدّاد، وقّفت، دفعت) تقريباً ١٠٠ دولار.

تمرين رقم ٢: استعمل الكلمات/العبارات التالية في جُمل كاملة

١. ممنوع

٢. مواصلات عامّة

٣. أمين

٤. سائق/راكب

٥. طريق

الدرس الأوّل

النصّ الأوّل–مشاهدة: باص، سرفيس، ولا تاكسي؟

كلمات جديدة

موقف	stop (bus stop)	رأيِك	your opinion
سريع	fast	منيح=كويس	
استنّى–يستنّى	to wait (for)	أمين	safe

أسئلة

١. في رأي فدوى، إيش المشكلة في سيّارات السرفيس وفي التاكسي؟ _____

٢. كم ساعة بياخذ الباص لعمّان؟ _____

٣. كم باص فيه من إربد لعمّان حسب فدوى؟ _____

النصّ الثاني–مشاهدة: إملي تحكي مع سائق التاكسي

كلمات جديدة

مادّة subject	نزل–ينزل to descend, come down
حبّ–يحبّ to love, to like	عِدّة several, a number of
	سَبَب (ج. أسباب) reason

أسئلة

١. من إمتى إملي في الأردن؟ ـــــــــــــــــــــــــــــــ

٢. ليش إملي قالت: أنا نزلت من بطن أمّي باحكي عربي؟ ـــــــــــــــــــــــــــــ

٣. ليش إملي بتتعلّم عربي؟ ـــــــــــــــــــــــــــــ

٤. إملي بتحبّ الأكل العربي، وإيش كمان؟ ـــــــــــــــــــــــــــــ

٥. وين إملي درست عربي؟ ـــــــــــــــــــــــــــــ

تمرين رقم ١ (شفهي في الصفّ): تكوين جمل وحوارات قصيرة.

أيش رأيك؟، لكن، كم (ساعة...)، لازم، تقريباً، أكيد، ممكن، أوّل شيء، بعدين، ليش بتتعلّم/ ي عربي؟

الدرس الثاني

النصّ الأوّل–مشاهدة: رايحة تشتغلي مع المخابرات؟

كلمات جديدة

اعتمد–يعتمد to depend on	درّس–يدرّس=علّم–يعلّم to teach
مَسيحيّ Christian	خلّص–يخلّص to finish, complete
دين religion	مُخابرات intelligence services
عيب shameful	تدريس=تعليم teaching
	حسَب according to, depending on

تعابير

وزارة الخارجيّة (State Department (Ministry of Foreign Affairs

دراسات عُليا higher, graduate studies

أسئلة

١. إيش رايحة تعمل إملي بعد ما تخلّص دراسة العربي؟ ــــــــــــــــــ

٢. في رأي إملي، أيّ تخصّص سهل وأيّ تخصّص صعب؟ ــــــــــــــــــ

٣. حسب إملي، كم عدد العرب في أمريكا؟ ــــــــــــــــــ

٤. حسب إملي، كم عدد المسلمين في أمريكا؟ ــــــــــــــــــ

٥. في رأي سائق التاكسي، الحكي عن الدين شيء خاصّ أو لأ؟ ــــــــــــــــــ

النصّ الثاني–مشاهدة: التاكسي المميّز

كلمات جديدة

عادي ordinary		سامَح–يسامِح to forgive	
فرق difference		دوش–يدوِّش to make someone dizzy	
وقَّف–يوقِّف (to stop (someone		مُستحيل impossible	
يبدو it seems		دائماً always	
فهم–يفهم to understand		دفَع–يدفع to pay	
		عدّاد counter, meter	

أسئلة

١. كم بتدفع إملي للتاكسي عادةً (usually)؟ ــــــــــــــــــ

٢. ليش هذا التاكسي أغلى؟ ــــــــــــــــــ

٣. إيش الفرق بين التاكسي العادي والتاكسي المميّز؟ ــــــــــــــــــ

٤. ليش سائق التاكسي قال لإملي: انتِ بتحكي عربي كويّس، لكن يبدو ما بتفهمي عربي كويّس!

ــــــــــــــــــ

٥. في رأيك، لازم إملي تدفع أربع دنانير وربع؟ ليش؟ ــــــــــــــــــ

تمرين رقم ١ (شفهي في الصفّ): تكوين جمل وحوارات قصيرة.

رايح(ة) يعمل/تعمل، وزارة الخارجيّة، بدّي أشتغل، سهل أو صعب؟، حسَب، مثلاً، فيه عرب؟
طبعاً، بسّ (لكن)، ما بنحب (ما باحبّ)، شيء خاصّ، عادي، مستحيل، شوف(ي)، أنظف،
أحسن، أغلى، أيش الفرق بين ... ؟ يبدو

الدرس الثالث

قراءة: مذكّرات إملي

يملك الكثير من الأردنيّين سيّارات خاصّة، ولكن أكثر الناس يستعملون المواصلات العامّة.

هناك ثلاثة أنواع من المواصلات في عمّان هي سيّارات السرفيس والباصات وسيّارات التاكسي.

أرخص هذه الأنواع الباصات العامّة. أكثر ركّاب هذه الباصات من الموظّفين الحكوميّين وطلاب المدارس والجامعات.

سيّارات التاكسي لونها أصفر، وهي أغلى من الباصات لكنّها أسرع. ولا تتوقّف مرّات كثيرة في الطريق مثل الباصات.

والنوع الأخير هو سيّارات السرفيس. هذه السيّارات أغلى من الباصات، لكنّها أرخص من سيّارات التاكسي. وهي تتوقّف كثيراً في الطريق مثل الباصات، لكنّها لا تأخذ وقتاً طويلاً لأنّ عدد الركّاب فيها قليل، أربعة أو خمسة ركّاب. مشكلة التدخين مشكلة كبيرة في السيّارات الأردنيّة.

الأسبوع الماضي أخذت تاكسي من وسط البلد الى الشقّة، كان في التاكسي لافتة مكتوب عليها "ممنوع التدخين". ولكن السائق أخرج سيجارة وبدأ يدخّن. عندما سألته كيف يدخّن وهناك لافتة تقول التدخين ممنوع، قال إنّ هذه ليست سيّارته وإنّ صاحب السيّارة وضع اللافتة، وهو مسؤول عنها.

كلمات جديدة

تَدخين	smoking	مَلَك-يملك	to own
لافتة	sign	استعمل-يستعمل	to use
سائق	driver	نوع (ج. أنواع)	type, kind
أخرج-يخرج	to take (something) out	حكومي	governmental
سيجارة	cigarette	توقّف-يتوقّف	to stop
عندما=لمّا	when	طريق	road
صاحِب	owner	وقت (وقت طويل a long time)	time
وضع-يضع	to put	راكِب (ج. رُكّاب)	passenger
مَسؤول	responsible	قَليل	little, few

تعبير

مُواصَلات عامّة public transportation

أسئلة

١.   ماذا يستعمل أكثر الناس للمواصلات في الأردن؟ _____

٢.   لماذا لا تأخذ سيّارات السرفيس وقتاً طويلاً مثل الباصات؟ _____

٣.   ماذا كُتب على اللافتة التي كانت في التاكسي؟ _____

٤.   ماذا سألت إملي سائق التاكسي؟ _____

٥.   ما رأيك في الذي فعله سائق التاكسي؟ _____

1.   What do most people use for transportation in Jordan?
2.   Why don't the service cars take a long time like buses?
3.   What was written on the sign that was in the taxi?
4.   What did Emily ask the taxi driver?
5.   What do you think of what the taxi driver did?

تمرين رقم ١: قارِن بين أنواع المواصلات الثلاثة التي تتحدّث عنها إملي.

Compare the three types of transportation that Emily discusses.

من يستعملها	السرعة	الأجرة	اللون	المواصلات
				سيّارات التاكسي
				الباصات
				سيّارات السرفيس

تمرين رقم ٢: رتّب الجمل التالية من ١ – ٧ حسب ما جاءت في النصّ.

(Arrange the sentences according to their order in the reading selection. The answer is provided for the first one.)

٢   الباصات العامّة أرخص أنواع المواصلات.

__   أكثر الناس في الأردن يستعملون المواصلات العامّة مثل الباصات وسيّارات السرفيس وسيّارات التاكسي.

__   سائق التاكسي دخّن سيجارة.

__   سيّارات السرفيس أرخص من سيّارات التاكسي.

__   سيّارات السرفيس أغلى من الباصات.

سيّارات السرفيس لا تأخذ وقتاً طويلاً مثل الباصات.

طلاب المدارس والجامعات في الأردن يركبون في الباصات وسيّارات السرفيس وسيّارات التاكسي.

الدرس الرابع

قواعد

٦. إيش رأيك؟

In spoken Arabic, the idiomatic equivalent of "what do you think?" is ؟أيش/شو رأيك. "I think" or "I believe" is generally expressed by في رأيي.

تمرين رقم ١

Take turns you and your partner asking and answering the following questions. Justify your answers by using لأنّ or بسبب. The main difference between لأنّ and بسبب is that لأنّ is followed by a sentence that starts with a noun or pronoun and بسبب is followed by a noun.

I study Arabic because I like the history of the Middle East	أدرس اللغة العربية لأني أحبّ تاريخ الشرق الأوسط.
I study Arabic because of the importance of the Middle East	أدرس اللغة العربية بسبب أهمّية الشرق الأوسط.

١. في رأيك، أي لغة أصعب، اللغة العربية أو اللغة الصينية؟

٢. في رأيك، أي فصل أحسن، فصل الشتاء أو فصل الصيف؟

٣. في رأيك، المواصلات العامة أحسن في أمريكا أو في أوروبا؟

٤. في رأيك، أي أكل أطيب، الأكل المكسيكي او الأكل العربي؟

٢. إنّ

A source of errors for speakers of English learning Arabic is in the use of the equivalent of English *that*. Consider the following two sentences:

1. She said *that* she uses public transportation.
2. This is the bus *that* I take every day.

The meaning of *that* in the first sentence is quite different from its meaning in the second. In Arabic, the first *that* is translated as إنّ, while the second is translated by الذي (اللي in فصحى). Here is an Arabic translation of the two English sentences above:

١. قالت انّها تستعمل المواصلات العامّة.

٢. هذا هو الباص الذي (اللي) أركبه كلّ يوم.

تمرين رقم ٢: ترجم الى الإنجليزيّة

قالت لي فدوى إنّ الحكومة الأردنيّة تملك هذه الباصات. ـــــــــــــــــــــــــــــــــــــ

قالت لي فدوى إنّ التدخين ممنوع في المواصلات العامّة. ـــــــــــــــــــــــــــــــــــــ

تمرين رقم ٣: ترجم الى العربيّة

1. I said to him that I do not smoke. ـــــــــــــــــــــــــــــــــــــ

2. This is the taxi that costs (يكلّف) more than the ordinary taxi. ـــــــــــــــــــ

3. إنّ/أَنّ

One variant of إنّ is أَنّ, which also means "that". The difference between the two is that إنّ is used after the verb قال, while أَنّ is used everywhere else.

تمرين رقم ٤

Fill in the blanks in the following with أَنّ or إنّ, التي, الذي:

١. أعتقد (I believe) ـــــــــــــــــ الباصات في لبنان رخيصة لكنها ليست نظيفة.

٢. الباصات ـــــــــــــــــ أركبها نظيفة لكن ليست سريعة.

(باصات is a non-human plural. Non-human plurals are treated grammatically as singular feminine nouns.)

٣. هذا هو الجامع ـــــــــــــــــ أريد زيارته في القاهرة.

٤. فكّر ـــــــــــــــــ الطالبة عربية لأنها تلبس كوفية.

٥. الأمتحان ـــــــــــــــــ نجحت فيه كان صعباً جداً.

٦. الوظيفة ـــــــــــــــــ أريد أن أحصل عليها في الحكومة الأمريكية.

٧. قال لي ـــــــــــــــــ شنطتي في مطار بيروت.

٨. سائق التاكسي ـــــــــــــــــ أخذني إلى المطار من أصل فلسطيني.

٩. أعرف ـــــــــــــــــ التدخين ممنوع في أماكن كثيرة مثل المطاعم والمكتبات.

١٠. هذه هي الجامعة ـــــــــــــــــ أريد أن أدرس فيها.

4. The Arabic sentence, word order, and agreement

Arabic sentences are of two general types: those with verbs and those without verbs. Sentences that have verbs are called *verbal sentences*, and sentences without verbs are generally referred to as *equational sentences*.

Equational sentences

Smoking is prohibited	التدخين ممنوع.

Note the absence of the equivalent of the English verb *to be*. The Arabic sentence literally translates as *The smoking prohibited*.

In an equational sentence that consists of an indefinite subject and an adverb or a prepositional phrase, the adverb or prepositional phrase precedes the subject:

There are three types of transportation.	هناك ثلاثة أنواع من المواصلات.
Among the problems which I faced [is] the problem of smoking.	من المشاكل التي واجهتها هي مشكلة التدخين.

Verbal sentences

There is a certain amount of flexibility in the word order of verbal sentences: it is common for a verb to precede or follow its subject. The following two word orders are grammatical, both meaning "Many Jordanians own private cars".

يملك الكثير من الأردنيّين سيّارات خاصّة.

الكثير من الأردنيّين يملكون سيّارات خاصّة.

(Do you remember why the first sentence has يملك while the second has يملكون؟)

Verb-object-subject order

An interesting word order in verbal sentences is observed when the object of a verb is a pronoun. The pronoun in such a case is attached to the verb, resulting in a verb-object-subject sequence. The following three sentences are all grammatical:

The students study in the universities the sciences of the Islamic religion and the Arabic language.	يدرس الطلّاب في الجامعات علوم الدين الإسلامي واللغة العربية.
The students study in them the sciences of the Islamic religion and the Arabic language.	يدرس الطلاب فيها علوم الدين الإسلامي واللغة العربية.
The students study in them the sciences of the Islamic religion and the Arabic language.	يدرس فيها الطلّاب علوم الدين الإسلامي واللغة العربية.

تمرين رقم ٥

Write six sentences, three nominal and three verbal using the words below. Make sure you provide the correct agreement, use the definite article ال with nouns and adjectives that need to be defined, and use the correct form of the verb in verbal sentences.

Nouns and adjectives	Verbs
طريق، أمين، خاصّ، موظّف، سيّارة، سائق، صاحب، مسؤول، فقير، طويل	وصل–يصل، نزل–ينزل، ساق–يسوق، درس–يدرس، عمل–يعمل

تمرين رقم ٦

Fill in the empty cells in the following table. All the verbs in the table are taken from the reading passage in Lesson 3.

Root Type	Stem	Root	Translation	Verb
			He owns	يملك
	استعمل		They use	يستعملون
			And they use it (her)	ويستعملها
assimilated	توقّف			تتوقّف
sound				تأخذ
				أخذت
		ك.و.ن		كان
	أخرج			أخرج
				وبدأ
				يدخّن
				سألته
				تقول
				قال
				وضَع

Sociolinguistic corner

It was mentioned earlier that فصحى has a case system for nouns and adjectives and that at this stage only a passive knowledge of this system is necessary. As was also pointed out before, the case system does not affect the meaning of words. So طويل and طويلاً are identical in meaning; they both mean "long". When you know more Arabic, you will be expected to know those few rules of the case and mood system that are essential for writing correct فصحى.

One of the more common manifestations of the case system is the suffix اً, which you have seen in common words like شكراً، عفواً، أهلاً وسهلاً. In addition to its frequent occurrence in such adverbs, it is frequently found in singular masculine indefinite nouns when they serve as the object of a verb or as a modifier of an object.

Translate the following two sentences.

They (taxi cabs) ...	وهي (سيّارات التاكسي) تتوقّف كثيراً.
	لكنّها لا تأخذ وقتاً طويلاً.

الدرس الخامس

كلمات الوحدة

to smoke	دخّن-يدخّن	to take (something) out	أخرج-يخرج
higher, graduate studies	دراسات عُليا	safe	أمين
to teach	درّس-يدرّس=علّم-يعلّم	to use	استعمل-يستعمل
to pay	دفَع-يدفع	to wait (for)	استنّى-يستنّى
to make someone dizzy	دوّش-يدوّش	to depend on	اعتمد-يعتمد
religion	دين	smoking	تَدخين
your opinion	رأيك	teaching	تدريس=تعليم
passenger (ج. رُكّاب)	راكِب	to stop	توقّف-يتوقّف
driver	سائق	to love, to like	حبّ-يحبّ
to forgive	سامَح-يسامِح	according to, depending on	حسَب
reason (ج. أسباب)	سَبَب	governmental	حكومي
cigarette	سيجارة	to finish, complete	خلّص-يخلّص
owner	صاحِب	always	دائماً

مَسيحيّ Christian	طريق road
مَلَك-يملك to own	عادي ordinary
مَمنوع prohibited, not allowed	عدّاد counter, meter
منيح=كويس	عدّة several, a number of
مُواصَلات عامّة public transportation	عندما=لمّا when
موقف stop (bus stop)	عيب shameful
نزل-ينزِل to descend, come down	فرق difference
نوع (ج. أنواع) type, kind	فهم-يفهم to understand
وزارة الخارجيّة State Department (Ministry of Foreign Affairs)	قَليل little, few
	لافتة sign
وضع-يضع to put	مادّة subject
وقت time (وقت طويل a long time)	مُخابرات intelligence services
وقّف-يوقِّف to stop (someone)	مَسؤول responsible
يبدو it seems	مُستحيل impossible

تمرين رقم ١: خمّن الكلمة (نشاط جماعي)

ممنوع، طريق، سيّارة سرفيس، باص، مواصلات عامّة، أمين، خاصّ، عامّ، راكِب، سائق، لافتة، توقّف-يتوقّف، نوع، دفع-يدفع، موظّف، حسَب، تدخين، التدخين ممنوع، ممنوع وقوف السيّارات

تمرين رقم ٢: حضّر في البيت، ناقش في الصفّ، ثمّ اكتب في البيت.

Prepare at home, discuss in class, and then write up a composition of about 50 words about one of the following topics:

1. You are planning a trip. Write in detail how you plan to get to your destination.
2. Describe the different transportation methods in your town. What is the best method in your opinion? What do most people use? Be sure to compare and contrast the fare/cost of each method.
3. Imagine yourself in a taxi or a bus in Jordan. The driver/another passenger wants to know why you are studying Arabic, what you plan to do after graduating, etc.

الوحدة رقم ١٤: الطقس

أهمّ كلمات الوحدة الجديدة

scarcity	قِلّة	to change	تغيّر – يتغيّر
little, few	قليل	dry	جافّ
amount	كَمِّية (ج. كميات)	mountainous	جَبَلي
evening, night	ليل	temperature	درجة الحرارة
rain	مطر	warm	دافئ
moderate, temperate	مُعتدل	humid	رَطب
daytime	نَهار	humidity	رُطوبة
to reach	وَصَل – يوصَل	flowers	زهرة (ج. زهور)
		desert-like	صحراوي

تمرين رقم ١

Describe each picture using as many words/phrases as necessary from the list above.

تمرين رقم ٢: إملأ الفراغات باستعمال الكلمات الجديدة

١.   الطقس في تكساس ـــــــــــــــــــ في الصيف.

٢.   وصلت درجة ـــــــــــــــــــ الى أكثر من ١٠٠ درجة فهرنهايت.

٣.   هناك ـــــــــــــــــــ كثيّر في مدينة سياتل.

٤.   الطقس في الليل أبرد من ـــــــــــــــــــ .

٥.   هناك ـــــــــــــــــــ كثيرة في فصل الربيع.

الدرس الأوّل

مشاهدة: الطقس في أمريكا

كلمات جديدة

تغيّر-يتغيّر to change	منطقة (ج. مناطق) region, area	هيّني! here I am!
لون (ج. ألوان) color	فصل season	رَطب humid
عنّا=عندنا	مُعتدل moderate, temperate	جافّ dry
زهرة (ج. زهور) flower	أحياناً sometimes	غَبي stupid
		قصدي I mean

تعابير

والله by God, I swear!	نفس الشيء the same thing
ما شاء الله! praise God, wow!	يا ألله! Oh God!

أسئلة

١.   ايش الولايات اللي عاشت فيها إملي؟ كيف الطقس فيها؟

٢.   كم شهر فيه ثلج في نيويورك، حسب إملي؟ من أي شهر لأي شهر؟

٣.   أيّ فصل بتحبّ إملي؟ ليش؟

٤.   اي فصل فدوى بتحبّ؟

٥.   أي فصل بيحبوا الناس في الأردن؟ ليش؟

تمرين رقم ١: اكتب فصول السنة

Write down in Arabic the season that corresponds to each picture.

		شتاء	

تمرين رقم ٢: حوار قصير

Ask your neighbor about the weather in his/her hometown or state. Use words like:

طقس، بارد، حامي/حارّ، جافّ، رطب، فصول السنة (صيف، شتاء، ربيع، خريف)، شهور السنة (كانون الثاني، شباط، الخ.)

الدرس الثاني

مشاهدة: الطقس في الأردن

كلمات جديدة

وَصَل-يوصَل	to reach	دائماً	always
بناية (ج. بنايات) building		هيك	like this
كِفّى-يكفّي	to be sufficient	نزل-ينزل	to fall
دُشّ	shower	مزبوط	correct
حرّ	heat	زيّ	like, such as

تعبير

يا ستّي my dear, my lady

أسئلة

١.   كيف الطقس في الربيع في مناطق العقبة والبحر الميّت؟

٢.   وين بينزل ثلج في الأردن؟

٣.   كيف الطقس في الصيف في المنطقة اللي ساكنة فيها إملي وفدوى؟

٤.   ايش المشكلة في رأي فدوى؟

٥.   ايش بتعمل إملي في أيّام الحرّ في أمريكا؟

تمرين: نشاط جماعي (احكي عن الطقس)

Get to know your neighbor better. Ask him/her where he/she is from, which city, state, etc. and ask about the weather there. Take notes of the answers. Then, on the basis of the notes, introduce that person to the rest of the class.

الدرس الثالث

(((قراءة: مذكّرات إملي

الطقس هنا ممتاز. عِشت في ولاية نيويورك وفي ولاية كولورادو وفي ولاية تكساس. في هذه الأيّام الطقس بارد في نيويورك وكولورادو، لكن دافئ في تكساس، ولكن لا أريد أن أفكّر في الصيف في تكساس، فهو حارّ جدّاً.

الأردنّ بلد صغير ولكن فيه عدّة أنواع من الطقس: في المناطق الجبلية في الشمال الطقس بارد قليلاً في الشتاء ومُعتدل في الصيف وممتاز جدّاً في الخريف والربيع، وفي المناطق الصحراوية في شرق البلاد الطقس حارّ جدّاً في الصيف، وفي الشتاء دافئ في النهار وبارد في الليل. وفي منطقة الغور والعقبة الطقس دافئ أكثر أيّام السنة، وحارّ في شهور الصيف.

المشكلة هنا هي قِلّة الماء، والماء قليل في منطقة الشرق الأوسط كلّها، وليس في الأردنّ فقط. الناس هنا لا يستعملون الماء مثل الأمريكيّين، هنا يستعملون كمّيات قليلة عند الغسيل والطبخ والحمّام. كثير من الناس يستحمّ مرّتين أو ثلاث مرّات في الأسبوع فقط. وعندما يطبخون ويغسلون الصحون والملابس يستعملون كمّيّات قليلة جدّاً من الماء.

كلمات جديدة

صحراوي	desert-like	عاش-يعيش	to live
نَهار	daytime	دافئ	warm
ليل	evening, night	حارّ=حامي	hot
قِلّة	scarcity	بَلَد (ج. بِلاد)	country
ماء=ميّة	water	عِدّة	several, a number of
كَمّية(ج. كمّيات)	amount	نوع (ج. أنواع)	kind, type
غسيل	washing	قليل	little, few
استحمّ-يستحِمّ	to take a shower	مُعتدل	moderate, temperate
استعمَل-يستعمِل	to use	جَبَلي	mountainous

تعبير

الشرق الأوسط the Middle East

أسئلة

١. كيف الطقس في كولورادو في هذا الوقت، حسب إملي؟

٢. كيف الطقس في الصيف في تكساس، حسب إملي؟

٣. كيف الطقس في المناطق الصحراويّة في الأردن؟

٤. ما هي المشكلة في الأردن، في رأي إملي؟

٥. ماذا تقول إملي عن استعمال الأردنيّين للماء؟

1. How does Emily describe the weather in Colorado at this time of year?
2. What is the weather like in the summer in Texas, according to Emily?
3. What is the weather like in the desert areas of Jordan?
4. What is the problem in Jordan, according to Emily's opinion?
5. What does Emily say about the way Jordanians use water?

تمرين رقم ١: أكمل الجدول التالي

الخريف	الصيف	الربيع	الشتاء	المنطقة
				الطقس (spanning)
				المناطق الجبليّة
x		x		المناطق الصحراويّة
				منطقة الغور والعقبة

تمرين رقم ٢: ابحث عن الكلمات المعرّفة في النصّ، كما في المثال، ثمّ أكمل الكلمات المُتقاطعة.

The following are definitions of some key words in the reading passage. Read the definitions, identify the words, as in the example, and then use the words to complete the puzzle below.

١. قبل الصيف وبعد الشتاء

٢. ليس بارداً وليس حارّاً

٣. حامي

٤. جمع "شهر"

٥. عكس "جنوب"

٦. منطقة منخفضة وحارّة في غرب الأردن

٧. سكن

٨. كثيراً

٩.   ليس كثيراً

١٠. من الساعة الثامنة في المساء إلى الساعة السادسة في الصباح

١١. من الساعة السادسة في الصباح حتى الساعة الثامنة في المساء

١.   بعد الصيف وقبل الشتاء   ربيع

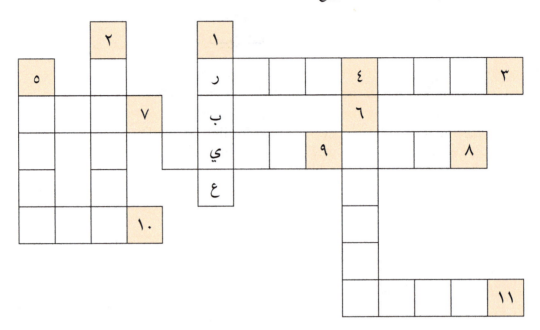

الدرس الرابع

قواعد

٥. ممكن يكون

In the brief discussion of equational sentences in Unit 13, it was noted that Arabic does not have the equivalents of the present forms of the English verb *to be* (*is* and *are*) in sentences like التدخين ممنوع (smoking is prohibited). The equivalents of *was* and *were* (كان، كانوا) are, of course, quite common: كان في التاكسي لافتة "there was a sign in the taxi".

The imperfect of كان, which is يكون, is often used to refer to future actions or states, particularly after ممكن and (فصحى in سوف) رايح.

Now translate the following sentences into English:

تمرين رقم ١

١.   خمس دقايق بيكون هون.

٢.   هذه رايحة تكون مشكلة كبيرة.

٣.   بيكون الطقس كثير حلو.

2. The forms of the Arabic verb

The thousands of verbs used in Arabic follow a surprisingly small number of patterns or forms. Some forms are quite common, others are rare.

While examples of 15 verb forms are found in Arabic, only twelve forms are considered productive in Modern Arabic, ten based on three-consonant roots and two on four-consonant roots. Only the nine most commonly used forms, all of which are based on three-consonant roots, will be introduced in this book.

Arab grammarians use the three-letter combination فعل to refer to the three letters of the root: ف for the first letter, ع for the second letter, and ل for the third. Western scholars of Arabic, on the other hand, use a system of roman numerals to refer to the different verb forms: I–X and Q1–Q2 (for verbs based on quadriliteral roots).

Form I

The most common verbal form in Arabic is Form I. It consists of the consonants of the three-consonant root and accompanying short vowels, as in كتب, كان, وصل, بدأ, درس, شرب, etc.

Other forms are constructed by modifying the structure of Form I in specific ways, such as doubling the second consonant, inserting ا between the first and second consonants of the root, adding a prefix, or a combination of these.

Different forms are generally, but not always, associated with certain meanings or grammatical functions, as will be shown below.

Form X

Verbs in Form X are distinguished by the prefix ست found before the root letters. The Form often has the meaning of doing something for oneself or thinking of something in relation to oneself.

Meaning/ grammatical function	Distinguishing feature	Examples	Shape		Form #
			Imperfect	Perfect	
No specific meaning	This form consists of the root letters and accompanying vowels	to study درس-يدرُس	يفعَل	فعَل	I
		to know عرَف-يعرِف	يفعِل	فعَل	
		to drink شرِب-يشرَب	يفعَل	فعِل	
		to open فتح-يفتَح	يفعَل	فعَل	
Often implies doing something for oneself or thinking of something in relation to oneself	The sequence ست before the root letters	استغرَب-يستغرِب to think of as strange	يستفعِل	استفعَل	X

تمرين رقم ٢

For the following verbs, all taken from the reading passage of this unit:

a. Give a full English translation (of the verb and all suffixes and prefixes).
b. Identify the root (remember that الف or ى do not exist at the root level).
c. Identify the stem
d. Write down the form of the verb if it belongs to Forms I or X, using both فعل and the form number. One verb doesn't belong to either of the two forms, write "other" for it.

The first two are given as examples.

Form	Stem	Root	Translation	Verb
Form I ،فعل	عاش	ع.ي.ش	I lived	عِشت
	أراد	ر.ي.د	I want	أُريد
	استعمل			يستعملون
		ح.م.م		يستحمّ
				يطبخون
				يغسلون

الدرس الخامس

كلمات الوحدة

mountainous	جَبَلي	sometimes	أحياناً
partial	جُزئي	to take a shower	استحمّ–يستحمّ
hot	حارّ=حامي	to use	استعمَل–يستعمِل
condition	حالة	The Middle East	الشرق الأوسط
heat	حرّ	country	بلَد (ج. بلاد)
always	دائماً	building	بناية (ج. بنايات)
warm	دافئ	to change	تغيّر–يتغيّر
temperature	درجة الحرارة	dry	جافّ

لون (ج. ألوان) color		دُشّ shower	

color لون (ج. ألوان)   shower دُشّ

evening, night ليل   humid رَطب

praise God, wow! ‬ما شاء الله!   humidity رُطوبة

water ماء=ميّة   wind ريح (ج. رِياح)

correct مزبوط   flower زهرة (ج. زهور)

rain مطر   like, such as زيّ

moderate, temperate مُعتدل   desert-like صحراوي

region, area منطقة (ج. مناطق)   to live عاش-يعيش

to fall نزل-ينزل   several, a number of عدّة

relative نسبيّة   عنّا=عندنا

the same thing نفس الشيء   cloudy غائم

daytime نَهار   stupid غَبي

kind, type نوع (ج. أنواع)   غَدا=بُكرة

like this هيك   washing غسيل

here I am! هيّني!   season فصل (ج. فُصول)

by God, I swear! والله   I mean قصدي

to reach وَصَل-يوصَل   scarcity قلّة

Oh God! يا أَلله!   little, few قليل

my dear, my lady يا ستّي   to be sufficient كفّى-يكفّي

amount كَمّية(ج. كَمّيات)

تمرين رقم ١

Read the following local weather forecast and answer the following questions below.

درجات الحرارة و حالة الطقس في عمّان – الاردن	
اليوم: الخميس ١/٥	الليلة: الخميس ١/٥
مشمس	غائم
رياح جنوبيّة شرقيّة معتدلة. نشطة أحياناً.	رياح غربيّة معتدلة السرعة
درجة الحرارة الكُبرى: ١٥ درجة مئويّة	درجة الحرارة الصغرى: ٤ درجات مئويّة
الرطوبة النسبيّة: ٤٥٪	الرطوبة النسبيّة: ٩٥٪

الإثنين ١/٩ ماطِر	الأحد ١/٨ غائم جُزئي	السبت ١/٧ مُشمس	غداً (الجمعة ١/٦) غائم جُزئي	
٩	١٠	١٥	١٠	الكُبرى
٤	٤	٤	٢	الصُغرى

كلمات جديدة

غَداً=بُكرة	ريح (ج. رياح) wind
نسبيّة relative	درجة الحرارة temperature
جُزئي partial	حالة condition
	غائِم cloudy

1. For which city is this weather forecast?
2. What day and date is it today?
3. Describe today's temperature, relative humidity, and overall weather conditions.
4. What will the weather be like 4 days from today?
5. Where is the wind blowing from today?
6. What do you think الصغرى and الكُبرى mean?

Extra credit

7. What information do you know about the wind tonight?

تمرين رقم ٢: العكس (opposites)

Match the words in row ب with their opposites in row أ by writing the word under its opposite. The first one is given as an example.

مُشمس	صيف	حار	طويل	ليل	جافّ	كُلّ	احياناً	قليل	أ
								كثير	
قصير	بعض	ماطر	رطب	بارد	كثير	دائماً	نهار	شتاء	ب

تمرين رقم ٣

Word search: First give the meaning of each of the following words and then find it in the word puzzle below. Each letter could be used in all directions (up, down, left, right, etc.)

معقول	يستعمل	وصل	معتدل	فقط	نهار	رطوبة	زهور
							flowers
	تزرع	كمّيّة	بناية	قليلاً	إلا	استحمّ	قليل

ب	إ	ل	ص	ف	ر	و	ه	ز	ق
ن	ث	ج	ط	ك	ش	ص	س	ل	ط
ا	ذ	ي	ا	ج	د	ل	ي	ق	خ
ي	س	ص	ر	د	ظ	ل	ف	ح	ع
ة	ث	ة	ل	م	ع	ت	س	ي	ر
ا	ل	ي	ل	ق	ا	ل	إ	ط	ض
إ	ة	ل	د	ت	ع	م	و	ن	ة
ف	ل	و	ق	ع	م	ب	ه	ف	ي
ت	ع	ر	ز	ت	ة	ا	ز	ك	م
م	ح	ت	س	إ	ر	س	م	ش	ك

تمرين رقم ٤: حضّر في البيت، ناقش في الصفّ، واكتب في البيت.

Prepare at home, discuss in class, and then write up a composition of about 50 words about one of the following topics:

1. The weather in your town. How is it compared to where you live now. Be as detailed as possible.
2. Your favorite (مُفضّل) weather? Why?

الوحدة رقم ١٥: الرياضة والهوايات

أهمّ كلمات الوحدة الجديدة

لعِبْ-يلعب to play	غلب-يغلب to defeat, to win	تعرُّف knowing
لعبة game	فريق team	تفرّج-يتفرّج to watch
ماهِر skilled	فضّل-يفضِّل to prefer	تنس طاولة table tennis
مُشاهدة watching	كرة سلّة basketball	حبّ-يحبّ to like
مَشهور famous	كرة طائرة volleyball	رأى-يرى to see
مُفضّل favorite	كرة قدم soccer	رياضة sport
هواية (ج. هوايات) hobby	لاعِب player	لعب playing

تمرين رقم ١

وافق بين الكلمة أو العبارة والصورة: اكتب الكلمة (أو العبارة) تحت الصورة المناسبة

سباحة، تنس طاولة، كرة طائرة، كرة قدم عاديّة، كرة قدم أمريكيّة، كرة سلة

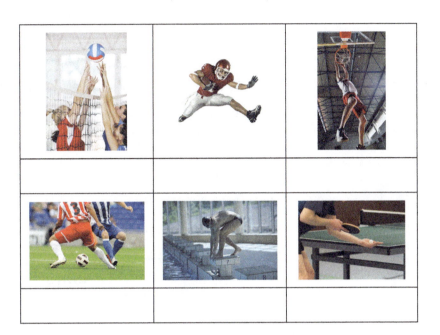

تمرين رقم ٢: (املأ الفراغات ثمّ ترجم الى الإنجليزيّة)، كما في المثال.

١.   أُفضّل (I prefer) ـــــــــــــــــ (ماهِر، مُشاهدة، مُفضل) الأفلام في السينما.

٢.   القراءة ـــــــــــــــــ (مشهور، هوايتي، فريق) المُفضلة.

٣.   مايكل جوردان ـــــــــــــــــ (لاعب، لعبة، يحب) كُرة سلّة مشهور.

٤.   كرة القدم ليست ـــــــــــــــــ كثيراً في أمريكا (مشهورة، رياضة، تفرّج).

٥.   هل هناك ـــــــــــــــــ (فريق، رأى، لعب) كرة طائرة للبنات في جامعتك؟

٦.   عندما كنت في المدرسة الثانويّة ـــــــــــــــــ (لعبت، لاعب، لعبة) كرة السلّة مع
ـــــــــــــــــ (هواية، فريق، تعرّف) المدرسة.

١.   أفضّل مشاهدة الأفلام في السينما.

I prefer watching movies in the movie theater.

الدرس الأوّل

مشاهدة: بتحبّي الرياضة؟

كلمات جديدة

كرة طائرة volleyball		حبّ–يحبّ to like	
تنس طاولة table tennis		رياضة sport	
كلّ اشي=كُلّ شيء		لعبة game	
كرة سلّة basketball		مُفضّل favorite	
اختلف–يختلف to differ		كرة قدم soccer	
عاديّ normal, ordinary		فريق team	
منتشرة widespread		لعب–يلعب to play	
		تفرّج–يتفرّج to watch	

أسئلة

١. أي لعبة فدوى بتحبّ؟ _____

٢. بتحبّ تلعبها أو تتفرّج عليها؟ _____

٣. إيش إملي بتحب تلعب؟ _____

٤. إيش اللعبة المنتشرة كثير في أمريكا؟ _____

٥. فدوى بتعرف شيء عن كرة القدم الأمريكيّة ؟ _____

تمرين رقم ١: ترجم الى الإنجليزية

١. كنت ألعب لمّا كنت صغيرة. _____

٢. كرة القدم الأمريكيّة. _____

٣. أكثر من كرة القدم العاديّة. _____

٤. كرة القدم العاديّة بدأت تنتشر. _____

تمرين رقم ٢: تكوين جمل وحوارات قصيرة

بتحبّ/ي، رياضة/لعبة مفضّلة، كرة القدم، كرة السلّة، كرة طائرة، كرة القدم الأمريكيّة، تنس طاولة، بدأت تنتشر

الدرس الثاني

قراءة: اعلانات للصداقة والتعارف والزواج

الاسم: س.م. الجنس: أنثى العمر: ٢٢ سنة الجنسيّة: كويتيّة المهنة: طالبة الهوايات: القراءة، مشاهدة الأفلام الأمريكيّة، السفر تريد التعرّف على شابّ، عمره ٢٥-٣٥ سنة، بهدف الصداقة والمراسلة	الاسم: محمد أبو الفول الجنس: ذكر العمر: ٢٨ سنة الجنسيّة: مصري المهنة: محاسب الهوايات: القراءة، السفر، مشاهدة الأخبار، لعب كرة القدم يريد التعرّف على فتاة عمرها ١٨-٢٥ سنة، بهدف الصداقة أو الزواج في المستقبل
الاسم: صالح محمد صالح الجنس: ذكر العمر: ٤٥ الجنسيّة: أردني المهنة: سائق سيّارة نقل الهوايات: الطبخ، لعب كرة السلّة، مشاهدة الأخبار على قناة العربيّة يريد التعرّف على فتاة مسلمة عمرها ٢٥-٤٥ بهدف الزواج	الاسم: رشا ت. الجنس: أنثى العمر: ٢٨ سنة الجنسيّة: سعوديّة المهنة: مساعدة مدير في بنك الهوايات: السفر، لعب تنس الطاولة تريد التعرّف على شباب وشابّات، كلّ الأعمار، بهَدَف الصداقة والزواج في المستقبل
الاسم: شادي غليون الجنس: ذكر العمر: ٢٤ الجنسيّة: سوري المهنة: مهندس الهوايات: السفر، الكتابة، لعب كرة القدم يريد التعرّف على شباب وشابّات بهدف المراسلة على الانترنت، وتبادل الأخبار والصور عن البلاد العربيّة	الاسم: منى ريحاوي الجنس: أنثى العمر: ١٩ الجنسيّة: لبنانيّة المهنة: طالبة الهوايات: القراءة، مشاهدة الأخبار، الطبخ تريد التعرّف على شابّ بهدف الصداقة والزواج في المستقبل

كلمات جديدة

فتاة=بنت	gender جنس
goal هدف	male ذكر
friendship صداقة	عُمر (ج. أعمار) age
مُستقبل future	هواية (ج. هوايات) hobby
مُراسلة correspondence	مُشاهدة watching
طبخ cooking	خبر (ج. أخبار) news
تبادل exchange	لعب playing
صورة (ج. صور) picture	تعرّف knowing

اسئلة

١. ما هي جنسيّة صالح محمد صالح؟ ماهي مهنته؟ _____

٢. ما هو جنس س.م.؟ _____

٣. ما هي هوايات محمد ابو الفول؟ كم عمره؟ _____

٤. لماذا يريد شادي غليون التعرُف على شباب وشابات؟ _____

٥. من يحبّ لعب كرة القدم؟ مشاهدة الأفلام الأمريكيّة؟ السفر؟ _____

٦. في رأيك، هل يجب على صالح محمد صالح التعرّف على منى ريحاوي؟ على شادي غليون؟ لماذا/لماذا لا؟ _____

1. What is the nationality of Salih Mohammed Salih? What is his occupation?
2. What is the gender of س.م.؟
3. What are Mohammed al-Fuul's hobbies? How old is he?
4. Why does Shadi Ghalyuun want to get to know other young men and women?
5. Who likes to play soccer? Watching American movies?
6. In your opinion, should Salih Mohammed Salih get to know Muna Rihawi? Shadi Ghalyuun? Why or why not?

تمرين: كتابة

اكمل الجدول التالي عن نفسك او عن شخص آخر

(Fill out the following table about yourself or someone else)

الإسم: _____

الجنس: _____

العُمر: _____

الجنسيّة: _____

المهنة: _____

الهوايات: _____

أُريد التعرّف على _____ بهدف _____

الدرس الثالث

قراءة: مُذكّرات إمِلي

قبل أسبوعين ذهبت أنا وفدوى ورانية الى مكّة مول واشترينا طاولة تنس. ووضعناها في غرفة الجلوس، مكان الأوراق والكتب والصحون وكاسات الشاي.

مفاجأة كبيرة! قبل ما اشترينا الطاولة قالت رانية إنّها لم تلعب تنس الطاولة في حياتها، فهي لا تحبّ الرياضة، حتى على التلفزيون.

لعبْت مع فدوى، وكانت رانية تتفرّج. ثمّ قالت إنّها تريد أن تتعلّم كيف تلعب. علّمتها قوانين اللعبة وكيف تلعبها. بعد أسبوع فقط بدأت تَغلبني وتَغلب فدوى؛ أصبحت لاعبة ماهرة.

أمس زارتنا مُنى، أخت فدوى الممرّضة، ولعبْت معها. كانت لاعبة ممتازة، وقالت إنّها لعبت في فريق المدرسة عندما كانت في المدرسة الثانويّة. لعبت معها أكثر من ساعة أو ساعتين، وتعلّمت منها أشياء كثيرة. أعتقد أنّني سأغلب رانية عندما نلعب المرّة القادمة!

كلمات جديدة

to defeat, to win	غلب-يغلب	to put	وضع-يضع
player	لاعِب	paper	ورقة (ج. أوراق)
skilled	ماهِر	surprise	مُفاجَأة
to visit	زار-يزور	life	حياة
to think	أعتقد-يعتقد	even	حتى
will	سَ	to teach	علّم-يعلّم
coming/next time	قادِم	rule	قانون (ج. قوانين)
		to start	بدأ-يبدأ

تعابير

فهي (ف+هي)   for, because she

لم تلعب   she did not play

كانت رانية تتفرّج   Rania was watching

أسئلة

١.   لماذا ذهبت إملي وفدوى ورانية الى مكة مول؟ _____

٢.   لماذا لم تلعب رانية تنس الطاولة في حياتها؟ _____

٣.   ماذا علّمت إملي رانية؟ _____

٤.   هل تعلّمت رانية لعبة تنس الطاولة؟ _____

٥.   مَن هي مُنى؟ لماذا هي ماهرة في لعبة تنس الطاولة؟ _____

٦.   لماذا تعتقد إملي انها ستغلب رانية المرّة القادمة؟ _____

1. Why did Emily, Fadwa, and Rania go to Mecca Mall?
2. Why didn't Rania ever play table tennis in her whole life?
3. What did Emily teach Rania?
4. Did Rania learn how to play table tennis?
5. Who is Muna and why is she very skilled in playing table tennis?
6. Why does Emily think she is going to beat Rania the next time?

تمرين رقم ١: اقرأ النصّ مرّة ثانية واملأ الفراغات.

Read the passage again and fill in the spaces in the following.

١.   ذهبت إملي وفدوى ورانية قبل _____ الى مكّة مول و _____ طاولة تنس.

٢.   قالت رانية إنّها لم _____ تنس الطاولة في حياتها.

٣.   علّمت إملي رانية _____ اللعبة وكيف تلعبها.

٤.   بعد أسبوع فقط فدوى أصبحت _____ _____ .

٥.   مُنى قالت انها لعبت في _____ المدرسة عندما كانت في المدرسة _____ .

٦.   إملي _____ مع مُني اكثر من _____ او _____ .

٧.   تعتقد إملي انها _____ رانية المرة القادمة.

تمرين رقم ٢

أكمل العبارات في العمود أ بما يناسبها في عمود ب، كما في المثال.

Create complete sentences by joining each phrase in the first column with the correct phrase from the second. Follow the example.

لاعبة ممتازة	اشترت إملي وفدوى	١
قوانين لعبة تنس الطاولة	بدأت رانية	٢
في غرفة الجلوس	تعلّمت إملي	٣
طاولة تنس	علّمت إملي رانية	٤
تغلب إملي وفدوى	قالت رانية	٥
إنها لا تحبّ الرياضة	كانت مُنى	٦
أشياء كثيرة من مُنى	وضعت إملي وفدوى طاولة التنس	٧

١. اشترت إملي وفدوى طاولة تنس.

الدرس الرابع

قواعد

١. Listing of names: أنا وفدوى ورانية

When listing a group of people including oneself, an Arabic speaker starts with himself/herself. So whereas in English you say: Fadwa, Rania, and I, in Arabic you say: I and Fadwa and Rania.

٢. بدأت تغلبني

The equivalent of English *I started to write*, which consists of a verb in the past tense and an infinitive, is بدأت أكتب, where the second verb is fully conjugated in the imperfect. A literal translation of بدأت أكتب is in fact *I started I write*.

   Now translate the following:

١.   بدأت تغلبني وتغلب فدوى.

٢.   ولكن السائق أخرج سيجارة وبدأ يدخّن.

3. Verb forms

Forms II and V

Form II is distinguished by the doubling of the root's middle letter and often has a causative meaning. Form V is often the passive or reflexive of Form II.

So علِمَ (Form I) is translated as "he became aware, he knew". علّم (Form II) has the meaning of "he taught" or "made someone know", and تعلّم (Form V) means "he taught himself, he learned".

Meaning/ grammatical function	Distinguishing feature	Examples	Shape		Form #
			Imperfect	Perfect	
Often causative of Form I verbs	Doubling of the middle root consonant	to teach علّم-يُعلّم	يُفعِّل	فعّل	II
Often passive/ reflexive of II	Doubling of the middle root consonant and the prefix ت	تعلّم-يتعلّم to teach oneself, learn	يتَفعّل	تَفعّل	V

تمرين رقم ١

Fill in the empty cells in the table. All the verbs are taken from مذكّرات إملي, and belong to Forms I, II, and V.

Form and #	Stem	Root	Translation	
Form I، فعل	ذهب	ذ.ه.ب	I went	ذهبت
		و.ض.ع		ووضعناها
				تلعب
				لعبْت
		ك.و.ن		وكانت
	تفرّج			تتفرّج
			She learns	تتعلّم
			I taught her	علّمتها
			She plays it (her)	تلعبها
			She defeats me	تَغلبني
				وتَغلّب
		ز.و.ر		زارتنا
				ولعبْت
				وتعلّمْت
			I will defeat	سأغلب
				نلعب

Sociolinguistic corner

While in شامي verbs are negated by ما regardless of their tense (ما راح، ما بيروح), فصحى uses different particles to negate the different tenses. Past tense verbs are negated with ما or لم. When ما is used, the verb is not changed:

he did not travel   ما سافر   he traveled سافر

When لم is used the verb is changed to the imperfect:

he did not travel   لم يسافر   he traveled سافر

(The change from سافر to لم يسافر is similar to the change in English from *traveled* to *did not travel*.)

Now translate the following sentence into English:

قبل ما اشترينا الطاولة قالت رانية إنّها لم تلعب تنس الطاولة في حياتها، فهي لا تحبّ الرياضة، حتى على التلفزيون.

فُصحى	شامي
ذهبت	رُحت
وضعناها	حطّيناها
لم تلعب	ما لعبت
لا تحبّ	ما بتحبّ
ثمّ	بعدين
تريد أن تتعلّم	بدها تتعلّم
فقط	بسّ
أصبحت	صارت
أمس	مبارح
عندما	لمّا
سأغلب	رايح أغلب

Sociolinguistic corner

الدرس الخامس

كلمات الوحدة

for, because she فَهي	to think أعتقد-يعتقد
coming/next time قادِم	to differ اختلف-يختلف
rule (ج. قوانين) قانون	to start بدأ-يبدأ
Rania was watching كانت رانية تتفرّج	exchange تبادُل
basketball كرة سلّة	knowing تعرُّف
volleyball كرة طائرة	to watch تفرّج-يتفرج
soccer كرة قدم	table tennis تنس طاولة
كلّ اشي=كُلّ شيء	gender جنس
player لاعِب	to like حبّ-يحبّ
playing لِعب	even حتى
to play لعِبْ-يلعب	life حياة
game لعبة	news (ج. أخبار) خبر
she did not play لم تلعب	male ذكر
skilled ماهِر	to see رأى-يرى
correspondence مُراسلة	sport رياضة
future مُستقبل	to visit زار-يزور
watching مُشاهدة	friendship صداقة
famous مَشهور	picture (ج. صور) صورة
surprise مُفاجَأة	cooking طبخ
favorite مُفضّل	normal, ordinary عاديّ
widespread مُنتشرة	to teach علّم-يعلّم
goal هدف	age (ج. أعمار) عمر
hobby (ج. هوايات) هواية	to defeat, to win غلب-يغلب
paper (ج. أوراق) ورقة	فتاة=بنت
to put وضع-يضع	team فريق
	to prefer فضّل-يفضّل

تمرين رقم ١: خمّن الكلمة (نشاط جماعي)

سباحة، تنس طاولة، كرة طائرة، الجري (running)، كرة قدم عاديّة، كرة قدم أمريكيّة، كرة سلة

تمرين رقم ٢: اقرأ وأجب على الأسئلة

الإسم: راشيم رايت (Rasheim Wright)
تاريخ الولادة: ١٩٨١/٧/٢١
مكان الولادة: الولايات المُتحدة الأمريكيّة
الطول: ١٩٣ سم (٦،٤ قدم)
الوزن: ٩٥ كيلوغرام (٢٠٩ باوند)
الجنسيّة: أردني وأمريكي
رقم القميص: ٥
الجامعة: دستركت اوف كولومبيا، أمريكا
الهوايات: السفر، القراءة، المُراسلة وتبادل الصور، مُشاهدة الرياضة خصوصاً كرة السلّة وكرة القدم الأمريكيّة

"زين"
فريق كُرة سلّة
الأردن

Credit: FIBA
Rasheim Wright (Jordan)

١.   ما اسم اللاعب في الصورة؟ كم رقم قميصه؟

٢.   ما جنسيته؟ اين وُلد؟ كم عمره؟

٣.   ما هي الرياضة التي يلعبها؟ أين؟

٤.   كم طوله؟ كم وزنه؟

٥.   أذكر هواياته.

٦.   ما اسم الفريق؟

تمرين رقم ٣: شفهي: اسأل زميلك وسجّل النتائج.

Ask your classmate about his/her favorite sport, write down the results, and report them to the rest of the class.

١.   ايش رياضتك المفضّلة؟

٢.   بتلعب أو بتتفرّج عليها؟

٣.   ايش فريقك المفضّل؟

٤.   مين لاعبك المفضّل؟

٥.   في رأيك، ايش اللعبة الأكثر انتشار (most widespread) في أمريكا؟ في أوروبا؟ في آسيا؟ في إفريقيا؟ في أمريكا اللاتينية؟

تمرين رقم ٤: (كتابي في البيت)

اكتب عن لاعبك المُفضل (اسم الرياضة والفريق، عمره/ها، رقم القميص، هل كان مع فريق آخر من قبل، من اي جامعة، _____)

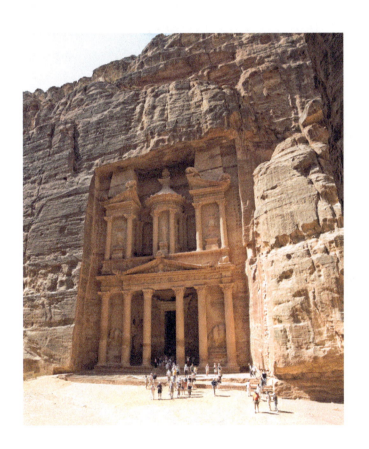

أهمّ كلمات الوحدة الجديدة

مقهى (ج. مقاهي) café	رأى–يرى to see	أعجب–يُعجِب to please
مِنطَقة (ج. مَناطِق) region	رئيسي main	بلد (ج. بِلاد) country
هادئً quiet	رحلة trip	تغيّر–يتغيّر to change
وافَق–يوافِق to agree	زار–يزور to visit	ثقافة culture
وقع–يقع to be located	مَشهور famous	دخل–يدخل to enter

تمرين رقم ١: (املأ الفراغات وترجم الى الإنجليزيّة)

Fill in the blanks in the following sentences by using one of the words in parentheses and then translate the whole sentence into English.

١. بيت الطلاب على الشارع _____ . (الرئيسي، رحلة، ثقافة)

٢. _____ اوروبا الصيف الماضي. (وافق، زرت، وقع)

٣. كانت _____ من كاليفورنيا لنيو يورك طويلة.(الرحلة، بلد، مقهى)

٤. هناك _____ قريب من الجامعة؟ (هادئ، مشهور، مقهى)

٥. _____ مدينة إثاكا في وسط ولاية نيو يورك. (رأى، تقع، تغيّر)

٦. الطقس جيّد (كويس) لكن سَوفَ (will) _____ بعد شهر او شهرين. (يتغيّر، دخل، أعجب)

٧. أريد شقّة في _____ هادئة ورخيصة. (بلد، رحلة، منطقة)

الدرس الأوّل

مشاهدة: عمان الغربيّة مثل أمريكا

كلمات جديدة

عاجِب	pleasing	بصراحة	honestly, in all honesty
مقهى (ج. مقاهي)	café/coffee house	واسع	wide
مجنون	crazy	شركة (ج. شركات)	company
حضارة	civilization	بلد (ج. بِلاد)	country
سنة (ج. سنين)	year	ثقافة	culture
آثار	ruins	مختلف	different
قلعة	citadel, fortress	غريب	strange

تعابير

كأنّ   as if

مش معقول!   not possible/unthinkable

قال ..... قال   this is nonsense

سؤال

Make a list of things that Emily and Fadwa like and dislike about عمّان الغربيّة and وسط البلد.

	عمّان الغربيّة		وسط البلد	
	بتحبّ	ما بتحبّ	بتحبّ	ما بتحبّ
فدوى				
إملي				

تمرين: تكوين جمل وحوارات قصيرة

ولّا لأ، عاجب (عاجبني/عاجبك، الخ.)، انت مجنون/ة، أصلاً، وسط البلد، أحسن، كلّ هذا، كلّ الناس، عمّان الغربيّة، مش معقول، سوق الخُضار

الدرس الثاني

النصّ الأوّل–مشاهدة: زرتِ مدن غير عمّان وإربد؟

كلمات جديدة

زار–يزور to visit		يوناني Greek	
مدينة (ج. مُدُن) city		عمود (ج. أعمدة) column	
غير other than		منطقة (ج. مَناطِق) region	
مكان (ج. أماكن) place		مبني built	
قديم old		سبح–يسبَح to swim	

تعبير

من الحامض للحلو all kinds (literally, from the sour to the sweet)

اسئلة

١.   إملي زارت مُدن غير عمان وإربد؟ ليش/ليش لأ؟

٢.   وين الآثار القديمة حسب سائق التاكسي؟

٣.   العقبة بعيدة عن البتراء؟

٤.   كيف الطقس في العقبة؟

٥.   إملي ممكن تسبح في العقبة هلّا (في شهر اذار)؟

٦.   كيف منطقة عجلون؟

تمرين: تكوين جمل وحوارات قصيرة

حَسَب، غير، بتحبّ تشوف/بتحبّي تشوفي، والله ما باعرف، كمان، زَيّ هيك، بعيد عن، ممكن تروح/ي، ممكن تسبح/تسبحي، هُناك

النصّ الثاني–قراءة: جرش

الموقع والسكّان

تَقع جرش في منطقة جبليّة على بُعد حوالي ٥٠ كيلومتراً شمال عمّان عاصمة الأردن على الطريق الرئيسي بين عمان وإربد. وهي مشهورة بآثارها اليونانيّة والرومانيّة الكثيرة.

جرش مدينة صغيرة؛ عدد سكانها حوالي ٤٠ الف نسمة، منهم عدد كبير من الشركس.

يمرّ من جرش نهر صغير اسمه "وادي الدير". تقع مدينة جرش الحديثة شرق النهر وتقع الاثار القديمة في الغرب.

تاريخ جرش

جرش مدينة قديمة، وقد أصبحت مدينة مشهورة في زمن الإسكَندر الكبير في القرن الرابع قبل الميلاد (ق.م.). في القرن الخامس الميلادي كان أكثر سكان جرش مسيحيّين.

دخل الفُرس جرش في سنة ٦١٤ ميلاديّة ثُمّ دخلها العرب المسلمون في سنة ٦٣٦م.، وأصبحت جزءاً من الدولة العربيّة الإسلاميّة.

وصول الشركس الى جرش

في سنة ١٨٧٨ وصلت مجموعات من الشركس الى جرش وبنوا بيوتاً فيها. والشركس لاجئون مسلمون هربوا من جبال القوقاز نتيجة غزو الجيش الروسي لبلادهم في القرن التاسع عشر.

كلمات جديدة

قَرْن	century	مَوقِع	location
ميلادي	A.D.	طَريق	road
دخَل–يدخل	to enter	رئيسي	main
فُرس	Persians	مَشهور	famous
جُزء	part	نسمة	souls
مجموعة	group	مرّ–يمرّ	to pass through
لاجئ (ج. لاجئُون)	refugee	نَهر	river
جبل (ج. جبال)	mountain	حَديث	modern
هرَب–يهرُب	to flee	قديم	old
نتيجة	(as a) result	زَمَن	time, era
غزو	invasion	الإسكَندر	Alexander
جَيش	army	ميلاد	birth

أسئلة

١. أين تقع جرش؟

٢. بماذا هي مشهورة؟

٣. كم عدد سكّان جَرَش؟

٤. ما اسم النهر الذي يمرّ من جرش؟

٥. أين تقع جرش الجديدة (الحديثة)؟

٦. متى أصبحت (صارت) جرش مدينة مشهورة؟

٧. ماذا كان دين اكثر سكان جرش في القرن الخامس الميلادي؟

٨. في أي سنة دخل العرب المسلمون جرش؟

٩. متى وصل الشركس الى جرش؟

١٠. لماذا هرب الشركس من بلاد القوقاز؟

1. Where is Jerash located?
2. What is it famous for?
3. What is the population of Jerash?
4. What is the name of the river that passes through Jerash?
5. Where is the New Jerash located?
6. When did Jerash become famous?
7. What was the religion of most people in Jerash during the fifth century A.D.?
8. When did the Muslim Arabs enter Jerash?
9. When did the Circassians arrive in Jerash?
10. Why did the Circassians flee the Caucuses?

تمرين رقم ١: املأ الفراغات (.Fill in the blanks without looking at the reading text)

١.   تقع جرش _____ حوالي ٥٠ كيلو متراً شمال عمّان.

٢.   يزيد عدد _____ جرش على أكثر من ٤٠ ألف _____.

٣.   تقع مدينة جرش _____ شرق نهر وادي الدير، أمّا _____ القديمة فهي في الغرب.

٤.   دخل العرب _____ جرش في _____ ٦٣٦ ميلاديّة واصبحت جزءاً من _____ العربيّة والإسلاميّة.

٥.   الشركس _____ مسلمون هربوا من جبال القوقاز.

٦.   دخل الإسكندر الكبير مدينة جرش في _____ الرابع قبل _____.

الدرس الثالث

(((قراءة: مذكّرات إملي

هربت من مكدونالدز وستاربكس وكنتاكي فرايد تشكن! أفضّل سوق الخضار القديم في عمّان على عمّان الغربيّة المملوءة بالمطاعم والمقاهي والمولات الغربيّة. تفكّر صاحباتي الأردنيّات أنّني مجنونة.

في سيّارة السرفيس التي ركبتها الى جرش اليوم، سألني السائق لماذا جئت الى الأردن وماذا أعجبني فيها. عندما قلت له إنّني أحبّ منطقة وسط البلد في عمّان ولا أحبّ عمّان الغربيّة أعجبه ذلك كثيراً، وقال إنّه لا يحبّ عمّان الغربيّة أبداً، فَقَد كانت تلك المناطق مزارع ومناطق مفتوحة، وكانت جميلة جدّاً ونظيفة وهادئة. أمّا الآن فهي مملوءة بالسيّارات والبنايات العالية، وكلّ شيء فيها أغلى من وسط البلد بكثير.

كانت رحلتي الى جرش ممتعة جدّاً، رأيت الآثار اليونانيّة القديمة ومشيت أكثر من أربع ساعات. كان الطقس جميلاً جدّاً، دافئاً ومشمساً. هذا شيء جميل جدّاً في الأردن في هذه الأيّام، طقس دافئ ومشمس كلّ يوم تقريباً. يقولون إنّ الطقس سَوفَ يتغيّر بعد شهر أو شهرين ويصبح حارّاً. هذا ليس مهمّا لي، لأنّني سأكون في ريف نيويورك في ذلك الوقت.

كلمات جديدة

مُمتِع enjoyable, fun	مَزرَعة (ج. مَزارِع) farm	فضّل-يفضّل to prefer
سَ، سَوفَ will	مَفتوح open	مَملوء full
مُهم important	هادِئ quiet	مجنون crazy
ريف countryside	عالي high	أعجب-يُعجِب to please
ذلك that	رِحلة trip	منطقة (ج. مناطق) region

تعبير

أمّا ... فـ   as for

أسئلة

١.   ماذا يستغرب الناس من إملي في الأردن؟

٢.   لماذا لا يحبّ سائق السيّارة عمّان الغربيّة؟

٣.   ماذا فعلت (did) إملي في جرش؟

٤.   ما هو الشيء الجميل في الأردن الذي تتحدّث عنه أملي؟

٥.   ما هو الشيء الذي ليس مهمّاً لإملي؟ لماذا؟

1.   What do people in Jordan find strange about Emily?
2.   Why doesn't the man who was with Emily in the car like West Amman?
3.   What did Emily do in Jerash?
4.   What is the beautiful thing in Jordan that Emily discusses?
5.   What is Emily not concerned about? Why?

تمرين رقم ٢: رتّب الجمل التالية من ١ – ٨ حسب ما جاءت في النصّ، كما في المثال، رقم ١.

(Arrange the sentences according to their order in the reading selection. The first one is given as an example.)

___   استمتعت إملي بزيارة جرش.

___   تغيّر الطقس ليس مهمّاً لإملي.

___   تكلّمت إملي مع سائق التاكسي.

١   إملي لا تحبّ عمّان الغربيّة.

___   سائق التاكسي لا يحبّ عمّان الغربيّة.

___   سافرت إملي إلى جرش بالتاكسي.

___   في عمّان الغربيّة مطاعم ومقاهي أمريكيّة.

___   كانت مناطق عمّان الغربيّة جميلة.

الدرس الرابع

قواعد

٦. قد + الفعل الماضي

Remember that when قد is followed by a verb in the perfect tense, it simply affirms that the action has taken place. Now translate the following two sentences:

جرش مدينة قديمة، وقد أصبحت مدينة مشهورة في زمن الإسكَندر الكبير في القرن الرابع قبل الميلاد (ق.م.).

فقد كانت تلك المناطق مزارع ومناطق مفتوحة، وكانت جميلة جدّاً ونظيفة وهادئة.

2. The imperfect of assimilated verbs in فصحى

As was pointed out earlier, three-letter roots whose first element is و, such as وقع "to be located", وصل "to arrive, reach", and وجد "to find", are called *assimilated*. One characteristic of verbs derived from these roots is that they lose the initial و in the imperfect form of the verb in فصحى. This explains the form تقع "it/she is located", which is the imperfect form of وقع.

تمرين رقم ١

Give the correct form of the verbs between parentheses:

١. (وقع) العراق شرق سوريا.

٢. أين (وقع) الأمارات العربية؟

٣. (وقف) السيّارة عند الإشارة الحمراء (red sign, light)، ولكن الباص لم (وقف).

٤. أي ساعة (وصل) الطالبة الجديدة أمس؟

٥. عندما ذهبت الى المستشفى فحصني الطبيب و(وصف) لي دواءً (medicine).

٦. الأولاد الصغار (وقع) كثيراً عندما يتعلّمون المشي.

3. مسلمون / مسلمين، مسيحيّون / مسيحيّين

In the sentences كان أكثر سكان جرش مسيحيّين and الشركس لاجئون مسلمون both مسيحيّين and مسلمون have a plural suffix. In fact, it is the same suffix with two variants. If the noun is in the nominative case (if it is the subject or predicate of a sentence or if it modifies a noun in the nominative case), it has the ون ending; if it is the object of a verb or a preposition it has the ين ending. You will learn more about the case system as you learn more Arabic, particularly as your need for writing Arabic increases. For now, remember that

مسلمون and مسلمين are two variants of the same word with no difference in meaning, as are مسيحيّون and مسيحيّين.

4. More on word order

In the discussion of the Arabic sentence in previous lessons, it was pointed out that there are different types of sentences and different types of word orders in the sentence. Identify the verb and the subject in each of the following sentences. Three of the sentences have two subject-verb combinations.

تمرين رقم ٢

١. تقع جرش في منطقة جبليّة.

٢. جرش مدينة صغيرة.

٣. يمرّ من جرش نهر صغير.

٤. تقع مدينة جرش الحديثة شرق النهر وتقع الاثار القديمة في الغرب.

٥. في القرن الخامس الميلادي كان أكثر سكان جرش مسيحيّين، وفي هذا القرن بُني فيها عدد من الكنائس.

Extra credit

٦. في سنة ١٨٧٨ وصلت مجموعات من الشركس الى جرش وبنوا بيوتاً فيها.

5. أمّا ... ف

The structure أمّا ... ف, in the sentence أمّا الآن فهي مملوءة بالسيّارات والبنايات العالية, translates as: As for now, it is full of cars and high buildings. أمّا and ف constitute one structure, so when you see أمّا look for ف, which will be prefixed to a word that follows it in the sentence.

تمرين رقم ٣

Complete the following sentences with a أمّا ... ف clause. The first sentence is given as an example.

١. أخي يحبّ اللغات، ...
أخي يحبّ اللغات، أمّا أنا فأحب العلوم.

٢. أنا أفضّل أن أدرس في الصباح، أمّا أبي ...

٣. فدوى تريد السفر إلى جرش، ...

٤. الطقس في "سياتل" دائماً ماطر، ...

٥. في أمريكا يأكل كثير من الناس لحم الخنزير، ...

٦. أعجبتني بيروت كثيراً، ...

6. Verb forms: Forms III and IV

Meaning/ grammatical function	Distinguishing feature	Examples	Shape		Form #
			Imperfect	Perfect	
Often has an "associative" meaning	ا between the first and second root letter	ساعَد–يُساعِد to help	يُفاعِل	فاعَل	III
Often causative of I	اُ before the first root letter in the perfect and the ضمّة on the imperfect prefix	أرجَع–يُرجِع to return something	يُفعِل	أفعَل	IV

تمرين رقم ٤

Fill in the empty cells in the table. All the verbs are taken from the reading passages of this unit, and belong to Forms I, II, III, IV, and V.

Form	Stem	Root	Translation	Verb
فعل ،Form I	دخل	د.خ.ل	He entered it	دخلها
				وأصبحت
			She arrived	وصَلت
				هربوا
				هربْت
	فضّل			أفضّل
				تفكّر
				ركبته
				سألني
أفعَل ،Form IV				أعجبني
		ق.و.ل		قلت
	أحبّ	ح.ب.ب		أحبّ
				أعجبه
		و.ف.ق		ووافق

Form	Stem	Root	Translation	Verb
				وقال
			He likes	يُحبّ
				وكانت
		م.ش.ي		ومشيت
				يقولون
	تغيّر			سيتغيّر
				ويصبح
				سأكون
Extra credit				
		و.ق.ع		تَقع

Sociolinguistic corner

ذلك ، تلك

The words ذلك (pronounced *dhaalika*) and تلك (pronounced *tilka*) are فصحى demonstrative pronouns that can be translated as "that" in English. The first is used to refer to masculine singular nouns, and the second to feminine singular nouns and non-human plural nouns.

تِلكَ المناطِق	those areas
ذلك الوقت	that time

Note the following:

1. Arabic uses the definite article in such constructions, while English does not.
2. Because مناطق "areas" is a non-human plural noun, it takes the feminine singular form of the demonstrative pronoun.

The following table shows the differences between فصحى and شامي in the use of the demonstrative pronouns. (مذكّر = masculine, مؤنّث = feminine)

شامي	فصحى		
هذا	هذا	مذكر	قريب (close objects)
هذه	هذه	مؤنّث	
هذاك	ذلك	مذكر	بعيد (far objects)
هذيك	تلك	مؤنّث	

الدرس الخامس

كلمات الوحدة

strange	غريب	ruins	آثار
invasion	غزو	to please	أعجب-يُعجِب
other than	غير	as for	أمّا ... ف
Persians	فُرس	Alexander	الإسكَندر
to prefer	فضّل-يفضّل	honestly, in all honesty	بصراحة
this is nonsense	قال ... قال	country	بلد (ج. بلاد)
old	قديم	to change	تغيّر-يتغيّر
century	قَرْن	culture	ثقافة
citadel	قلعة	mountain	جبل (ج. جبال)
as if	كأن	part	جُزء
refugee	لاجئٌ	army	جَيش
built	مبني	modern	حَديث
group	مجموعة	civilization	حضارة
crazy	مجنون	to enter	دخل-يدخل
different	مختلف	that	ذلك
city	مدينة (ج. مُدُن)	to see	رأى-يرى
to pass through	مرّ-يمرّ	main	رئيسي
farm	مَزرَعة (ج. مَزارِع)	trip	رِحلة
not possible, unthinkable!	مش معقول!	countryside	ريف
famous	مَشهور	to visit	زار-يزور
open	مَفتوح	time, era	زَمَن
café, coffee house	مقهى (ج. مقاهي)	to swim	سبح-يسبَح
place	مكان (ج. أماكن)	year	سنة (ج. سنين)
enjoyable, fun	مُمتِع	company	شركة (ج. شركات)
full	مَملوء	road	طَريق
all kinds (literally, from the sour to the sweet)	من الحامض للحلو	pleasing	عاجِب
		high	عالي
region	منطقة (ج. مناطق)	column	عمود (ج. أعمدة)

هادئ quiet	مُهم important
هرَب–يهرُب to flee	موقع location
واسع wide	ميلاد birth
وافَق–يوافِق to agree	ميلادي .A.D
وقع–يقع to be located	نتيجة (as a) result
يوناني Greek	نسمة souls
	نَهر river

تمرين رقم ١: ما هو الجمع؟

الجمع	المُفرد	الجمع	المُفرد
	صاحبة		منطقة
	بلد		مجموعة
	مول		بيت
	مزرعة		لاجئ
	سيارة		مسلم
	بناية		جبل
	مكان		مقهى
	شارع		مطعم

تمرين رقم ٢: رتّب الكلمات وكوّن جُملاً كاملة، ثم ترجم الى الإنجليزيّة.

Rearrange the following words to create meaningful sentences then translate your sentences into English. The first sentence is given as an example.

١. الى مُمتعة كانت جرش جدّاً رحلتي.

كانت رحلتي الى جرش ممتعة جدّاً.

٢. من السفر المُفضلة هواياتي.

٣. امريكا مقاهي مشهورة خصوصاً ستاربكس في كثيراً.

٤. على ١٥٤ رقم بيتي الرئيسي وهو الشارع.

٥. في دولة جنوب غرب عربيّة آسيا الأردن.

٦.   اطول نهر في نهر العالم النيل.

٧.   حيّ جبل عمّان قديم عمّان في مدينة.

٨.   جرش تقع مدينة الحديثة شرق القديمة الاثار في النهر الغرب وتقع.

تمرين رقم ٣: خمّن الكلمة (نشاط جماعي)

بِناية، طريق، جيش، جبل، آثار، يوناني، نهر، مملوء، مفتوح، مقهى، مزرعة، وافَق-يوافِق، زار-يزور

تمرين رقم ٤: احكي واكتب

حضّر في البيت، ناقش في الصفّ، واكتب في البيت.

Prepare at home, discuss in class, and then write up a composition of about 50 words about one of the following topics:

١.   مدينة زُرتها أو مدينة تحبّ أن تزورها.

٢.   دولة الأردن.

الوحدة رقم ١٧: زيارة فلسطين

اهمّ الكلمات الجديدة

شُعور feeling		أزعَج-يزعِج to bother	
ضيف (ج. ضيوف) guest		أصل origin	
طَعْم taste		إزعاج bothering	
عطشان thirsty		اعتُبِر-يُعتَبَر to be considered	
قدّم-يقدّم to offer		بلغ-يبلغ to amount to	
كرِه-يكرَه to hate		دفع-يدفُع to pay	
مَسؤول responsible		رفَض-يرفُض to refuse	
نازِل staying		ساعَد-يُساعِد to help	
لَطيف nice, kind		شعر-يشعر to feel	

تمرين: املأ الفراغات وترجم الجمل.

Fill in the blank spaces, then translate the sentences into English.

١. الطقس في سان فرانسسكو _____ (عطشان، لطيف، مسؤول) كلّ أيّام السنة تقريباً.

٢. _____ (رفضت، نزلت، قدّمت) في فندق قريب من السوق لكن _____ (رفض، بلغ، أزعجني) صوت (noise, sound) السيارات.

٣. أنا _____ (أصلي، عطشان، دفعت) من مدينة سان فرانسيسكو.

٤. أخذت تاكسي من المطار و_____ (دفعت، بلغت، قدّمت) ٢٥ دولار فقط.

٥. أحب الثلج لكن _____ (أشعر، أكره، أدفع) البرد!

٦. _____ (يبلغ، نازل، اعتبر) عدد سكّان سوريا حوالي ٢٤ مليون نسمة.

الدرس الأوّل

مشاهدة: انتَ أصلك من نابلس؟

كلمات جديدة

ضيف (ج. ضيوف) guest	أصل origin
نازِل staying	مُخيَّم (ج. مُخيَّمات) camp
إجا-ييجي to come	خِدمة service
أزعَج-يزعِج to bother	دَعوة invitation
	إزعاج bothering

اسئلة

١. من وين سائق التاكسي في الأصل؟

٢. وين سكن جدّ سائق التاكسي وأبوه؟

٣. ايش في مخيّم "بلاطة" غير بيوت السكن؟

٤. كيف الخدمات في المخيّم بالمقارنة (in comparison) بالخدمات في نابلس؟

٥. ايش قال سائق التاكسي عن الكنافة النابلسيّة؟

٦. ايش قال عن "المسخّن"؟

٧. وين إملي رايحة تاكل مسخّن؟ مع مين هي رايحة؟

٨. أي نوع فندق بدها إملي؟

تمرين: تكوين جمل وحوارات قصيرة

لا والله، أصل، أجا وسكن، أشياء زيّ هيك، كلّ الخدمات، اللي، ما فيه أحسن/أحسن من ... ، سمع بـ ... ، بلا ... بلا بطّيخ، أحسن مسخّن، رايح ييجي/يفتّش، ما باعرف، رخيص وقريب

الدرس الثاني

قراءة: مدينة نابلس

مقدّمة

مدينة نابلس من أكبر المُدن الفلسطينية. يزيد عدد سكّانها على ١٢٠ ألف نسمة. أكثر سكّان نابلس مسلمون، وهناك أقلّيّة من المسيحيّين وأقلّيّة من السَمَرة. تُعتَبَر نابلس العاصمة التجاريّة لفلسطين، وفيها آثار قديمة كثيرة.

الموقع

تقع نابلس في شمال فلسطين على بعد حوالي سبعين كيلومتراً شمال مدينة القدس وحوالي أربعين كيلومتراً شرق البحر الأبيض المتوسّط. وهي مبنيّة على جَبَلَين هُما "عيبال" و "جرزيم".

الطقس

الطقس في نابلس حارّ وجافّ في الصيف وبارد وماطر في الشتاء. ويبلغ متوسّط درجة الحرارة في الصيف ٢٦ درجة، وفي الشتاء ٨ درجات مئويّة.

مساجد ومستشفيات ومدارس كثيرة

في نابلس مساجد ومستشفيات ومدارس كثيرة ومكتبة عامّة تُعتَبَر أكبر مكتبة في الضفّة الغربيّة. وفي نابلس أيضاً تقع جامعة النجاح، وهي أكبر جامعة فلسطينيّة.

مخيّمات اللاجئين

تقع ثلاثة مخيّمات للاجئين الفلسطينيين بالقرب من نابلس. وهذه المخيّمات هي مخيّم عين بيت الما، ومخيّم بلاطة، ومخيّم عسكر.

تاريخ نابلس

بُنيت نابلس قبل أكثر من ٢٠٠٠ سنة. وقد ذُكرت في التوراة باسم "شيخِم"، وتقول التوراة إنّ سيّدنا ابراهيم عليه السلام مرّ بمدينة شيخم في طريقه الى بلاد كنعان. وكانت نابلس مركزاً تجارياً هامّاً بين مصر والجزيرة العربيّة وباقي بلاد الشام.

فتح العرب المسلمون المدينة في سنة ٦٣٦ م.

اثار نابلس

من آثار مدينة نابلس المشهورة قبر يوسف، وبئر يعقوب، والمدرّج الروماني الذي بُني في القرن الثالث الميلادي.

كلمات جديدة

لاجئ	refugee	مُسلم (ج. مُسلمون)	Muslim
ذُكر	to be mentioned	أقلّيّة	minority
التوراة	the Torah	مَسيحي (ج. مَسيحيّون)	Christian
كنعان	Canaan	سَمَرة	Samaritans
باقي	remaining, rest	تجاري	commercial
فتح–يفتَح	to conquer (open up)	هُما	they are (dual)
قَبر	grave, tomb	جافّ	dry
بئر (ج. آبار)	well	ماطر	rainy
أعتُبِر–يُعتَبَر	to be considered	متوسّط	middle, average
بلغ–يبلغ	to amount to	مسجد (ج. مساجد)	temple/place of worship
		مُخيّم (ج. مُخيّمات)	camp

تعابير

يزيد على exceeds more than

على بعد at a distance

درجة حرارة temperature (degree of heat)

عليه السلام peace be upon him (referring to the prophet Mohammed)

الجزيرة العربيّة the Arabian Peninsula

بلاد الشام Greater Syria

أسئلة

١.   ما هو عدد سكّان نابلس؟

٢.   ما هي الأقلّيّات غير المسلمة التي تعيش في نابلس؟

٣.   أين تقع نابلس؟

٤.   على ماذا بُنيت نابلس؟

٥.   كيف الطقس في نابلس في الشتاء؟

٦.   ما هي أهم معالم (landmarks) نابلس القديمة والحديثة؟

٧.   أيّة مخيّمات لاجئين تقع بالقرب من نابلس؟

٨.   ما هو اسم نابلس في التوراة؟

٩.   ما هي المناطق (البلاد) التي كانت نابلس مهمّة في تجارتها؟

١٠. متى دخل العرب المسلمون نابلس؟

تمرين رقم ١: أيّة معلومة (piece of information) غير موجودة في النصّ؟

One of the following pieces of information is not found in the text. Which one is it?

١.   الطقس في نابلس جافّ في الصيف.

٢.   يعيش في نابلس مسلمون ومسيحيّون وسمَرة.

٣.   تقع نابلس شمال القدس.

٤.   في نابلس أكبر مكتبة عامّة في الضفّة الغربيّة.

٥.   يقع مخيّم بلاطة بالقرب من نابلس.

٦.   سيّدنا إبراهيم بنى مدينة نابلس.

٧.   مدينة نابلس هي نفس مدينة شيخم.

٨.   كانت نابلس مركزاً تجاريّاً وهي الآن مركز تجاري.

٩.   يوجد في نابلس آثار رومانيّة.

تمرين رقم ٢: املأ الفراغات

١.   ـــــــــ   ـــــــــ عدد سكان نابلس ـــــــــ ١٢٠ ألف نسمة.

٢.   ـــــــــ   ـــــــــ نابلس عاصمة فلسطين التجاريّة.

٣.   نابلس ـــــــــ على ـــــــــ هُما "عيبال" و"حرزيم".

٤.   الطقس في نابلس ـــــــــ و ـــــــــ في الشتاء و ـــــــــ و
     ـــــــــ في الصيف.

٥.   المكتبة ـــــــــ في نابلس ـــــــــ أكبر ـــــــــ في الضفّة الغربيّة.

٦.   كانت ـــــــــ مركزاً ـــــــــ هاماً بين ـــــــــ والجزيرة العربيّة و
     ـــــــــ بلاد الشام.

٧.   تقع ـــــــــ النجاح في نابلس وهي أكبر جامعة في فلسطين.

٨.   في نابلس آثار ـــــــــ كثيرة.

٩.   بالقرب من نابلس ـــــــــ مخيمات للاجئين الفلسطينيين.

١٠. دخل ـــــــــ ـــــــــ مدينة نابلس في سنة ٦٣٦ م.

١١. بُني المدّرج الروماني في ـــــــــ ـــــــــ ـــــــــ الميلادي.

الدرس الثالث

(((قراءة: مذكّرات إمِلي

شعور غريب. أوّل مرّة في حياتي أدخل مخيّم لاجئين. كنت قد رأيت مخيّمات اللاجئين في الأردن، ولكنّي كنت أخاف أن أدخلها. كنت أفكّر أنّ الفلسطينيين في المخيّم سوفَ يكرهونني لأنّني أمريكية ولأنّ أمريكا تساعد إسرائيل. وفي نظرهم، إسرائيل هي المسؤولة عن وضعهم.

ولكنّ المخيّم لا يختلف كثيراً عن الأحياء الفقيرة في كثير من مُدُن العالم الثالث، في الهند ونيجيريا والمكسيك.

كما قلت، كنت أفكّر أن أهل المخيّم سيكرهونني لأنّني أمريكية، ولكن عائلة محمود أبو الرزّ، سائق التاكسي الذي ركبت معه من الجسر، كانت لطيفة جدّاً. المشكلة لم تكن أمريكا أو إسرائيل أو اللاجئين، ولكن كثرة الأكل والشرب. عندما وصلت الى بيت محمود دان قدّموا لنا عصير برتقال. كان الطقس حارّاً وكنت عطشانة جدّاً. بعد العصير جاء الشاي، ثمّ الغداء: مسخّن دجاج. أوّل مرّة في حياتي أكلت مسخّن دجاج. ولا أكذب إذا قلت انّ المسخّن أطيب أكلة أكلتها في

حياتي. أكلت حتى شبعت، ولكن قالوا "لا، لازم تاكلوا كمان". وأكلت حتى شعرت أن معدتي ستنفجر. ولكن، والحمد لله، لم تنفجر معدتي. ثمّ شربنا قهوة وبيبسي ورجعنا مع محمود الى الفندق. عند الفندق حاولت أن أدفع لمحمود أجرة التاكسي، ولكنّه رفض، لأنّنا ضيوف، حسب قوله.

كلمات جديدة

قدّم-يقدّم to offer		شُعور feeling	
عطشان thirsty		خاف-يخاف to be scared	
كذب-يكذب to lie		كرِه-يكرَه to hate	
شبِع-يشبع to be full		ساعَد-يساعِد to help	
شعر-يشعر to feel		نظر view	
انفجَر-ينفجِر to burst, explode		مَسؤول responsible	
حاوَل-يحاوِل to try		وَضْع situation	
دفع-يدفع to pay		حَيّ (ج. أحياء) quarter (of a city), neighborhood	
رفَض-يرفُض to refuse		كما as	
ضيف (ج. ضيوف) guest		جسر bridge	
		لَطيف nice, kind	

تعبير

لم تكن was not

أسئلة

١.   لماذا كانت إملي تخاف أن تدخل مخيّمات اللاجئين؟

٢.   لماذا ذُكرت الهند في النصّ؟

٣.   مَن هو محمود أبو الرزّ؟ كيف عاملت (treated) عائلته إملي؟

٤.   ماذا كانت المشكلة؟

٥.   ما هو المسخّن؟ ماذا تقول إملي عنه؟

٦.   هل أخذ محمود أجرة التاكسي من إملي؟ لماذا؟

تمرين: رتّب الجمل التالية من ١–٩، حسب ما جاء في نصّ القراءة.

__٢__   أمريكا تساعد إسرائيل.

____   المخيّمات مثل الأحياء الفقيرة في الهند.

____   حاولت إملي أن تدفع أجرة التاكسي.

ـــ   رفض محمود أن يأخذ الأجرة من إملي.

ـــ   شربت إملي الشاي.

ـــ   شربت إملي العصير.

ـــ   شربت إملي القهوة.

ـــ   كانت إملي تخاف أن تدخل المخيّمات.

ـــ   كانت المشكلة الأكل والشرب.

الدرس الرابع

قواعد

١. لم يكُن

As was pointed out earlier, لم is a فصحى particle used to negate verbs in the perfect tense. When it is used to negate the verb كان and other hollow verbs in Form I, the middle vowel is dropped.

كان he was   لم يكن he was not   (لم + يكون based on)

2. Verb forms: Forms VII and VIII

In شامي Form VII is the typical passive form. So while كتب translates as "he wrote" انكَتَب translates as "it was written". Form VIII had a similar function in older forms of Arabic, but the passive meaning is not transparent any more.

Meaning/ grammatical function	Distinguishing feature	Examples	Shape		Form #
			Imperfect	Perfect	
Passive of I	ن before the first root letter	انكَسَر–ينكسِر to be broken	ينفَعِل	انفَعَل	VII
Historically passive/ reflexive of I	ت between first and second root letters	اشتغل–يشتغل to work	يَفتَعِل	افتَعَل	VIII

تمرين

Fill in the empty cells in the table. All the verbs are taken from the reading passages of this unit, and belong to Forms I, II, VII, and VIII.

Form	Stem	Root	Translation	Verb
Form I ،فعل	زاد	ز.ي.د	It (he) exceeds	يزيد (على)
			And it amounts	ويبلغ
				وتقول
				وكانت
Form I ،فعل				أدخل
				كنت
			I am afraid	أخاف
				أدخلها
				أفكّر
		ك.ر.ه	They hate me	يكرهونني
		خ.ل.ف		يختلف
				وصلت
				أكذب
				أكلتها
				شبعت
				قالوا
				ستنفجر
				تنفجر
				شربنا
				ورجعنا
Extra credit				
				تقع
				قلت

Sociolinguistic corner

1. As was pointed out earlier, فصحى has an *internal* passive formation rule like بَنى-بُني, which is absent in شامي. A Form I verb is changed to Form VII to express the passive meaning. So the equivalent of "it (she) was built" is rendered in فصحى as بُنِيَت, but in شامي as انبَنَت. (The final ي of the root is dropped when the suffix ـَت is attached.)

تمرين

Fill in the empty cells in the following table and then answer the question below.

	Passive		Active
شامي	فصحى		
انبَنى	بُنِي		بَنى
	فُتِح		فَتَح
	سُمِح		سَمَح
			دَفَع
			رَفَض
			كَتَب

How is the internal passive expressed in فصحى؟

2. While شامي has dual only in nouns, فصحى has a dual form for verbs, nouns, adjectives, and pronouns. So هُمّ in شامي stands for "they" and can refer to two or more people or objects, فصحى uses هُما to refer to two and هُم to refer to more than two persons or objects.

الدرس الخامس

كلمات الوحدة الجديدة

to be considered	اعتُبَر-يُعتَبَر	to bother	أزعَج-يزعِج
the Torah	التوراة	origin	أصل
the Arabian Peninsula	الجزيرة العربيّة	minority	أقلّيّة
to burst, explode	انفجَر-ينفجِر	to come	إجا-يجي
well	بِئر	bothering	إزعاج

باقي remaining, rest

بلاد الشام Greater Syria

بلغ-يبلُغ to amount to

تجاري commercial

جافّ dry

جسر bridge

حاوَل-يحاول to try

حَيّ (ج. أحياء) quarter (of a city)

خاف-يخاف to be scared

خِدمة service

درجة حرارة temperature (degree of heat)

دَعوة invitation

دفع-يدفع to pay

ذُكِر to be mentioned

رفَض-يرفُض to refuse

ساعَد-يساعِد to help

سَمَرة Samaritans

شبع-يشبع to be full

شعر-يشعر to feel

شُعور feeling

ضيف (ج. ضيوف) guest

عطشان thirsty

على بعد at a distance

عليه السلام peace be upon him (referring to the prophet Mohammed)

فتح-يفتَح to conquer (open up)

قَبر grave, tomb

قدّم-يقدّم to offer

كذب-يكذِب to lie

كره-يكرَه to hate

كما as

كنعان Canaan

لاجىئ refugee

لَطيف nice, kind

ماطِر rainy

متوسّط middle, average

مُخيَّم (ج. مُخيّمات) camp

مَسؤول responsible

مسجد (ج. مساجد) temple/place of worship

مُسلم (ج. مُسلمون) Muslim

مَسيحيّ (ج. مَسيحيّون) Christian

نازل staying

نظر view

هُما they are (dual)

وَضْع situation

يزيد على exceeds more than

تمرين رقم ۱

Word search. Find each word in the puzzle below and give its meaning in English:

ئ	ج	ل	ا	ف	ا	خ	ض	ب	ا	ر	ش
ا	و	ع	ف	د	ي	ط	ل	م	س
ن	ع	ل	ز	ا	ن	ش	ا	ل	ك	س	ا
ه	ر	ب	و	ا	و	ع	ص	ت	ا	م	ع
ه	م	ر	ف	ظ	ر	ب	ض	ي	ف	د

ما	ضيف	لاجئ	هُم	في	مكتب	شراب
	رفض	ساعد	هرب	عن	لطيف	او
		نازل	دفعوا	شعر	خاف	لا

تمرين رقم ٢: ابحث عن الكلمة المعرّفة في نصّي القراءة.

The following are definitions of some key words in the two reading passages. Read the definitions, identify the words, and use them to complete the puzzle below.

١. كتاب اليهود المقدّس

٢. فيها كتُب كثيرة

٣. عكس "يُحبّ"

٤. هرب من بلاده ويعيش في بلد آخر

٥. أجزاء (parts) المدينة

٦. عكس "أكثريّة"

٧. عكس "غني"

٨. قال "لا"

٩. عكس "رطب"

١٠. لم يشرب منذ وقت طويل

١١. يُعطي الأجرة لسائق التاكسي

١٢. فوق (above, over) النهر ويربط أحياء المدينة

١٣. عكس "بارِد"

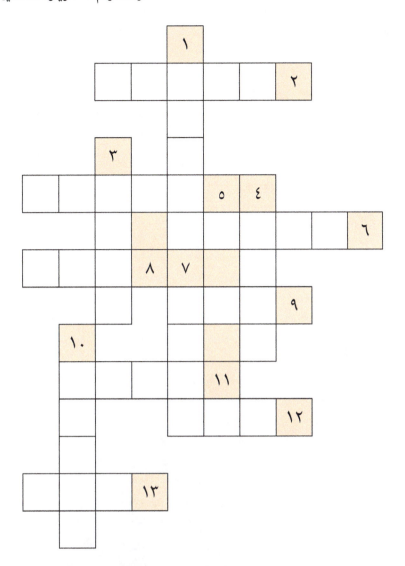

تمرين رقم ٣: حضّر في البيت، ناقش في الصفّ، واكتب في البيت.

Prepare at home, discuss in class, and then write up a composition of about 50 words about one of the following topics:

١.   مُعاملة (treatment) سائق التاكسي محمود أبو الرّز لإملي.

٢.   ماذا تعرف عن مشكلة فلسطين؟

٣.   مدينة القدس.

٤.   الأكل الفلسطيني.

الوحدة رقم ١٨: زيارة لبنان

أهمّ كلمات الوحدة الجديدة

مُتأخر late	شاطىء beach	أجنبي (ج. أجانب) foreign
متحف (ج. متاحف) museum	شاعر poet	استقلال independence
مصرف (ج. مصارِف) bank	شركة (ج. شركات) company	بقي–يبقى to remain
نعسان sleepy	صديق friend	حُكم control, ruling
هامّ important	قرية village	حكم–يحكم to rule
هدية (ج. هدايا) gift	للأسف unfortunately	رجع–يرجع goes back to

تمرين رقم ١: املأ الفراغات

١.   كانت الرحلة طويلة، لكن نمت طول الوقت لأني كنت _____ (هامّ، نعسان، مُتأخر).

٢.   "مايا أنجلو" _____ (شاعرة، مهندسة، شركة) أمريكيّة مشهورة.

٣.   صديقي مُحاسب في _____ (مصرف، شاطئ، متحف).

٤.   في بيروت عدد كبير من الشركات _____ (الأجنبيّة، المشويّة، قرية).

٥.   كان _____ (هامّة، استقلال، شاطئ) امريكا في سنة ١٧٧٦.

تمرين رقم ٢

Using the clues below write the correct word to complete the puzzle.

١.   صاحب

٢.   مدينة صغيرة

٣.   من دولة أخرى

٤.   يكتب شعر

٥.   بنك

٦.   جذر حكومة

الدرس الأوّل

النصّ الأوّل-مشاهدة: أهلاً وسهلاً بيكِ في بيروت!

كلمات جديدة

هَيدا=هذا	to arrive	وصل-يوصل	هَيدا=هذا
خَيّ=أخ	other than	غير	
تمام good, all well	sleepy	نعسان	
وينه=وين هو	to go, go out	ضهر-يضهَر=راح-يروح=طلع-يطلَع	
تأخّر-يتأخّر to be late	to eat dinner	تعشّى-يتعشّى	

تعابير

كيفِك؟=كيف حالك؟	الحمد لله عَ السلامة!, Thank God for your safe arrival,
مش بطّال not bad	glad you made it safely!
طول الوقت the whole time	May God keep you safe! الله يسلمك!

اسئلة

١.   مين نبيل؟

٢.   ليش دان مش مع إملي؟

٣.   كم شنطة عند إملي؟

٤.   ليش ما كانت رحلة إملي صعبة؟

٥.   ايش إملي ونبيل ونادية رايحين يعملوا بعد ما يروحوا للفندق؟

النصّ الثاني-مشاهدة: شو بتحبّوا تاكلوا؟

كلمات جديدة

أَكلة dish, something to eat

مازة (ج. مازات) appetizer

مَشوي (ج. مَشاوي) grilled food

كبّة، شاورما، فتّوش، تبّولة names of dishes

نعنع mint

تعابير

أشتقنا لك we missed you

عَ راسي وعيني I will be happy to (lit. on my head and eyes)

أسئلة

١. مين مع إملي في المطعم؟

٢. ايش إملي طلبت تاكل؟ نادية؟ نبيل؟

٣. اي نوع شاي طلبت إملي تشرب؟

النصّ الثالث: مشاهدة: شو حابّة تشوفي بلبنان؟

كلمات جديدة

قلعة citadel		أخبار news	
ماشي=كويّس	منيح=كويّس good, well	
أتّفق–يتفق to agree		ماضي past, last	
		سهل plain, meadow	

تعابير

زيّ ما تركتيني as you left me

شو حابّة تشوفي؟ What would you like to see?

اسئلة

١. اي ساعة نادية ونبيل رايحين بيجوا للفندق؟

٢. ايش بدها تشوف إملي في لبنان؟

٣. وين رايحين بكرة؟ بعد بكرة؟

تمرين رقم ١: تكوين جمل وحوارات قصيرة

الحمد لله ع السلامة، الله يسلّمك، هذا ... ، كيفَك/كيفِك، تمام، غير، كيف كان ... ؟ اشتاق–يشتاق، وأنا كمان، لو سمحت، ع راسي وعيني، زَيّ=مثل، المرّة الماضية، كيف شفت/شفتِ ... ؟ ماشي

تمرين رقم ٢: أحكي في الصفّ

Create a dialogue with your neighbor in which one of you acts the role of a waiter and the other a customer in a restaurant in an Arab country.

الدرس الثاني

قراءة: بيروت

مُقدّمة

بيروت عاصمة لبنان وأكبر مدينة فيه. يزيد عدد سكانها على مليون نسمة.

تقع في غرب الدولة على الساحل الشرقي للبحر الأبيض المتوسط، وهي المركز الثقافي والتجاري في البلاد، ومركز الحكومة ايضاً.

مركز ثقافي واقتصادي هامّ في الشرق الأوسط والعالم العربي

بيروت من أهمّ المراكز الثقافيّة في منطقة الشرق الأوسط والعالم العربي، وفيها عدد من الجامعات المشهورة مثل الجامعة الأمريكيّة في بيروت والجامعة اللبنانيّة وجامعة بيروت العربيّة. تُعتَبَر بيروت أيضاً من أهمّ مراكز التجارة والاقتصاد في الشرق الأوسط. وفيها عدد كبير من المصارِف والشركات اللبنانية والأجنبية.

تاريخ بيروت

يرجع تاريخ بيروت الى أكثر من خمسة آلاف سنة، ويرجع اسمها الى كلمة "بروت" (beroth) الفينيقيّة، التي تعني آبار (جمع بئر).

احتلّ الرومان بيروت في سنة ٦٤ ق.م. وأصبحت مدينة هامّة في دولتهم. وفي نهاية القرن الثاني وبداية القرن الثالث الميلادي كانت مدرسة القانون في بيروت من أشهر مدارس القانون في بلاد الرومان.

دخل العرب المسلمون بيروت في القرن السابع الميلادي، وأصبحت جزءاً من الدولة العربيّة الإسلاميّة . وفي سنة ١١١٠ احتلّها الصليبيّون، وبقيت تحت حكمهم الى سنة ١٢٩١ عندما دخلها المماليك. وفي سنة ١٥١٦ أصبحت جزءاً من الدولة العثمانيّة، وبقيت كذلك حتى هزيمة الدولة العثمانية في الحرب العالميّة الأولى. وبعد العثمانيين دخلها الفرنسيون وحكموها الى سنة ١٩٤٣، وهي سنة استقلال لبنان.

كلمات جديدة

المماليك the Mamluks		ساحل coast	
عُثمانيّ Ottoman		اقتصادي economic	
كذلك that way		هامّ important	
هزيمة defeat		مصرف (ج. مصارِف)=بَنك (ج. بُنوك) bank	
استقلال independence		شركة (ج. شركات) company	
رجع–يرجع goes back to		بئَر (ج. آبار) well	
احتلّ–يحتلّ to occupy		جزء (ج. أجزاء) section, part	
بقي–يبقى to remain		الصليبيّون the Crusaders	
حكم–يحكم to rule		تحت under	
		حُكم control, rule	

تعبير

الحرب العالميّة الأولى World War I

أسئلة

١.   اين تقع بيروت؟ كم عدد سكانها؟

٢.   ماهي الجامعات المشهورة في بيروت؟

٣.   كم عمر بيروت؟

٤.   مامعنى كلمة بيروت؟ ماهو اصل الكلمة؟

٥.   لماذا تُعتبر بيروت من اهمّ المدن في العالم العربي؟

٦.   من احتل بيروت في سنة ٦٤ ق.م.؟

٧.   متى دخل العرب المسلمون بيروت؟

٨.   من حكم بيروت في سنة ١١١٠؟ سنة ١٢٩١؟ سنة ١٥١٦؟

٩.   من دخل بيروت بعد الحرب العالميّة الأولى؟

١٠. متى كان استقلال لبنان؟

تمرين رقم ١: ترجم الى الإنجليزيّة

١. بيروت من أهمّ المراكز الثقافيّة في منطقة الشرق الأوسط والعالم العربي.

٢. تُعتَبَر بيروت أيضاً من أهمّ مراكز التجارة والاقتصاد في الشرق الأوسط.

تمرين رقم ٢: املأ الفراغات

١. تقع بيروت على _____ البحر الأبيض المتوسط.

٢. _____ تاريخ بيروت الى أكثر من خمسة آلاف سنة.

٣. _____ الرومان بيروت في سنة ٦٤ ق.م. وأصبحت مدينة _____ في دولتهم.

٤. أصبحت بيروت جزءاً من الدولة العربيّة الإسلاميّة في القرن _____ _____.

٥. دخل _____ بيروت في سنة ١٢٩١م.

تمرين رقم ٣

أكمل كلّ واحدة من العبارات في عمود أ بما يناسبها في عمود ب، كما في المثال.

ب	أ	
من الدولة العربيّة الإسلاميّة في القرن السابع	هناك علاقة (relationship) بين	١
في سنة ١٩٤٣	من جامعات بيروت المشهورة	٢
في سنة ١٢٩١	في بيروت عدد كبير من	٣
هامّ في الشرق الأوسط	دخل المماليك بيروت	٤
حتى الحرب العالميّة الأولى	بيروت مركز ثقافي	٥
المصارف والشركات الأجنبيّة	بقيَت بيروت جزءاً من الدولة العثمانيّة	٦
الجامعة اللبنانيّة	استقلّ لبنان	٧
اسم بيروت وكلمة "بئر"	أصبحت بيروت مدينة هامّة	٨
في زمن الرومان	أصبحت بيروت جزءاً	٩

١. هناك علاقة بين اسم بيروت وكلمة "بئر".

الدرس الثالث

قراءة: مذكّرات إِملي

كانت زيارتي للبنان ممتعة، لكن قصيرة. نزلت في الفندق لأن بيت صديقتي نادية صغير. بعد وصولي، أكلنا العشاء في مطعم. أنا ونادية طلبنا كبّة مشويّة مع فتّوش ونبيل طلب شاورما وتبّولة.

في اليوم الثاني مشينا في شوارع بيروت، وجلسنا في مقهى على الشاطئ ودخّنا النرجيلة ... حتى ساعة متأخرة من الليل.

يوم الأربعاء ذهبنا بالسيّارة الى الجنوب، وزرنا ميناء صيدا، وقلعة صيدا، ومتحف الصابون. ثمّ ذهبنا الى سوق صيدا القديم، واشتريت بعض الهدايا لأهلي وأصحابي في أمريكا.

يوم الخميس زُرنا منطقة البقاع. أكلنا الغداء (سمك وبطاطا مقليّة وسلطة خضار) في مطعم على نهر البردوني، ثم زرنا آثار "بعلبك" الرومانية. وفي الطريق زرنا قرية "بشرّي" التي وُلد فيها الكاتب والشاعر اللبناني المشهور جبران خليل جبران.

يوم الجمعة زرنا مدينة جبيل، وهي مدينة تاريخية على الساحل، فيها الكثير من الآثار القديمة والمقاهي والمطاعم، وأكلنا الغداء هناك.

كما قلت، كانت زيارتي للبنان قصيرة، أسبوع واحد فقط. كنت أريد أن أزور طرابلس، ومغارة "جعيتا"، و"الباروك" ... في الرحلة القادمة إن شاء الله.

كلمات جديدة

مَقليّ	fried	صديق (ج. أصدِقاء)=صاحِب (ج. أصحاب)	friend
قرية	village	شاطىء	beach
شاعر	poet	مُتأخر	late
للأسف	unfortunately	متحف (ج. متاحف)	museum
مَغارة	cave	صابون	soap
		هدية (ج. هدايا)	gift

اسئلة:

١. لماذا لم تنم إملي في بيت نادية؟

٢. ماذا أكلت إملي وشربت في العشاء اليوم الأول؟

٣. ماذا فعلت (= عملت did) إملي في اليوم الثاني (يوم الثلاثاء)؟

٤. ماذا فعلت إملي يوم الأربعاء؟

٥. ما هي "بشرّي"؟ لماذا ذُكرت في المُذكرات؟

٦. أين أكل نبيل ونادية وإملي الغداء يوم الجمعة؟

٧. ما هي الأشياء التي لم تزرها إملي في لبنان؟ لماذا لم تزرها في هذه الرحلة؟

تمرين رقم ١: رتّب الجمل من ١ – ١٠ حسب ما جاءت في النصّ.

___ في اليوم الرابع، تغدوا في منطقة البقاع.

___ إملي اشترت هدايا لأهلها واصحابها من سوق صيدا القديم.

___ في اليوم الثالث (الأربعاء) سافروا الى الجنوب.

___ في اليوم الأول، أكلت إملي العشاء في مطعم مع نادية ونبيل.

___ نزلت إملي في فندق لأن بيت نادية صغير.

___ زاروا آثار بعلبك الرومانية.

___ ذهبوا لمقهى على الشاطئ ودخّنوا النرجيلة.

___ زاروا قرية بشري التي وُلد فيها الشاعر جبران خليل جبران.

__١__ كانت زيارة إملي للبنان ممتعة لكن قصيرة.

___ زاروا متحف الصابون.

تمرين رقم ٢: ابحث عن الكلمات المعرّفة في النصّ، كما في المثال، ثمّ أكمل الكلمات المُتقاطعة.

The following are definitions of some key words in the reading passage. Read the definitions, identify the words, as in the example, and then use the words to complete the puzzle below.

١. منتشرة في الشرق الأوسط ويدخّنها الناس بدل السجاير

٢. عكس "شرق"

٣. وجبة نأكلها في الظهر

٤. قديمة

٥. اشترت منه إملي هدايا لأهلها

٦. بجانب البحر

٧. عكس "طويل"

٨. شارع

٩. يعرفه كثير من الناس

١٠. نطبخ فيه

١١. نشرب فيه القهوة

مِثال

١. منتشرة في الشرق الأوسط ويدخّنها الناس بدل السجاير　　النرجيلة

	١
	ا
	ل
	ن
	ر
	ج
	ي
	ل
	ة

الدرس الرابع

قواعد

Verb forms: summary

Meaning/grammatical function	Distinguishing feature	Shape		Form #
No specific meaning	Root letters and accompanying vowels	يفعَل، يفعِل، يفعُل	فعَل، فعِل، فعُل	I
Often causative of I	Doubling of the middle root consonant	يُفعِّل	فعَّل	II
Often has an "associative" meaning	ا between the first and second root letter	يُفاعِل	فاعَل	III
Often causative of I	ا before the first root letter in the perfect and the ضمّة on the imperfect prefix	يُفعِل	أفعَل	IV
Often passive/reflexive of II	Doubling of the middle root consonant and the prefix ت	يتَفعَّل	تَفعَّل	V
Passive of I	ن before the first root letter	ينفَعِل	انفَعَل	VII
Historically passive/ reflexive of I	ت between first and second root letters	يَفتَعِل	افتَعَل	VIII
Often implies doing something for oneself or thinking of something in relation to oneself	The sequence ست before the root letters	يستفعِل	استفعَل	X

تمرين: املأ الفراغات

Fill in the empty cells in the following table. All the verbs are taken from the reading passages of this unit.

Form	Stem	Root	Translation	Verb
			She is located	تقع
	اعتبر		She is considered	تُعتَبَر
				يرجع
		ح.ل.ل		احتلّ
				وأصبحت
				كانت
				احتلّها
				وبقيت
				دخلها
				وحكموها
				نزلت
		م.ش.ي		مشينا
				وجلسنا
	دخّن			ودخّنّا
				ذهبنا
				واشتريت
فعل، Form I				زرنا
	أراد			أريد
			I visit	أزور

Sociolinguistic corner

One thing that you may have realized by now is that the majority of words and grammatical structures are shared by شامي and فصحى. There are of course differences in the pronunciation of most words, but such differences are minor and systematic. The word طريق, for

example, is pronounced by many شامي speakers with a همزة or g in place of the ق of فصحى.
But this is a phenomenon that you can pick up quickly without the need to learn the
two pronunciations as two separate words. The following table shows the same sentence
expressed in both language varieties. Can you identify the differences?

وفي الطريء زرنا ضيعة بشرّي اللي انولد فيها الكاتب والشاعر اللبناني المشهور جبران خليل جبران.	وفي الطريق زرنا قرية بشرّي التي وُلد فيها الكاتب والشاعر اللبناني المشهور جبران خليل جبران.

الدرس الخامس

كلمات الوحدة

حابّ (شو حابّة تشوفي؟	to agree أتّفق-يتفق
What would you like to see?)	foreign (ج. أجانب) أجنبي
control, rule حُكم	news أخبار
to rule حكم-يحكم	we missed you أشتقنا لك
خيّ=أخ	dish, something to eat أكلة
goes back to رجع-يرجع	to occupy احتلّ-يحتلّ
as you left me زي ماتركتيني	independence استقلال
coast ساحل	economic اقتصادي
plain, meadow (ج. سُهول) سهل	World War I الحرب العالميّة الأولى
beach شاطىء	the Crusaders الصليبيّون
poet شاعر	the Mamluks المماليك
company (ج. شركات) شركة	well (ج. آبار) بئر
soap صابون	to remain بقي-يبقى
friend صديق (ج. أصدقاء)=صاحِب (ج. أصحاب)	to be late تأخّر-يتأخّر
to go, go out ضهَر-يضهَر=راح-يروح=طلع-يطلَع	under تحت
I will be happy to عَ راسي وعيني	to eat dinner تعشّى-يتعشّى
(lit. on my head and eyes)	good, all well تمام
Ottoman عُثمانيّ	section, part (ج. أجزاء) جزء

مَشوي (ج. مَشاوي) grilled food	other than غير
مصرف (ج. مصارِف)=بَنك (ج. بُنوك) bank	قرية (ج. قُرى) village
مَغارة cave	قلعة citadel
مَقليّ fried	كبّة، شاورما، فتّوش، تبّولة
منيح=كويّس good, well	names of dishes
نعسان sleepy	كذلك that way
نعنع mint	كيفِك؟=كيف حالك؟
هامّ important	للأسف unfortunately
هدية (ج. هدايا) gift	مازة (ج. مازات) appetizer
هزيمة defeat	ماشي=كويس
وصل-يوصل to arrive	ماضي past, last
وينُه=وين هو	مُتأخر late
	متحف (ج. متاحف) museum

تمرين رقم ١

Circle the word that does not belong in each group.

مقهى	هدية	مطعم	١. مكتبة
فول	فلوس	مصرف	٢. بنك
مازة	مشوي	مكتوب	٣. مقلي
حمّام	تعبان	نعسان	٤. جوعان
ساحل	كاتب	مهندس	٥. شاعر
لحم	نعنع	عسل	٦. سُكر
يفطر	يتعشى	يلعب	٧. يتغدى
قريبة	مدينة	قرية	٨. دولة
متحف	ساحل	شاطئ	٩. بحر

Extra credit

عالميّة	تجارة	اقتصاديّة	١٠. ثقافيّة

تمرين رقم ٢

استعمل الكلمات التاليّة في جُمل كاملة:

١. هدية _____

٢. هامّ _____

٣. مصرف _____

٤. صديق _____

٥. مُتأَخِّر _____

٦. رجع _____

٧. تعشّى-يتعشّى _____

تمرين رقم ٣: كلمات متقاطعة

	١	٢	٣	٤	٥	٦	٧	٨	٩	١٠
١										
٢										
٣										
٤										
٥										
٦										
٧										
٨										
٩										
١٠										

عمودي		أفقي	
جمع بئر؛ جمع مصرف	١.	الحرب العالميّة ـــــــ؛ نسكن فيه	١.
إسم الحرف "ل"	٢.	ندخل الغرفة منه	٢.
إسم الـــــــ لو سمحتِ؛ انا ـــــــ مدينة نيويورك	٣.	في عائلتي اب وـــــــواخ واخت؛ كان ـــــــ أمريكا سنة ١٧٧٦	٣.
نشرب فيه قهوة	٤.	ـــــــ أبي هنري؛ عكس "أيوا"	٥.
جذر "ملابس"	٥.	جذر "شُكراً"	٧.
أخ إملي الصغير(معكوسة)؛ مهنة (profession) جبران خليل جبران وتي إس إليوت.	٦.	إسم أخت فدوى التي تدرس التوجيهي	٩.
شراب (معكوسة)	٨.	دخّنّتها إملي ونادية ونبيل	١٠.
الاسم الـ ـــــــ لو سمحت!	٩.		

تمرين رقم ٤: حضّر في البيت، ناقش في الصفّ، واكتب في البيت.

Prepare at home, discuss in class, and then write up a composition of about 50 words about one of the following topics:

١. لبنان أو دولة عربيّة أخرى.

٢. زيارة لدولة عربيّة.

الوحدة رقم ١٩: زيارة سوريا

أهمّ كلمات الوحدة الجديدة

سهل	easy	أجمل	most beautiful
شَعب (ج. شُعوب)	people	أعجب-يُعجب	to please
شكر-يشكر	to thank	أكيد	certainly
عدد	number	ألطَف	gentler, kinder
قُرب	near	إداري	administrative
محفظة	wallet	انسرق-ينسرق	to get stolen
مَعالم	landmarks	بنفسي	by myself
مَنظر	scene, sight	ساعَد-يُساعِد	to help
نسي-ينسى	to forget	سرَق-يسرِق	to steal

تمرين: املأ الفراغات

١.   في رأيي الخريف _____ (أجمل، أعجب، أكيد) فصل في السنة!

٢.   أين المكتب _____ (منظر، الإداري، عامّ) في الجامعة؟

٣.   ضيّعت _____ (محفظتي، عدد، بنفسي) في الباص.

٤.   من _____ (قُرب، معالم، شعب) مدينة نيويورك المشهورة تمثال الحرّية (Statue of Liberty).

٥.   _____ (شكر، ساعد، نسيت) كتاب اللغة العربيّة في شقتي.

٦.   تقع ولاية أريزونا بـ _____ (القُرب، ألطف، سهل) من الحدود المكسيكيّة.

٧.   يزيد _____ (شعب، نسمة، عدد) الطلاب في الصف على أكثر من خمسين طالب.

الدرس الأوّل

النصّ الأوّل–مشاهدة: بكم الفلافل؟

كلمات جديدة

الشام=دمشق	حضارة civilization
أعجب–يعجب to please	خسّ lettuce
نسي–ينسى to forget	

تعابير

على شانِك! for you!	عن جدّ seriously
ببلاش free, for nothing	زمان صار لِك ... ؟ have you been a long time ... ?

أسئلة

١.   بكم سندويشة فلافل حسب بائع الفلافل؟

٢.   كم دفعت إملي؟ ليش؟

٣.   فيه اثار قديمة في امريكا حسب إملي؟

النصّ الثاني-مشاهدة: أكيد محفظتي انسرقت

كلمات جديدة

انسرق-ينسرق	to get stolen	محفظة	wallet
ايّاها	it (her)	سرَق-يسرِق	to steal

(See grammar note below.)

شكر-يشكر   to thank

تعبير

ما عليكِ   don't worry about it

اسئلة

١.   ايش ضيعت إملي؟

٢.   إملي وجدت الشيء اللى ضيعته؟ وين؟

٣.   كيف شكرت إملي سائق التاكسي؟

٤.   ليش إملي قالت بائع الفلافل راجل طيب؟

Notes

1.   دمشق is commonly referred to by Syrians and Arabs from neighboring countries as الشام, the same way that القاهرة is referred to by Egyptians as مصر.
2.   The verb عجب (Form I) is used alongside أعجب (Form IV) with the same meaning, "to please". So عجبتك الشام؟ literally translates as *Did Damascus please you?* However, idiomatically, it is better translated as *Did you like Damascus?*
3.   You may have noticed that the preposition على is often abbreviated to عَ. Both forms are often used by the same person in the same situation. The فلافل seller thus uses على شانك and ع شانك with the same meaning "for you" (lit. for your sake).
4.   The word ايّاها consists of the "carrier" إيّا and the attached pronoun ها "it, her". The carrier إيّا is used when there is a sequence of two object pronouns. For example, when the two objects in the following sentence are replaced by pronouns, the direct object is attached to إيّا.

أعطيت أحمد الكتاب.   I gave Ahmad the book.

أعطيته إيّاه.   I gave it to him (lit. I gave him it).

تمرين: تكوين جمل وحوارات قصيرة

على شانَك/شانِك (ع شانَك/ع شانِك)، من وين، مش من هون، زمان صار لِك/لَك، غير، عجب/
أعجَب، سندويشة فلافل، محفظة، جواز سفر، كان معي، لاقى/يلاقي، فلوس، جوعان، ما بدّك
ايّاه/ايّاها؟

الدرس الثاني

قراءة: دمشق

مقدّمة

دمشق عاصمة سوريا وأكبر مدينة فيها. وهي المركز الإداري والتجاري والثقافي في البلاد. تقع
في جنوب غرب الدولة قُرب الحدود اللبنانية، ويمُرّ منها نهر "بَرَدى". يزيد عدد سكان دمشق
على مليون وخمسمئة ألف نسمة.

تاريخ دمشق القديم

دمشق من أقدم المُدن في العالم، ويرجع تاريخها الى الألف الثالث قبل الميلاد (ق.م.). وقد
احتلّها المصريّون في القرن الخامس عشر ق.م.، وفي حوالي سنة ١٠٠٠ ق.م. دخلها الملك
"داوود"، ثمّ احتلّها الآشوريون والبابليّون والفُرس واليونان والأنباط والرومان. وفي نهاية القرن
الرابع الميلادي كان أكثر سكّان دمشق مسيحيّين.

الفَتْح الإسلامي

فتَح العرب المسلمون دمشق سنة ٦٣٦ م.، وأصبحت عاصمة الدولة العربيّة الإسلاميّة في زمن الدولة الأمويّة. وفي سنة ٧٥٠ م. أصبحت بغداد عاصمة الدولة الإسلاميّة، ولكن بقيت دمشق مدينة هامّة في الدولة الإسلاميّة.

الدولة العثمانيّة

كانت دمشق جزءاً من الدولة العثمانية من سنة ١٥١٦ حتى الحرب العالميّة الأولى. وبعد هزيمة الدولة العثمانيّة في تلك الحرب دخلها الجيش الفرنسي، وبقي فيها حتى استقلال سوريا عن فرنسا في شهر نيسان سنة ١٩٤٦.

مَعالم دمشق المشهورة

من معالم دمشق المشهورة سوق الحميديّة؛ والجامع الأموي، الذي يرجع تاريخه الى القرن التاسع قبل الميلاد؛ وقَبر صَلاح الدين الأيّوبي، القائد المُسلم المعروف؛ وعدد من المدارس القرآنيّة القديمة والكنائس والمتاحف والحمّامات العامّة.

كلمات جديدة

قَبر	grave	فتح–يفتح	to open up, conquer	إداري	administrative
قائد	leader	زمن	era, time period	قُرب	near
عدد	number	هزيمة	defeat	الآشوريون	the Assyrians
قرآنيّة	Quranic	جيش	army	البابليّون	the Babylonians
كنيسة (ج. كنائس)	church	مَعالم	landmarks	الفُرس	the Persians
عامّ	public	مشهور	famous	اليونان	the Greeks
				الأنباط	the Nabataeans

اسئلة

١. اين تقع دمشق؟ كم عدد سكانها؟

٢. من احتل دمشق في القرن الخامس عشر ق.م.؟

٣. ماهي المجموعات التي دخلت دمشق؟

٤. متى دخل العرب المسلمون دمشق؟

٥. ماذا حدث في سنة ٧٥٠ م.؟

٦. من احتل دمشق بعد الحرب العالميّة الأولى؟

٧. أذكر معالم دمشق المشهورة؟

٨. لماذا ذُكر اسم القائد المُسلم صلاح الدين الأيوبي؟

تمرين رقم ١: املأ الفراغات

١. تقع دمشق في ــــــــــــــ ــــــــــــــ سوريا.

٢. احتل ــــــــــــــ دمشق في القرن الخامس عشر ق.م.

٣. ــــــــــــــ سوريا عن فرنسا في شهر نيسان سنة ١٩٤٦.

٤. من معالم دمشق المشهورة ــــــــــــــ و ــــــــــــــ و ــــــــــــــ.

٥. كانت دمشق ــــــــــــــ من الدولة العثمانية من ــــــــــــــ ١٥١٦ حتى الحرب ــــــــــــــ الأولى.

تمرين رقم ٢: رتّب الجمل من ١ – ٩ حسب ما جاءت في النصّ، كما في المثال، رقم ١.

(Arrange the sentences according to their order in the reading selection. The first one is given as an example.)

ـــــ احتلّ المصريون دمشق.

ـــــ استقلّت سوريا.

ـــــ دخل الجيش الفرنسي دمشق.

ـــــ دخل الملك داوود دمشق.

ـــــ دمشق مدينة قديمة.

١ سوريا قريبة من لبنان.

ـــــ فتح المسلمون دمشق.

ـــــ في القرن الرابع كان أكثر سكّان دمشق مسيحيين.

ـــــ هُزمت الدولة العثمانيّة في الحرب العالميّة الأولى.

الدرس الثالث

قراءة: مذكّرات إملي

سوريا! أجمل بلد، ألطف ناس، وأطيب أكل! لكن ... حكومة وشرطة وجيش ومخابرات وخوف في كلّ مكان. الكلّ يخاف من الحكومة والشرطة والمخابرات.

سمعت وقرأت عن "ستالين" و "ماو تسي تونغ" و "كم ال سونغ"، ولكن ما رأيت روسيا والصين وكوريا الشماليّة بنفسي. مسكينة سوريا الجميلة، مسكين الشعب السوري اللطيف!

في اليوم الثاني من زيارتي كنت أمشي في شارع من شوارع دمشق الرئيسيّة. وقفت سيّارة عند الإشارة الضوئيّة، ولكن عندما حاول سائقها أن يتقدّم الى الأمام، لم تشتغل السيّارة، وبقيت في وسط الشارع عند الإشارة. كانت سيّارة قديمة جدّاً.

بعد قليل وصلت سيّارة شرطة، ونزل شرطي منها وذهب الى السيّارة الواقفة. كنت أفكّر أنّه سيساعد سائقها... ولكنّه أخرج السائق وبدأ يضربه ضرباً شديداً... منظر مؤلم.

لذلك كانت زيارتي لسوريا قصيرة، يومين فقط. كنت أريد أن أبقى فيها أسبوعاً، ولكن منظر سائق السيّارة والشرطي يضربه ... لم يكن سهلاً عليّ أن أبقى في سوريا يوماً آخر.

كلمات جديدة

مَنظر	scene, sight	أجمل	most beautiful
مُؤلِم	painful	ألطَف	gentlest, kindest
سهل	easy	مُخابَرات	intelligence service
عليّ	to me	خَوف	fear
آخر	another	بنفسي	by myself
تقدّم-يتقدّم	to move forward	مسكين (!)	poor (as in oh, poor guy!)
ساعَد-يُساعِد	to help	شعب (ج.شُعوب)	people
ضرب-يضرِب	to hit	واقف	standing

تعابير

إشارة ضوئيّة traffic light

ضربه ضرباً شديداً he hit him harshly (literally: he hit him severe hitting)

أسئلة

١. ماذا قالت إملي عن سوريا والشعب السوري والأكل السوري؟

٢. لماذا ذكرت روسيا والصين وكوريا الشماليّة؟

٣. ماذا حدث في اليوم الثاني من زيارة إملي لدمشق؟

٤. كم يوماً بقيت إملي في سوريا؟ لماذا؟

تمرين رقم ١: أكمل كلَّ واحدة من العبارات في عمود أ بما يناسبها في عمود ب، كما في المثال.

كوريّة قديمة	الكلّ يخاف من
عند الإشارة الضوئيّة	بدأ الشرطي
في شارع رئيسي	بقيت السيّارة
في كلّ مكان	حكومة وشرطة
كوريا الشماليّة والصين	كانت سيّارة
الحكومة والمخابرات	كنت أمشي
من السيّارة	ما رأيت
يضرب السائق	نزل الشرطي

١. الكلّ يخاف من الحكومة والمخابرات.

تمرين رقم ٢: ابحث عن الكلمات المعرّفة في النصّ، كما في المثال، ثمّ أكمل الكلمات المتقاطعة.

١.   عكس "صعب"
٢.   لونها أحمر أو أخضر أو أصفر وموجودة في الشارع
٣.   سبعة أيّام
٤.   حَكم الاتّحاد السوفييتي في القرن العشرين
٥.   طيّبة أو جيّدة
٦.   قُدّام
٧.   وقفت عند الإشارة الضوئيّة
٨.   بدّي
٩.   عكس "طويل"
١٠. ليست جديدة أو حديثة
١١. شارع كبير ومهمّ في المدينة
١٢. شُفت

مثال

١. عكس "صعب"   سهل

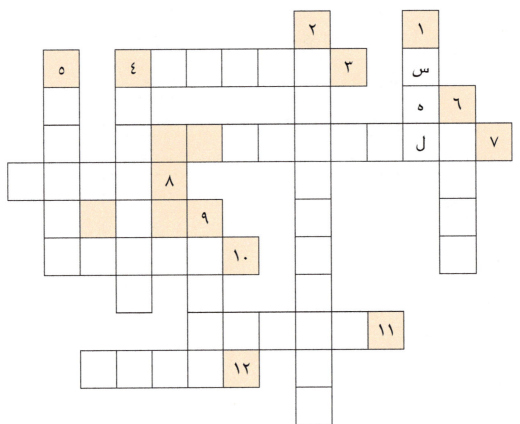

الدرس الرابع

قواعد

كنت أريد

When كان (and its derivatives) is followed by a verb in the imperfect tense, then it has the meaning of past continuous or past habitual action.

Now translate the following sentences:

تمرين رقم ١

١. في اليوم الثاني من زيارتي كنت أمشي في شارع من شوارع دمشق الرئيسيّة.

٢. كنت أفكّر أنّه سيساعد سائقها.

٣. كنت أريد أن أبقى فيها أسبوعاً.

تمرين رقم ٢

Change the verbs in parentheses from present to past time, using كان (+ the imperfect form of the verb). The first sentence is given as an example.

١. (أريد) أن أدرس في الشرق الأوسط لكن أبي (يرفض).
كنت أريد أن أدرس في الشرق الأوسط، لكن أبي رفض.

٢. (يحب) أن يزور سوريا، لكن الأحوال (لا تسمح).

٣. (تركب) الباص الساعة السابعة كل يوم حتى تذهب إلى المدرسة.

٤. (نقضي we spend) شهور الصيف في بيت جدّي في الجبل.

٥. (يفكّرون) أن كل البلاد العربية صحراوية!

٦. أبي (يعمل) في شركة هندسة في وسط البلد.

تمرين رقم ٣

Fill in the empty cells in the following table (أكمل الجدول التالي). All the verbs are taken from the listening and reading material of this unit.

Form	Stem	Root	Translation	Verb
أفعل، IV	أعجب		She pleased you	أعجبتك
				أعجبتني
	نسي			أنساها
			They steal	يسرقوا
				يزيد
		ح.ل.ل		احتلّها
				وأصبحت
	خاف			يخاف
			I walk	أمشي
				حاوَل
				يتقدّم
				تشتغل

Form	Stem	Root	Translation	Verb
				أفكّر
				سيساعد
	أخرَج			أخرج
	أراد		I want	أريد
	بقي		I remain, stay	أبقى

الدرس الخامس

كلمات الوحدة

حضارة	civilization	ايّاها	it (her)
خسّ	lettuce	آخر	another
خَوف	fear	أجمل	most beautiful
زمان صار لِك ... ؟	have you been	أعجب-يعجب	to please
	a long time ... ?	ألطَف	gentlest, kindest
زمن	era, time period	إداري	administrative
ساعَد-يُساعِد	to help	إشارة ضوئيّة	traffic light
سرَق-يسرق	to steal	الآشوريون	the Assyrians
سهل	easy	الأنباط	the Nabataeans
شعب (ج. شُعوب)	people	البابليّون	the Babylonians
شكر-يشكرُ	to thank	الشام=دمشق	
ضرب-يضرب	to hit	الفُرس	the Persians
ضربه ضرباً شديداً	he hit him harshly (lit. he	اليونان	the Greeks
	hit him severe hitting)	انسرق-ينسرق	to get stolen
عامّ	public	ببلاش	free, for nothing
عدد	number	بنفسي	by myself
على شانِك!	for you!	تقدّم-يتقدّم	to move forward
عليّ	to me	جيش	army

مُخابَرات intelligence service	عن جدّ seriously
مسكين poor (as in oh, poor guy!)	فتح–يفتح to open up, conquer
مشهور famous	قائد leader
مَعالم landmarks	قَبر grave
مَنظر scene, sight	قرآنيّ Qur'anic
مُؤلِم painful	قُرب near
نسي–ينسى to forget	كنيسة (ج. كنائس) church
هزيمة defeat	ما عليكِ don't worry about it
واقف standing	محفظة wallet

أغنية

(كلمات: منذر يونس، غِناء: جواد إياد قبها)

(هديّة إلى السيّد نديم صاحب Ned's Pizza، أحسن بيتسا وفلافل في ولاية نيويورك.)

'ala dal'uuna w-'ala dal'uuna	على دلعونة وعلى دلعونة
We don't want cheese or macaroni	ما بدنا جبنة ولا معكرونة
We want to eat only at your place	ما بدنا ناكل الّا من عندك
Even if it was a piece of bread and an olive.	لو كانت خبزة وحبّة زيتونا.
O Uncle Yousef, you with the great qualities,	يا عمّو يوسف يا ابو الشمايل،
We've come to you to eat *falaafil*.	جينا لَعندك ناكل فلافل.
We've tried the *hummus* in the whole world,	جرّبنا الحمّص في العالم كلّه،
The *hummus* of this restaurant doesn't have an equal.	حمّص هالمطعم ما له مثايل.
Not to forget *baba* (*ghannouj*) and the green salad	ما ننسى البابا والسلطة الخضرا،
And grilled chicken covering the tables.	والجاج المشوي مغطّي الطوايل.
More than seven (dollars) I will not pay,	أكثر من سبعة مش رايح أدفع،
(Even) if you brought the police riding the purebred horses.	لو جِبت الشرطة فوق الأصايل.

تمرين رقم ١: خمّن الكلمة (نشاط جماعي)

Group activity (guess the word): one student describes a word, gives an example, or draws an object and the other students guess it.

جيش، فلافل، مخابرات، كنيسة، محفظة، إشارة ضوئية، ضرب-يضرب، سرق-يسرق، جامِع، سائق تكسي، مسكين، لطيف

تمرين رقم ٢: حضّر في البيت، ناقش في الصفّ، واكتب في البيت.

Prepare at home, discuss in class, and then write up a composition of about 50 words about one of the following topics:

١. دولة عربيّة لم تقرأ عنها في هذا الكتاب

(An Arab country you have not read about in this book.)

2. An experience where something was stolen from you.
3. Was Emily right in leaving Syria after two days only?
4. You are traveling in the Middle East. Send a postcard to a friend. Tell him/her what you liked or did not like. Use أعجب.

أكتب لك من مدينة ... في ...

أعجبني/أعجبتني ... لكن الأسعار/الطقس، السيّارات، الخ.

الوحدة رقم ٢٠: زيارة مصر

أهمّ كلمات الوحدة الجديدة

أَهَمّيّة importance	فاهِم understood
اتّصل-يتّصل to call	قريب (ج. أقارِب) relative
استأجَر-يستأجر to rent	مبلغ sum, amount
اكتشف-يكتشف to discover	مزح-يمزَح to jest, make jokes
تحدّث-يتحدّث to talk (about something)	مُغنّي singer
جيب (ج. جُيوب) pocket	مُمتِع enjoyable, fun
حدّد-يحدّد to limit	مُناسب suitable
ردّ-يردّ to answer	مواصلات transportation
زَحمة crowdedness	نتَج-ينتُج to result
سبب reason	هادي quiet
ضحك-يضحك to laugh	

تمرين رقم ١: املأ الفراغات

١. مَن الذي _____ (نتج، اكتشف، اتصل) أمريكا فعلاً؟

٢. _____ (ردّ، مزح، تحدّث) رئيس الدولة عن (أهمّية، مواصلات، مُغني) التعليم في المجتمع.

٣. استأجرت إملي شقة _____ (سبب، مبلغ، مُناسبة) لها.

٤. أحب مدينة نيويورك، لكن لا أحب _____ (قريب، زحمة، شركة) السيارات.

٥. كانت الفلوس في _____ (جيبي، مُغني، زحمة) لكن ضيعتها!

٦. محمد يحبّ الموسيقى _____ (الكبيرة، الكثيرة، الهادئة) مثل الموسيقى الكلاسيكية أكثر من "روك أند رول"!

٧. السباحة رياضة _____ (مُمتعة، مُشكلة، مغنّي) وجيدّة للصحة.

٨. أريد أن _____ (أدفع، أضحك، استأجر) سيارة لمّدة اسبوع.

الدرس الأوّل

النصّ الأوّل–مشاهدة: رايحة فين النهار دا؟

كلمات جديدة[1]

فاضي	empty	فاهم	understanding, having understood
هادي	quiet	مواصلات	transportation
عربيّة=سيّارة		زَحمة	crowdedness
حاجة	something	بُصّي=شوفي	

[1] A number of words in the dialogues of this lesson are typical Egyptian words, as shown in the "sociolinguistic corner" below.

تعابير

صباح النور والفُل=صباح الخير

على فين النهار دا؟ to where (are you going) today?

أرجوك=لو سمحت please

أسئلة

١. لوين إملي رايحة؟

٢. عن ايش إملي بِدها تسأل سائق التاكسي؟

النصّ الثاني–مشاهدة: الدنيا كلّها زحمة

كلمات جديدة

جاب–يجيب to bring		ليه=ليش	
مراة=زوجة		هنا=هُنا=هون	
عمّ paternal uncle		دُنيا=عالَم world	
خالّ maternal uncle		حلّ solution	
بقي–يبقى=صار–يصير to become		حدّد–يحدّد to limit	
أصل origin		أهل (ج. أهالي) folks	
اتولد–يتولد=انولد–ينولد to be born		صعيدي (ج. صعايدة) Sa'idi, a person	
دا=هذا this		from Upper Egypt	
		سَبب reason	

تعابير

تشرّفنا I am delighted (or honored) to have met you

ما فيش=ما فيه there is not

معانا=مَعنا with us

أسئلة

١. ليش إملي في مصر؟

٢. وين فيه زحمة حسب السائق؟

٣. ايش سبب الزحمة في رأيِ السائق؟ ليش؟

٤. من وين السائق أصلاً؟

٥. وين انولد؟

٦. ليش سائق التاكسي أعطى رقم تلفونه لإملي؟

تمرين

Create a dialogue similar to the one in the video clip, where one speaker uses شامي and the other مصري. Some helpful words and expressions:

اليوم/النهار دا، مش فاهم، وين رايح/رايح فين، على عيني وراسي، الأخ/الأخت من وين/
فين، زحمة، مشاكل المواصلات، ولا شيء/ولا حاجة، ابن خال، ابن عمّ، خدمات، شكراً جزيلاً،
مع السلامة

الدرس الثاني

متحف القاهرة

قراءة: القاهرة

مقدّمة

القاهرة عاصمة مصر وأكبر مدينة فيها. وهي أكبر مدينة في العالم العربي وإفريقيا. وهي
العاصمة الإداريّة والتجاريّة والثقافيّة في البلاد.

الموقع والمساحة

تقع القاهرة على نهر النيل في شمال مصر، وتُحيط بها الصحراء من الشرق والجنوب والغرب.
وتبلغ مساحتها حوالي ٤٥٠ كيلومتراً مربّعاً.

السكّان

يزيد عدد سكّان القاهرة على ثمانية ملايين نسمة، ويزيد عدد سكّانها مع المناطق المُحيطة بها على
١١ مليون نسمة. أكثر سكّان القاهرة من المسلمين السُنّة، ولكن هناك أقلّية كبيرة من المسيحيّين
الأقباط. يرجع أصل الأقباط الى المسيحيّين الذين سكنوا القاهرة قبل وصول المسلمين في القرن
السابع الميلادي.

أحياء القاهرة

تقع أحياء القاهرة الإسلاميّة على الضفّة الشرقيّة لنهر النيل وتمتدّ من الشمال الشرقي الى الجنوب الشرقي. وهذه الأحياء مشهورة بشوارعها الضيّقة وأسواقها ومساجدها القديمة. الى الجنوب من أحياء القاهرة الإسلاميّة تقع منطقة مصر القديمة، التي يسكنها أقباط القاهرة. ويقع فيها المتحف القبطي وعدد من الكنائس القبطيّة.

مشاكل المُواصلات والسكَن

القاهرة مركز الحَياة في مصر، ويُسَمّيها المصريّون "مصر" لأهمّيّتها في حياتهم. فهي مركز الحكومة والثقافة والتِجارة والاقتصاد والمُواصلات في البلاد. ويجيء لها المصريّون من المناطق الأخرى من أجل الخدمات والوظائف. وينتج عن ذلك مَشاكل كثيرة في المواصلات والسَكن.

كلمات جديدة

اقتَصاد	economy	صحراء	desert
مُواصَلات	transportation	مُحيط	surrounding
وَظيفة (ج. وَظائف)	job	اقليّة	minority
احاط–يحيط	to surround	الأقْباط	the Copts
نتَج–ينتُج	to result	حَيّ (ج. أَحْياء)	neighborhood
مِن أجل	for (the sake of)	ضفّة	bank (of a river)
نهر النيل	the Nile River	ضَيّق	narrow
		أهَمّيّة	importance

أسئلة: اكتب صحّ أو خطأ (true/false)

١.   القاهرة أكبر مدينة في إفريقيا.

٢.   القاهرة هي العاصمة الثقافيّة لمصر.

٣.   تحيط الصحراء بالقاهرة من كلّ الجهات (الشرق والغرب والشمال والجنوب).

٤.   يبلغ عدد سكّان القاهرة مع المناطق المحيطة بها حوالي ٨ ملايين نسمة.

٥.   عاش الأقباط في القاهرة قبل وصول المسلمين.

٦.   توجد الأحياء الإسلاميّة في القاهرة على الضفّة الشرقيّة من نهر النيل والأحياء القبطيّة على الضفة الغربيّة.

٧.   توجد أسواق قديمة في الأحياء الإسلامية في القاهرة.

٨.   يسمّي المصريون مصر القاهرة.

٩.   يُغادر (leave) المصريّون القاهرة الى المناطق الأخرى للبحث عن عمل.

١٠. في القاهرة مشاكل في المواصلات والسكن.

تمرين رقم ١: ابحث عن الكلمات المعرّفة في النصّ ثمّ أكمل الكلمات المُتقاطعة.

١. يصلّي فيها المسيحيّون

٢. حارات أو أجزاء من المدينة

٣. الناس الذين يعيشون في دولة أو مدينة

٤. أهمّ مدينة في الدولة

٥. عكس "واسع"

٦. يصلّي فيه المسلمون

٧. من أكبر أنهار إفريقيا

٨. أكثر المسيحيّين في مصر

٩. حارّة وجافّة وليس بها ماء

١٠. عكس "أكثريّة"

١١. توجد فيه أشياء قديمة

١٢. سيّارات التاكسي وسيّارات السرفيس والباصات

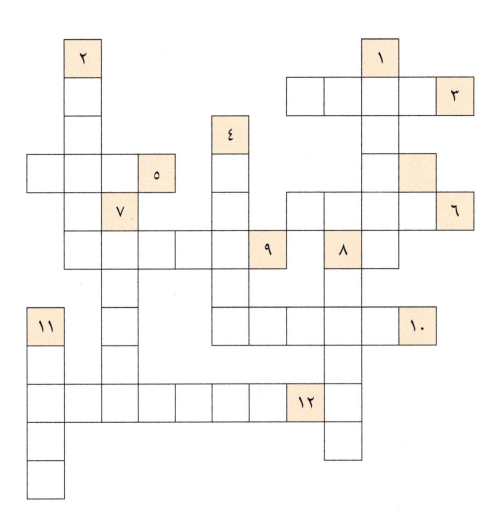

تمرين رقم ٢: أين الجملة غير الصحيحة؟

كلّ الجمل التالية صحيحة حسب النصّ الّا جملة واحدة. أي جملة غير صحيحة؟

All the following statements are correct according to the reading passage above, except one.
Which statement is incorrect?

١. القاهرة مركز المواصلات في مصر.

٢. تقع القاهرة في شمال مصر.

٣. سكن الأقباط مصر قبل المسلمين.

٤. عدد المساجد في القاهرة أكبر من عدد الكنائس.

٥. عدد سكّان القاهرة والمناطق المحيطة بها أكثر من ١١ مليون نسمة.

٦. في الأحياء الإسلاميّة في القاهرة شوارع ضيّقة.

٧. يسكن أقباط القاهرة في مصر القديمة.

٨. يسمّي المصريون القاهرة "مصر".

٩. يقع المتحف القبطي في مصر القديمة.

تمرين رقم ٣: ارسم خريطة بسيطة للقاهرة حسب المعلومات في النصّ وتحدّث عنها
مع زميلك في الصفّ.

Draw a simple map of Cairo and then describe it to your partner in class. Be sure to include
the different neighborhoods and other landmarks such as the Nile, etc.

الدرس الثالث

قراءة: مذكّرات إمِلي

كانت رحلتي للقاهرة مُمتعة جداً. طقس جميل طول الوقت: دافئ ومشمس. في اليوم الاول
استأجرت تاكسي وزرت قلعة صلاح الدين الأيوبي. أخذت الرحلة حوالي ساعة بسبب الزحمة.
سائق التاكسي قال لي اسمه محمد واسم والده عبد الحليم حافظ واسم أمه أمّ كلثوم! طبعاً كان
يمزح، فعبد الحليم حافظ مُغنّي مصري مشهور وأم كلثوم مغنّية مشهورة أيضاً.

سألت محمّد عن مشاكل الزحمة في القاهرة، فقال، وهو يمزح، إنّ سبب مشكلة الزحمة هو أهل
الصعيد الذين يجيئون الى القاهرة، ثم تجيء زوجاتهم وأولادهم وكلّ أقاربهم.

في طريقي من القلعة إلى الفندق اكتشفت أنّني ضيّعت "موبايلي". فتّشت عليه في شنطتي وفي جيوبي وفي شنطتي مرة أخرى ولكنّي لم أجده، فقرّرت أن اتّصل برقمي. ردّ عليّ رجل وقال إنّه سيُرجع الموبايل اذا دفعت له "مبلغ مناسب"! زعلت كثيراً.

عندما التقيت بالرجل ورأى أنّني طالبة فقيرة، ضَحك وأعطاني الموبايل، ثم دعاني لأشرب الشاي ونتحدّث عن أمريكا.

يوم الجمعة زرت عائلة محمد سائق التاكسي وأكلت الفول معهم. في رأيي ليس هناك أكلة أطيَب من الفول المُدمّس المصري!

كلمات جديدة

اتّصل–يتّصل	to call	مُمتعة	enjoyable, fun
ردّ–يردّ	to answer	استأجَر–يستأجِر	to rent
رجّع–يُرجّع	to return something	مزح–يمزح	to jest, make jokes
مبلغ	sum/amount	والد=أب	father
مناسب	suitable	مُغنّي	singer
ضحك–يضحك	to laugh	قريب (ج. أقارِب)	relative
دعى–يدعى	to invite	اكتشف–يكتشف	to discover
تحدّث–يتحدّث	to talk (about something)	جيب (ج. جُيوب)	pocket

تعابير

لم أجده   I did not find it

فول مُدَمّس   Egyptian dish (fava beans with olive oil, spices, etc.)

أسئلة

١. كيف كانت رحلة إملي للقاهرة؟

٢. ماذا فعلت إملي في اليوم الأول؟ ماهي الأماكن التي زارتها؟

٣. كم ساعة اخذت الرحلة؟ لماذا؟

٤. من هما عبد الحليم حافظ وأُم كلثوم؟ لماذا ذُكروا في النصّ؟

٥. ماذا حدث لموبايل إملي؟

٦. ماذا فعلت إملي عندما اكتشفت انها ضيّعت موبايلها؟

٧. لماذا غضبت إملي؟

٨. كيف استرجعت (retrieve) إملي الموبايل؟

٩. ماذا فعلت إملي يوم الجمعة؟

تمرين: رتّب الجمل من ١ – ١٠، حسب ما جاءت في النصّ.

___ إملي أكلت فول مدمّس.

___ اتّصلت إملي برقم الموبايل.

___ زارت إملى قلعة صلاح الدين الأيّوبي.

___ ضحك الرجل الذي وجد الموبايل.

___ ضيّعت إملي "موبايلها".

___ طقس القاهرة ممتاز.

___ عرف الرجل أنّ إملي طالبة فقيرة.

___ قال الرجل إنّه يريد فلوساً من إملي.

___ قال سائق التاكسي إنّ أهل الصعيد سبب مشاكل الزحمة.

___ قال سائق التاكسي إنّ اسم أبيه عبد الحليم حافظ.

الدرس الرابع

قواعد

أكمل الجدول التالي

Form	Stem	Root	Translation	Verb
			I ask you	اسألك
	تشرّف		We were honored	تشرّفنا
	تغدّى			تتغدى
				ونتكلّم
				يسكنها
				وينتج
I				يمزح
				سألت
	جاء	ج.ي.ء		يجيئون
		ك.ش.ف		اكتشفت

Form	Stem	Root	Translation	Verb
				ضيّعت
II				فتّشت
			So I decided	فقرّرت
			He will return (something)	سيُرجع
	أعطى			وأعطاني
			And we converse, talk	ونتحدّث
Extra credit (hint: all three verbs belong to the same form.)				
	امتدّ	م.د.د		وتمتدّ
				التقيت
		و.ص.ل		اتّصل

Looking up words in the dictionary

Now that you know the verb form numbers, you have all the tools to look up words in an Arabic dictionary.

The first step in looking up a word is to identify its root. To get to the root, all affixes and modifications of the stem need to be removed. Let's take two words found in this unit as examples, one a verb and another a noun: سأفكّر and والامتحانات.

The context and the structure of the word سأفكّر (the prefix س, the imperfect subject marker أ for "I") show that it is a verb. Another two pieces of information that you need to know are the root of سأفكّر and its form. Recognizing roots of words is a skill that takes time and practice, but as you learn more Arabic you will find it easier to recognize roots. Once you can identify the root of the word as ف.ك.ر and its form as Form II, you will be able to find its meaning in the dictionary.

The word والامتحانات, on the other hand, has the structure of a noun. The definite article and the plural ending are clear indications of that. To find the root, follow steps 1–3:

1. Remove the prefix و, the definite article ال, and plural suffix ات. The result is امتحان.
2. Remove the vowels. Since four-letter roots are quite rare, we can assume that one consonant in the sequence is not part of the root (an affix).
3. Decide which of the four letters is an affix:
   - ح is never an affix
   - ن at the end of a noun can be a number suffix; but in this case, we have already removed the plural suffix ات. Therefore, ن is likely to be part of the root.
   - You are left with two possibilities: م and ت, both of which can be affixes in the positions they are in. ت.ح.ن or م.ح.ن. Try looking both of them up in the dictionary: ت.ح.ن or م.ح.ن. You will not find ت.ح.ن. Therefore the root of أمتحان is م.ح.ن.

Weak roots, i.e. *assimilated, hollow, lame,* and *doubled* are harder to recognize than sound roots. But the more Arabic you know, the easier it will be to recognize relationships among families of words and the root of each family. The following hints may be helpful:

1. The consonants of a root generally stay stable from one form to another in the same family. If you look at the words طيران, طيّارة, طارت you will notice that the consonants ط and ر stay the same. This is an indication that they are part of the root. The alternation between ي and ا is typical of hollow roots.

2. Remember that ا and ى cannot be part of the root. In the root form, the ا and ى are either و or ي. After taking out all suffixes and prefixes and arriving at the form طار, you need to figure out whether the root form of ا is ي or و. You can for the most part tell whether a verb derives from و or ي by looking at the other members of the family: for example, طيّارة and يطير are derived from the same root as طار, and both include ي. It is therefore likely that the root of طار is طير, not طور.

3. Certain consonants cannot be a part of an affix and hence have to be a part of the root. These consonants include, غ, ع, ظ, ط, ص, ز, ر, ذ, د, خ, ح, ج, ث, and ق. Some consonants like ب, ف, ل, occur as prefixes but not as suffixes; the consonant ـه occurs as a suffix only.

تمرين

Figure out the root form of the ا in the following verbs: نام، مشى، كان، قال، حكى

Hint: think of related words that you already know such as verb conjugations in the imperfect and related nouns.

Sociolinguistic corner

شامي	مصري
اليوم	النهار دا
وين	فين
ما فيه	ما فيش
هون	هِنا
زوجته	مراته
يصير	يبقى
ما كان	ما كانش
شيء	حاجة
انولدت	اتولدت
هذا	دا
ونحكي	ونتكلّم

الدرس الخامس

كلمات الوحدة

to answer رَدّ-يرُدّ	أرجوك=لو سمحت please
crowdedness زَحمة	أصل origin
reason سبب	أهل (ج. أهالي) folks
صباح النور والفُل=صباح الخير	أهَمِّيّة importance
desert صحراء	اتّصل-يتّصل to call
Sa'idi, a person صعيدي ج. صعايدة	اتولد-يتولد=انولد-ينولد to be born
from Upper Egypt	to surround احاط-يحيط
to laugh ضحك-يضحك	to rent استأجَر-يستأجر
bank (of a river) ضِفّة	economy اقتصاد
narrow ضَيِّق	minority اقليّة
عربيّة=سيّارة	to discover اكتشف-يكتشِف
to where (are you going) على فين النهار دا؟	the Copts الأقْباط
this morning?	بُصّي=شوفي
paternal uncle عَمّ	to become بقي-يبقى
empty فاضية	to talk (about something) تحدّث-يتحدّث
understanding, having understood فاهِم	I am delighted (or honored) تشرّفنا
Egyptian dish (fava beans with فول مُدمّس	to have met you
olive oil, spices, etc.)	to bring جاب-يجيب
relative (ج. أقارِب) قريب	pocket (ج. جُيوب) جيب
I did not find it لم أجده	something حاجة
ليه=ليش	to limit حدّد-يحدّد
there is not ما فيش=ما فيه	solution حَلّ
sum/amount مبلغ	neighborhood (ج. أحْياء) حَيّ
surrounding مُحيط	maternal uncle خالّ
مراة=زوجة	this (Egyptian) دا
to jest, make jokes مزح-يمزح	to invite دعى-يدعي
with us معانا=مَعنا	دُنيا=عالَم
singer مُغنّي	to return something رجّع-يُرجّع

the Nile River نهر النيل	for (the sake of) مِن أَجل
quiet هادي	suitable مناسب
(Egyptian) هِنا = هُنا = هون	transportation مُواصَلات
job (ج. وَظائف) وَظيفة	to result نتَج–ينتُج

تمرين رقم ١

Rearrange the letters to create words, and then translate the words into English. All the words you will create were introduced in this unit.

١. ت م ل ا ص و ل ا _____

٢. س ا م ن ب _____

٣. ر ص م _____

٤. ا ا ه ر ة ق ل _____

٥. ب ل غ م _____

٦. ض ك ح _____

٧. ت ف م ح _____

٨. ه ر ن _____

٩. ف ل و _____

١٠. ز م ة ح _____

تمرين رقم ٢

Word Search: Find the following words in the box and then translate them into English. You can go from left to right, right to left, and from the top down.

فاهم مزح ممتع نتج صحراء هادية وظيفة غضب أب

غ	ض	ب	ص	ح	ر	ا	ء
ح	أ	ب	ة	ف	ي	ظ	و
م	د	ه	د	ا	ي	ة	ن
ز	ص	د	ف	ا	ه	م	ت
ح	ي	ر	ع	ت	م	م	ج

تمرين رقم ٣: ابحث في القاموس (Look up in the dictionary)

Look up the following words in the dictionary:

Meaning	Root	
_____	_____	١. القاهرة
_____	_____	٢. المواصلات
_____	_____	٣. مُحيط
_____	_____	٤. حليم
_____	_____	٥. حافِظ

تمرين رقم ٤

Now look up the following words, all of which appear in the next unit:

يصدّقون، كلّموني، تعوّدوا، متديّنون، صحوْت، المؤذّن، المزعج، يستغربون، متديّنة

Extra credit

أحبّ، يؤمنون، ومحلّات، الأذان

تمرين رقم ٤: حضّر في البيت، ناقش في الصفّ، واكتب في البيت.

Prepare at home, discuss in class, and then write up a composition of about 50 words about one of the following topics:

١. دولة عربيّة لم تقرأ عنها في هذا الكتاب

(An Arab country you have not read about in this book.)

٢. مشاكل الزحمة والمواصلات في مدينة كبيرة مثل نيويورك، لندن، عمّان، القاهرة، بغداد، الخ.

أهمّ كلمات الوحدة الجديدة

ثَورة (ج. ثورات) revolution		أزعج-يُزعِج to bother, disturb	
دَور role		أعتبر-يعتبر to consider	
رجا-يرجو to hope		كَفى-يَكفي to suffice	
رَغمَ أنّ in spite of		أمام ahead, in front of	
شَخصي personal		آمَن-يُؤمِن to believe	
صعوبة (ج. صعوبات) difficulty		اختلاف (ج. اختلافات) difference	
علاقة (ج. علاقات) relationship		استطاع-يستطيع to be able	
مُجتمَع society		استغرب-يستغرب to find strange	
مُزعِج disturbing, bothersome		انتهى-ينتهي to end	
مشروع (ج. مشاريع) project		تحسّن-يتحسّن to improve	
واجه-يواجِه to face		تفاجأ-يتفاجأ to be surprised	

تمرين ١: املأ الفراغات

Use the words above to fill in the blanks. Pay special attention to gender and number agreements. Some words can be used more than once.

١. أريد أن _____ لغتي العربيّة ولذلك السبب سوف أسافر الى دولة عربيّة في الصيف.

٢. هناك _____ ثقافيّة واجتماعيّة كثيرة بين _____ العربي والمجتمع الأمريكي.

٣. من الأشياء التي لم أعرفها قبل دراسة اللُغة العربية _____ الدين في
_____ العربي.

٤. الشيءُ _____ كان الأسئلة الكثيرة التي يسألها الناس عن العُمر والدين والزواج
، أسئلة أعتبرها _____.

٥. أرجو أن _____ _____ الأمريكيّة العربيّة أكثر وأكثر.

٦. أحب دراسة اللُغة العربيّة لكن كانت هناك _____ قليلة في بداية السنة.

الدرس الأوّل

))) قراءة: انطِباعات إملي (١)

أربعة شهور. أربعة شهور عِشت في العالم العربي وتعلّمت الكثير: عن الشعب العربي، عن الثقافة العربيّة، الكَرَم العربي، والأَكل العربي، كما تحسّنت لغتي العربيّة كثيراً.

في البداية كانت هناك صعوبات كثيرة، فرغم أنّني كنت أتكلّم العربيّة، في التاكسي وفي المطعم وفي الفندق وفي المكاتب الحكوميّة، فقد كانت هناك اختلافات ثقافيّة وأشياء كثيرة لا يتعلّمها الطالب في الصفّ.

كنت قد تعلّمت العاميّة والفصحى قبل وصولي إلى الأردن–العاميّة للحديث اليومي، والفصحى في القراءة والكتابة وفي فهم الأخبار–ولذلك كان سهلاً أن أتحدّث مع الناس. وقد واجه الطلاب الذين درسوا الفصحى فقط صعوبات أكثر منّي لأنّهم لم يستطيعوا التحدّث مع الناس في البداية، لأنّ العرب لا يستعملون الفصحى في الحديث.

أكبر مشكلة واجهتها في البداية هي أنّ الكثير من الأردنيين وخصوصاً الشباب يحبّون التكلّم بالإنجليزيّة. ولكن كلّما كلّموني بالإنجليزيّة جاوبت بالعربيّة حتى تعوّدوا أن يكلّموني بالعربيّة طول الوقت.

من الأشياء التي لم أعرفها قبل وصولي إلى الأردن دور الدين في المجتمع العربي. كنت قد درست أنّ أكثر العرب مسلمون وأنّ هناك أقليّات مسيحيّة، ولكن لم أدرس أنّ أكثر الناس متديّنون، يؤمنون بالله والجنّة والنار، ويصومون في شهر رمضان ويصلّون، وخصوصاً يوم الجمعة.

كلمات جديدة

كلَّم-يكلِّم to speak to	كَرَم hospitality
جاوب-يجاوب to reply, to answer	تحسَّن-يتحسَّن to improve
تعوَّد-يتعوَّد to get used to something	صعوبة (ج. صعوبات) difficulty
دَور role	رَغمَ أنّ in spite of
مُتديّن religious	إختِلاف (ج. إختِلافات) difference
آمَن-يُؤمِن to believe	حديث conversation
جنة heaven	فهم understanding
نار fire, hell	لذلك for that reason
صام-يصوم to fast	واجه-يواجه to face
صلّى-يصلّي to pray	استطاع-يستطيع to be able
رمضان Islamic month of fasting	تَكلُّم = حَكي speaking
	كُلَّما = كُلّ + ما whenever

أسئلة

١. ماذا تعلّمت إملي خلال الأربعة شهور؟

٢. لماذا واجه الطلاب الذين درسوا العربيّة في جامعات أخرى صعوبات أكثر في نظر إملي؟

٣. متى تُستعمل الفصحى؟

٤. لماذا كان التحدث مع الناس سهلاً بالنسبة لإملي؟

٥. ما هي المشاكل التي واجهتها إملي في الأيّام الأولى؟

٦. كيف حلّت إملي المشكلة؟

٧. ماذا تعلّمت إملي عن دور الدين في المجتمع العربي؟

٨. ماهي الاشياء الجديدة التي تعلمتها إملي عن دور الدين في العالم العربي؟

تمرين رقم ١: أكمل كلّ واحدة من العبارات في عمود أ بما يناسبها في عمود ب.

ب	أ
مشاكل كثيرة	تعلّمت الكثير عن
في المجتمع الأمريكي	تعلّمت في الجامعة
في التاكسي والمطعم والفندق	كنت أتكلم العربيّة
خصوصاً يوم الجمعة	هل هناك دور كبير للدين

ب	أ
بين العالم العربي والعالم الغربي	هناك اختلافات ثقافيّة كثيرة
الشعب العربي والثقافة العربيّة	واجه الطلاب
التحدّث باللغة الإنجليزية	يحبّ الشباب الأردنيون
أنّ أكثر العرب مسلمون	يصلّي أكثر الناس

تمرين رقم ٢: ما هو عكس كلّ من الكلمات التالية؟ (كل الإجابات موجودة في النصّ.)

نهاية، سهولة، قليل، بَعد، صَعب، أقلّ، أكثريّة، النار

الدرس الثاني

قراءة: انطِباعات إملي (٢)

تفاجأَت كثيراً في أوّل ليلة نمتها في عمّان فقد صحوت مبكراً على صوت المؤذّن. لم أعرف في البداية ماذا كان الصوت، وخفت كثيراً، ولم أنَم جيّداً، ولكن بعد مدّة قصيرة تعوّدت على صوت المؤذّن ولم يُزعجني أبداً.

ولكن المُزعج كان الأسئلة الكثيرة التي يسألها الناس عن الدين. سألوني مثلاً: هل أنا مسيحيّة أو يهوديّة، وما رأيي في الدين الإسلامي. كانوا يستغربون عندما قُلت لهم انّني لست متديّنة ولا أفكر في الدين كثيراً. هم يفكّرون بالدين ويتحدّثون عنه كثيراً.

ربّما كانت أصعب مشكلة هي مشكلة الأكل. فالأكل العربي طيّب جدّاً، وخصوصاً المنسف والمسخّن والكبّة والفول والكنافة والبقلاوة. المشكلة هي أنّ في هذه الأكلات دُهن أو سكّر كثير. وهي موجودة في البيوت والمطاعم ومحلّات الحلويات، وهي رخيصة أيضاً. كل أنواع الطعام، المطبوخ وغير المطبوخ، أرخص من أمريكا بكثير. لذلك زاد وزني كثيراً (لن أقول كم أصبح وزني الآن!)

عندما دعاني أصحابي الى بيوتهم كان عليّ أن آكل وأشرب الكثير. وقد مرضت مرّة أو مرّتين من كثرة الأكل.

اشتريت أنا وفدوى ورانية طاولة تنس ولعبنا في الشقّة، وكان ذلك ممتعاً، وقد تحسّن لعبي كثيراً، ولكن رياضة تنس الطاولة لا تكفي لتخفيف الوزن.

كلمات جديدة

استغرَب–يستغرِب	to find strange	تفاجأ–يتفاجأ	to be surprised
ربّما	perhaps	صحا–يصحو	to wake up
دُهن	fat	مُبكّر	early
مَطبوخ	cooked	صَوت (ج. أصوات)	sound, voice
زاد–يزيد	to increase	مُؤذّن	the Mu'adhdhin, the one who calls for prayer
وَزن	weight	أزعج–يُزعِج	to bother, disturb
كَفى–يَكفي	to suffice	مُزعِج	disturbing, bothersome

تعبير

تخفيف الوزن   weight loss, reduction

أسئلة

١. لماذا تفاجأت إملي في أوّل ليلة نامتها في عمّان؟

٢. ماذا أزعج إملي أكثر من المؤذّن؟

٣. ما هي مشكلة الأكل التي تتكلّم عنها إملي؟

٤. كيف كان الطعام الرخيص مشكلة؟

٥. لماذا مرضت إملي أكثر من مرة عندما دعاها أصحابها الى بيوتهم؟

٦. مَن اشترى طاولة تنس؟ لماذا؟

تمرين رقم ١: رتّب الجمل من ١ – ١٠ حسب ما جاءت في النصّ.

___ إملي لا تفكّر في الدين أبداً.

___ اشترت إملي وفدوى ورانية طاولة تنس.

___ الأسئلة التي سألها الناس عن الدين أزعجت إملي كثيراً.

___ الأكل في الأردن أرخص من الأكل في أمريكا.

___ الأكل مشكلة كبيرة.

___ العرب يفكّرون بالدين كثيراً.

___ تعوّدت إملي على صوت المؤذّن.

___ خافت إملي كثيراً.

___ صحَت إملي على صوت المؤذّن.

___ مرضت إملي من كثرة الأكل.

تمرين رقم ٢

Match the words in column ج, all taken from the reading selections of the first two lessons of this unit, to their definitions in column أ by writing each word next to its definition in column ب. Follow the example.

ج	ب	أ
استغرب	فول	أكلة منتشرة كثيراً في مصر
العامّيّة		اعتقد أنّ هذا شيء غريب
الفصحى		الساعة الخامسة أو السادسة في الصباح
تحسّن		اليهوديّة والمسيحيّة والإسلام
دين		دُكّان
يتكلّم		زاكي
صعوبة		صار أحسن
طيّب		عكس "سهولة"
فول		قام من النوم
مؤمن		لغة الحديث بين العرب
مبكّر		لا يأكل ولا يشرب طول النهار
محلّ		يؤمن بالله والجنّة والنار
صحى		يحكي
يصوم		يستعملها العرب للقراءة والكتابة

الدرس الثالث

))))

قراءة: انطِباعات إملي (٣)

كلمة أخيرة

قبل سفري الى البلاد العربيّة، كنت قد قرأت وسمعت أن العرب يكرهون أمريكا. لذلك كنت أفكّر أنّهم سيكرهونني. ولكنّي وجدت أنّهم لا يكرهون الشعب الأمريكي أبداً، ولا يكرهون أمريكا أبداً. على العكس، الكثير منهم، وخصوصاً الشباب، يحلُمون بالهجرة أو السفر الى أمريكا والدراسة في جامعاتها والعيش في مدنها مثل نيويورك وشيكاغو وبوستن وواشنطن.

لكنّهم يكرهون سياسة الحكومة الأمريكيّة لأنّها تدعم الحكومة الإسرائيليّة، ولأنّها كانت تدعم الحكومات العربيّة الدكتاتوريّة. ولكن الوضع تغيّر الآن، بعد الربيع العربي والثورات العربيّة. فالحكومة الأمريكيّة الآن ساعدت الشعب العربي ضدّ الحكومات الدكتاتوريّة؛ في تونس ومصر وليبيا وسوريا.

أرجو أن تتحسّن العلاقات الأمريكيّة العربيّة أكثر وأكثر. سأرجع إن شاء الله، وأعيش في بلد عربي لمدّة سنة أو أكثر. رغم أنّني عشت هذه المدّة في الأردن، وزرت فلسطين ولبنان وسوريا ومصر، وأشعر أنّني أفهم لغة الشرق العربي جيّداً، فقد سمعت الكثير عن بلاد المغرب وشعوبها. أريد أن أزور ليبيا وتونس والجزائر والمغرب.

بعد سنتين سأفكّر في هذا المشروع، وأقرّر أين سأسافر، ولكن الآن لا أرى أمامي الا الدراسة والامتحانات والواجبات التي لا تنتهي.

كلمات جديدة

رجى–يرجي	to want/hope	كرِه–يكرَه	to hate
علاقة (ج. علاقات)	relationship	حلِم–يحلُم	to dream
شعب (ج. شعوب)	people	هِجرة	immigration
مشروع (ج. مشاريع)	project	عيش=سكن	living
واجب (ج. واجبات)	homework	سِياسة	policy, politics
أمام	ahead, in front of	وَضع	situation
انتهى–ينتهي	to end	ثورة (ج. ثورات)	revolution
		ضدّ	against

تعابير

كلمة اخيرة last word

أسئلة

٣.   ماذا سمعت وقرأت إملي في الصحف الكبيرة وقنوات التلفزيون الرئيسيّة؟

٤.   ماذا تعلّمت خلال رحلتها في الأردن عن ذلك؟

٥.   ماذا يكره العرب حسب إملي؟

٦.   كيف تغيّر الوضع؟

٧.   أين ستعيش إملي عندما ترجع الى العالم العربي؟

٨.   لماذا لا يمكنها السفر والعيش هناك الآن؟

تمرين رقم ١: أين الجملة غير الصحيحة؟

كلّ الجمل التالية صحيحة حسب النصّ الّا جملة واحدة. أي جملة غير صحيحة؟

١.   الحكومة الأمريكيّة ساعدت الحكومات الدكتاتورية العربيّة.

٢.   الحكومة الأمريكية ساعدت بعض الشعوب العربيّة.

٣.   العرب لا يكرهون الشعب الأمريكي.

٤.   إملي تريد زيارة ليبيا.

٥.   إملي تفهم لغة المغرب العربي جيّداً.

٦.   سوف ترجع إملي إلى العالم العربي.

٧.   عند إملي عمل كثير.

٨.   كثير من العرب يحبّون السفر الى أمريكا.

٩.   يحبّ كثير من العرب الدراسة في الجامعات الأمريكية.

١٠. يكره العرب سياسة الحكومة الأمريكية.

تمرين رقم ٢: ابحث عن الكلمات المعرّفة في النصّ وأكمل الكلمات المُتقاطعة.

١.   بدأت في تونس وانتقلت (moved) إلى مصر ثمّ ليبيا ثمّ سوريا

٢.   ليس مع

٣.   لا يحبّ

٤.   يساعد

٥.   ليس ديمقراطيّاً

٦.   يسكن

٧.   عكس "نهاية"

٨.   بعد الشتاء وقبل الصيف

٩.   عكس "مشرق"

١٠. تتصوّر أو تفكّر وهي نائمة

١١. دولة في شمال إفريقيا تُريد إملي زيارتها

١٢. جمع شعب

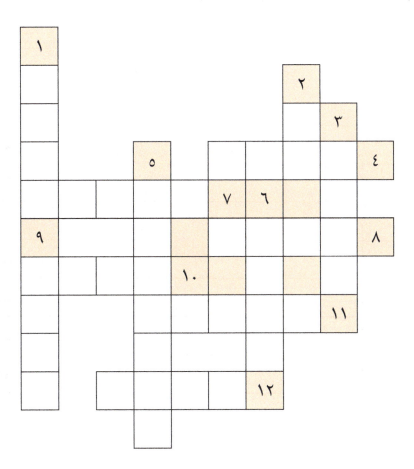

الدرس الرابع

قواعد

Verb form VI

In the perfect tense this form appears as تفاعل and in the imperfect as يتفاعل. The only example of this form found in the book is تفاجأت "I was surprised". Because of its rare occurrence in the language, it will not be included in tables and exercises on the forms of the verb.

تمرين رقم ١: أكمل الجدول

Fill in the empty cells in the following table. All the verbs in the table are taken from the readings of this unit and are all derived, i.e. there are no Form I verbs among them.

Form	Stem	Root	Translation	Verb
				تعلّمت
	تحسّن			تحسّنَت
			I speak	أتكلّم
				يتعلّمها
		و.ج.ه		واجهوا
				يستطيعوا
				يتحدّثوا
				يتكلّمون
				يستعمل
				أتحدّث
				كلّموني
				تعوّدوا
				يكلّموني
IV، أفعل	آمَن			يؤمنون
				تعوّدت
				يُزعجني
				أعتبرها
				يستغربون
				يفكّرون
				ويتحدّثون

Form	Stem	Root	Translation	Verb
				اشتريت
				تغيّر
				تتحسّن
				أريد
				سأفكّر
				وأقرّر
				سأسافر
				تنتهي
Extra credit				
				يحبّون

Noun patterns: active participles, passive participles, verbal nouns

As in the case of verbs, Arabic nouns (and adjectives) follow specific patterns of derivation which share similar meanings or grammatical functions. Whereas the number of verb patterns is limited to fourteen, the number of noun patterns is much higher. Some noun patterns are more common than others. Some of the most common noun types are participles and verbal nouns, which are derived regularly from certain verb patterns.

An active participle generally refers to the doer of an action, the passive participle the recipient or the result of the action, while the مصدر refers to the action itself. كاتب "writer", مكتوب "written", and كتابة "(the act of) writing" are an active participle, a passive participle, and a مصدر, respectively.

The following table provides a summary of the most common patterns of active participles, passive participles, and verbal nouns introduced in this textbook with reference to the verb forms from which they are derived. The verbal noun patterns derived from Form I are too numerous to list, while the patterns that are rare or of which examples are not found in the textbook will be marked with an "x" in the corresponding cell.

Verbal noun مصدر		Passive participle اسم مفعول		Active participle اسم فاعل		
many patterns		written مكتوب	مفعول	writer كاتب	فاعل	I
founding تأسيس	تَفعيل	مُؤَسَّسة foundation	مُفَعَّل	founder مُؤَسِّس	مُفعِّل	II
assistance مساعَدة	مُفاعَلة	x	x	helper مُساعِد	مُفاعِل	III
submitting إسلام	إفعال	x	x	Muslim مُسلِم	مُفعِل	IV
تخصّص specialization	تفعُّل	x	x	مُتَخصِّص specialist	مُتفعِّل	V
listening استماع	افتعال	x	x	listener مُستَمِع	مُفتعِل	VIII
renting استئجار	استفعال	x	x	tenant مُستأجِر	مُستفعِل	X

تمرين رقم ٢: أكمل الجدول

Method of derivation	Root	Stem	Noun or adjective
Verbal noun of Form VIII	خ.ل.ف	اختلاف	اختلافات
			سائق
Passive participle of Form II			موظَّف
Active participle of Form IV			مسلمون
			متديّنون
			مؤذِّن
		مُبكّر	مبكّراً
			مُسخَّن
			المطبوخ
			مُمتعاً
			المشروع
			والامتحانات

الدرس الخامس

كلمات الوحدة الجديدة

صام-يصوم	to fast	أزعج-يُزعِج	to bother, disturb
صحا-يصحو	to wake up	أمام	ahead, in front of
صعوبة (ج. صعوبات)	difficulty	آمَن-يُؤمِن	to believe
صلّى-يصلّي	to pray	إختِلاف (ج. إختلافات)	difference
صَوت (ج. أصوات)	sound, voice	استطاع-يستطيع	to be able
ضدّ	against	استغرب-يستغرب	to find strange
علاقة (ج. علاقات)	relationship	انتهى-ينتهي	to end
عيش=سكن	living	تحسّن-يتحسّن	to improve
فَهِم	understanding	تخفيف الوزن	weight loss, reduction
كَرَم	hospitality	تعوّد-يتعوّد	to get used to something
كره-يكرَه	to hate	تفاجأ-يتفاجأ	to be surprised
كَفى-يَكفي	to suffice	تكلّم-يتكلّم=حكى-يحكي	
كلمة اخيرة	last word	ثورة (ج. ثورات)	revolution
لذلك	for that reason	جاوب-يجاوب	to reply, to answer
مُؤذِّن،	the Mu'adhdhin,	جنة	heaven
the one who calls for prayer		حديث	conversation
مُبكّر	early	حلم-يحلُم	to dream
مُتديّن	religious	دُهن	fat
مُزعِج	disturbing/bothersome	دَور	role
مشروع (ج. مشاريع)	project	ربّما	perhaps
مَطبوخ	cooked	رجا-يرجو	to hope
نار	fire, hell	رَغمَ أنّ	in spite of
هِجرة	immigration	رمضان	Islamic month of fasting
واجب (ج. واجبات)	homework	زاد-يزيد	to increase
واجه-يواجه	to face	سِياسة	policy, politics
وَزن	weight	شخصي	personal
وَضع	situation	شعب (ج. شعوب)	people

تمرين: حضّر في البيت، ناقش في الصفّ، واكتب في البيت.

Prepare at home, discuss in class, and then write up a composition of about 50 words about one of the following topics:

أ.   خطّط لزيارة دولة عربيّة: لماذا تريد أن تزور هذه الدولة، مدّة الزيارة، ماذا تريد أن ترى، الخ.

Plan a visit to an Arab country. Explain why you want to visit it, for how long, what you want to see, etc.

ب.   لماذا تتعلّم العربيّة؟ Why are you learning Arabic?

ت.   المرحلة التالية في تعلّمك للغة العربيّة. The next stage in your study of Arabic.

ث.   أكتب فقرة تبدأ بواحدة من العبارات التالية: Write a paragraph starting with one of the following phrases/sentences:

- أربعة شهور عشت في العالم العربي وتعلّمت الكثير: عن الشعب العربي، عن ...
- تفاجأت كثيراً في أوّل ليلة ...
- ربّما كانت أصعب مشكلة هي مشكلة ...
- قبل سفري الى البلاد العربيّة، كنت قد قرأت وسمعت أن ...
- بعد سنتين سوف ...

Arabic–English Glossary

Words are arranged for the most part by root, except in the following cases, which are listed alphabetically:

1. Words which do not derive from three-letter roots
2. Proper names (like البابليون)
3. Expressions (like إن شاء الله)

Please note the following:

1. A diamond "◆" appears next to words that are found in فصحى but not in شامي, and a star "*" appears next to words that are found in شامي but not in فصحى.
2. The Roman numerals I–X next to verbs refer to verb form numbers.
3. The following abbreviations are used:

- جمع = ج "plural"
- f. = feminine
- m. = masculine
- s. = singular
- pl. = plural

أ

father		أب (ج آباء)
at all, never	أبداً	أ.ب.د
ruins	آثار	أ.ث.ر
to rent	استأجَر– يستأجر (X)	أ.ج.ر
fare, rent	أجْرة	
rent	إيجار	
Sunday	الأحد	أ.ح.د
brother, a friendly way of addressing a man		أخ (ج إخوة، إخوان)
sister, a friendly way of addressing a woman		أخت (ج أخوات)
to take	أخذ – يأخذ (I)	أ.خ.ذ
to be late	تأخّر– يتأخّر (V)	أ.خ.ر
last, latest, most recent	آخِر	
another	أخَر◆	
another (f.)	أخرى = ثانية	
last	أخير	
late	مُتأخّر	
literature	أدب	أ.د.ب
if	إذا	
therefore, in that case	إذَن	
the Mu'adhdhin, the one who calls for prayer	مُؤذِّن	أ.ذ.ن
hookah	أرجيلة = نرجيلة	
date, history	تاريخ	أ.ر.خ
teacher, professor		أستاذ (ج أساتذة)
look up under إن.ي	استنّى – يستنّى	
to be founded	تأسّس–يتأسّس (V)	أ.س.س
sorry	آسِف	أ.س.ف
name	إسم (ج. أسماء◆، أسامي*)	أ.س.م
Asia	آسيا	
we missed you	اشتقنا لَك	
traffic light	إشارة ضوئيّة	أ.ش.ر
visa	تأشيرة	
origin	أصل	أ.ص.ل

English		Arabic
Africa		إفريقيا
certainly	أكيد	أ.ك.د
to eat	أكل – يأكل	أ.ك.ل
food	أكْل	
dish, food	أكلة	
the Assyrians		الآشوريون
now		الآن◆ = هلّأ*
the Copts		الأقْباط
the Nabataeans		الأنباط
Alexander		الإسكَندر
minus, to, except		إلّا
the Babylonians		البابليّون
the Torah		التوراة
who, that, which (f.s.)		التي◆ = اللي*
thank God		الحمد لله
who, that, which (m.s.)		الذي◆
who, that, which (m.pl.)		الذين◆
Saturday		السبت
Damascus		الشام = دمشق
China		الصين
the Persians		الفُرس
Cairo		القاهرة
Jerusalem		القُدس
God knows		الله أعلَم
painful	مُؤلِم	أ.ل.م
the Mamluks		المماليك
the United States		الولايات المتحدة
to		إلى◆ = ل
the Greeks		اليونان
or (in direct and indirect questions)		أم◆ = أو
as for		أمّا ... ف◆
when?		امتى؟*
yesterday	أمس◆ = مبارِح*	أ.م.س

mother	أُم (ج. أُمّهات◆)	أ.م.م
ahead, in front of	أمام◆	
to believe	آمَن – يُؤمِن (IV)	أ.م.ن
safe	أمين	
that	أنّ	
God willing	إن شاء الله	
to	إن◆	
I	أنا	
you (m.s.)	انتَ	
you (f.s.)	انتِ	
to wait (for)	استنّى-يستنّى (X)*	أ.ن.ي
people, folks	أهل (ج. أهالي)	أ.ه.ل
welcome to you	أهلا (وسهلاً) فيك	
first	أوّل	أ.و.ل
the day before yesterday	أوّل أمس◆ = أوّل مبارِح*	
first time	أوّل مرّة	
which?	أيّ؟	
it (her)	إيّاها	
what is your opinion?	ايش رأيِك؟*	
what?	ايش؟* = شو؟*	
also	أيضاً◆ = كَمان*	
yes	أيوا*	

ب

well	بِئر (ج. آبار)	ب.ء.ر.
bus	باص	
free, for nothing	ببلاش*	
the Mediterranean Sea	البحر الأبيض المتوسط	ب.ح.ر.
the Red Sea	البحر الأحمر	
the Black Sea	البحر الأسود	
to start	بدأ – يبدأ (I)	ب.د.ء.
to want	بدّ (بدّه، بدها، الخ.)*	
exchanging	تبادُل◆	ب.د.ل.

it seems	يبدو	ب.د.و.
orange	بُرتُقال	
orange (color)	بُرتُقالي	
yesterday	مبارح*	ب.ر.ح.
the day before yesterday	أوّل مبارح* = أوّل أمس◆	
cold	بارِد	ب.ر.د.
cold	بَرْد	
only	بَسّ*	
simple	بسيط	ب.س.ط.
look!	بُصّ* = شوف*!	ب.ص.ص.
potatoes	بطاطا	
watermelon	بطّيخ	
belly, stomach	بَطن (ج. بطون)	ب.ط.ن.
after	بَعد	ب.ع.د.
afternoon	بعد الظُهر	
then	بعدين*	
far	بَعيد	
some	بَعض	
cow(s)	بَقَر	ب.ق.ر.
name of a dessert	بقلاوة	
to remain, stay	بقي – يبقى (I)	ب.ق.ي.
remaining, rest	باقي	
Bachelor's, B.A. degree	بكالوريوس	
tomorrow	بُكرة*	ب.ك.ر.
the day after tomorrow	بَعد بُكرة*	
early	مُبكّر	
nonsense (lit. no study no watermelon)	بلا دراسة بلا بطّيخ*	
without, no need for	بَلاش*	
country	بلَد (ج. بِلاد)	ب.ل.د.
local	بلَدي	
Greater Syria	بلاد الشام	
to amount to	بلغ – يبلُغ (I)	ب.ل.غ.
sum, amount	مبلغ	

balcony		بَلكونة
girl, daughter		بِنت (ج. بنات)
tomato		بَندورة
pants, trousers		بَنطلون
brown	بُنّي	ب.ن.ن.
was built	بُني ◆	ب.ن.ي.
building	بِناية (ج. بِنايات)	
built	مَبني	
spices	بِهارات	ب.ه.ر.
door	باب (ج. أبواب)	ب.و.ب.
house	بيت (ج. بيوت)	ب.ي.ت.
dormitory	بيت طُلاب	
white	أبيض	ب.ي.ض
eggs	بَيض	

ت

name of a vegetarian dish		تبّولة
commerce, trade, business	تِجارة	ت.ج.ر.
commercial	تجاري	
under		تَحت
museum	متحف (ج. متاحف)	ت.ح.ف.
to leave	ترَك – يترُك (I)	ت.ر.ك
ninth	تاسِع	ت.س.ع
nine	تسعة	
tired	تَعبان	ت.ع.ب.
apples	تُفّاح	ت.ف.ح.
you're most welcome; whatever pleases you		تكرم عينك *
that (f.)	تلكَ ◆	
great, perfect	تَمام	ت.م.م
totally, exactly, fully	تماماً	

ث

culture	ثقافة	ث.ق.ف.
third	ثالِث	ث.ل.ث.

Tuesday	الثلاثاء	
three	ثلاثة	
third	ثُلُث	
snow	ثَلَج (ج. ثلوج)	ث.ل.ج.
refrigerator	ثلّاجة	
then, and then	ثُمّ ◆ = بَعدين*	
eighth	ثامِن	ث.م.ن.
eight	ثمانية	
two	اثنين	ث.ن.ي.
two kilograms	اثنين كيلو*	
Monday	الإثنين	
second	ثانِي	
revolution	ثورة (ج. ثورات)	ث.و.ر.

ج

jacket	جاكيت	
mountain	جَبَل (ج. جبال)	ج.ب.ل.
mountainous	جَبَلي	
cheese	جِبن	ج.ب.ن.
grandfather	جَدّ	
very	جدّاً ◆ = كثير	
new	جَديد	ج.د.د.
to try something out	جرّب – يجرّب (II)	ج.ر.ب.
socks	جْرابات	
newspaper	جَريدة	ج.ر.د.
part, section	جُزء (ج. أجزاء)	ج.ز.ء.
partial	جُزئي	
the Arabian Peninsula	الجزيرة العربيّة	
bridge	جسر	ج.س.ر.
dry	جافّ	ج.ف.ف.
to sit down	جلس – يجلس (I)	ج.ل.س.
sitting	جالس	
Friday	الجُمعة	ج.م.ع.
mosque	جامع (ج. جوامع) = مَسجِد (ج. مساجد)	

university	جامِعة	
total	مجموع	
group	مجموعة	
beautiful	جميل = حلو	ج.م.ل.
republic	جُمهوريّة	ج.م.ﻫ.ر.
foreigner	أجنَبي (ج. أجانِب)	ج.ن.ب.
south	جنوب	
gender, sex	جِنس	ج.ن.س.
nationality, citizenship	جِنسِيّة	
crazy	مجنون	ج.ن.ن.
heaven, paradise	جنّة	
to reply, to answer	جاوب – يجاوب (III)	ج.و.ب.
neighbor	جار (ج. جيران)	ج.و.ر.
passport	جَواز سَفَر	ج.و.ز.
to come	جاء – يجيء◆ = أجا – ييجي* (I)	ج.ي.ء.
I came	جيت*	
to bring	جاب – يجيب* (I)	ج.ي.ب.
pocket	جيب (ج. جُيوب)	
army	جيش	ج.ي.ش.

ح

to love, to like	حبّ – يحبّ* (I)	ح.ب.ب.
would like, liking	حابّ = حابِب*	
until, in order to, even	حتّى	
to reserve	حجز – يحجِز (I)	ح.ج.ز.
to happen	حدث – يحدُث◆ (I)	ح.د.ث.
to talk (about something)	تحدّث – يتحدّث◆ (V)	
modern; conversation	حديث	
to border	حدّ – يحُدّ (I)	ح.د.د.
borders	حُدود	
to limit	حدّد – يحدِّد (II)	
It's not right! It's too much!	حَرام عليك!	
World War I	الحرب العالميّة الأولى	ح.ر.ب.

hot	حارّ ◆ = حامي	ح.ر.ر.
heat	حَرّ	
security, guarding	حِراسة	ح.ر.س.
according to, depending on	حَسَب	ح.س.ب.
accountant	مُحاسب	
better, the best	أحسَن	ح.س.ن.
to improve	تحسّن – يتحسّن (V)	
to obtain	حصل – يحصُل (على) (I)	ح.ص.ل.
presently, right away	حاضر	ح.ض.ر.
you, formal way of address	حضرتك	
civilization	حضارة	
to put	حَطّ – يحُطّ* (I)	ح.ط.ط.
stop, station	مَحطة	
wallet	مَحفظة	ح.ف.ظ.
to rule	حكم – يحكُم (I)	ح.ك.م.
control, rule	حُكم	
public, governmental	حُكومي	
to speak, narrate	حكى – يحكي	ح.ك.ي.
milk	حَليب	ح.ل.ب.
to occupy	احتلّ – يحتلّ (VIII)	ح.ل.ل.
solution	حَلّ	
shop	مَحَلّ (ج.محلّات) = دُكّان (ج. دكاكين)	
to dream	حلِم – يحلُم (I)	ح.ل.م.
pretty (sweet)	حلو	ح.ل.و.
sweets, desserts	حَلَويّات، حِلويّات	
red	أحمر	ح.م.ر.
to take a bath	استحمّ – يستحمّ (X) ◆	ح.م.م.
bathroom	حَمّام (ج. حمّامات)	
hot	حامي*	ح.م.ي.
something	حاجة	ح.و.ج.
to surround	أحاط – يُحيط (IV)	ح.و.ط.
surrounding	مُحيط	
to try	حاوَل – يحاوِل (III)	ح.و.ل.

condition	حالة	
impossible	مُستحيل	
sometimes	أحياناً	ح.ي.ن.
life	حياة	ح.ي.و.
city quarter, neighborhood	حَيّ (ج. أحياء)	

خ

news	خبر (ج. أخبار)	خ.ب.ر.
intelligence service	مُخابَرات	
bread	خُبز	خ.ب.ز.
service	خِدمة	خ.د.م.
to take (something) out	أخرَج – يخرِج (IV)	خ.ر.ج.
lamb	خَروف	خ.ر.ف.
fall, autumn	خَريف	
lettuce	خَسّ	
private	خاصّ	خ.ص.ص.
specialization, major	تخصُّص	
to specialize, to major	تخصَّص – يتخصَّص (V)	
specially	خصوصاً	
green	أخضَر	خ.ض.ر.
vegetables	خُضار	
engagement	خُطوبة	خ.ط.ب.
engaged	مَخطوب	
weight loss, reduction	تخفيف الوزن	خ.ف.ف.
to finish, complete	خلَّص – يخلِّص (II)*	خ.ل.ص.
that's sufficient, enough	خَلاص*	
to differ	اختلف – يختلف (VIII)	خ.ل.ف.
difference	اختلاف (ج. إختلافات)	
different	مُختلِف	
let me see	خلّيني أشوف*	
fifth	خامِس	خ.م.س.
five	خمسة	
Thursday	الخميس	

pork, pig		خَنزير
to be afraid	خاف – يخاف (I)	خ.و.ف.
afraid	خائِف◆ = خايِف*	
fear	خَوف	
frightening	مُخيف	
maternal uncle	خال (ج. أخوال)	خ.و.ل.
brother	خيّ* = أخ	
camp	مُخيَّم (ج. مُخيَّمات)	خ.ي.م.

د

this (Egyptian)	دا* = هذا	
chicken	دَجاج	
to enter	دخَل – يدخُل (I)	د.خ.ل.
to smoke	دخّن – يدخّن (II)	د.خ.ن.
smoking	تَدخين	
bicycle	درّاجة = بُسُكليت (بِسِكليت)	د.ر.ج.
temperature (degree of heat)	درجة حَرارة	
to study	درَس – يدرُس (I)	د.ر.س.
to teach	درّس – يدرّس = علّم – يعلّم (II)	
teaching	تدريس = تعليم	
study	دراسة	
higher, graduate studies	دراسات عُليا	
school	مَدرسة (ج. مدارس)	
secondary (high) school	المدرسة الثانوية	
shower	دُشّ	
straight	دُغري*	
to invite	دَعا – يدعو◆ (I)	د.ع.و.
invitation	دَعوة	
to pay	دفَع – يدفَع (I)	د.ف.ع.
warm	دافئً	د.ف.ي.
minute	دقيقة (ج. دقائق)	د.ق.ق.
Ph.D., doctorate	دكتوراه	
world	دُنيا = عالَم	د.ن.و.

fat	دُهن	د.ه.ن.
administrative	إداري	د.و.ر.
role	دَور	
director, manager	مُدير	
to make someone dizzy	دوَّش – يدوِّش* (I)	د.و.ش.
nation	دولة (ج. دُوَل)	د.و.ل.
always	دائماً	د.و.م.
without	بدون	د.و.ن.
religion	دين (ج. أديان)	د.ي.ن.
the Islamic religion	الدين الإسلامي	
religious	مُتديّن	
city	مدينة (ج. مُدُن)	
dinar (Jordanian currency)	دينار (ج. دنانير)	دينار (ج. دنانير)

ذ

male	ذكر (ج. ذكور)	ذ.ك.ر.
to remember	ذكَر – يذكُر (I)	
was mentioned	ذُكِر	
that, m.		◆ذلِك
to go	ذهَب – يذهب◆ = راح – يروح* (I)	ذ.ه.ب.

ر

head	رأس (ج. روس*، رؤوس◆)	ر.ء.س.
main, principal	رئيسي	
to see	رأى – يرى◆ = شاف – يشوف*	ر.ء.ي.
opinion	رأي	
in your opinion	في رأيك	
four	أربعة	ر.ب.ع
Wednesday	الأربعاء	
fourth	رابِع	
quarter	رُبع (ج. أرباع)	
spring	رَبيع	ر.ب.ع

English	Arabic (verb forms)	Root
perhaps		◆رُبّما
housewife		ربّة بيت
to return, go back to	رجع – يرجع (I)	ر.ج.ع.
to return something	رجّع – يُرجّع (II)	
man	رَجُل (ج. رجال)	ر.ج.ل.
for men	رِجالي	
to hope	رجا – يرجو◆	ر.ج.و.
please	أرجوك = لوسمحت	
trip	رِحلة	ر.ح.ل.
cheap	رخيص	ر.خ.ص.
to answer	ردّ – يرُدّ	ر.د.د.
rice	رُزّ	
to fail	رسب – يرسُب (I)	ر.س.ب.
correspondence	مُراسَلة	ر.س.ل.
humid	رَطب	ر.ط.ب.
humidity	رُطوبة	
in spite of		رَغَم أنّ
to refuse	رفَض – يرفُض (I)	ر.ف.ض.
to raise	رفع – يرفَع (I)	ر.ف.ع.
number	رقَم	ر.ق.م.
to ride	ركب – يركَب (I)	ر.ك.ب.
passenger	راكب (ج. رُكّاب)	
center	مَركَز (ج. مَراكِز)	ر.ك.ز.
Islamic month of fasting		رَمضان
to go	راح – يروح* (I)	ر.و.ح.
comfortable	مُريح	ر.ي.ح.
to rest	استراح – يستريح (X)	
wind	ريح (ج. رِياح)	
to want	أراد – يُريد (IV)◆ = بدّه، بدها، الخ.*	ر.ي.د.
sport	رياضة	ر.ي.ض.
countryside	ريف	ر.ي.ف.

ز

delicious, tasty		زاكي*
correct	مزبوط	ز.ب.ط.
crowdedness	زَحمة	ز.ح.م.
blue	أزرق	ز.ر.ق.
to bother	أزعَج – يزعِج (IV)	ز.ع.ج.
bothering	إزعاج	
disturbing, bothersome	مُزعِج	
to upset someone	أزعَل – يزعِل (IV)* = زعّل – يُزعِّل (II)*	ز.ع.ل.
upset	زَعلان*	
time, era	زَمَن	ز.م.ن.
have you been ... a long time?	زمان صار لك ... ؟*	
flower	زهرة (ج. زهور)	ز.ه.ر.
marriage	زَواج	ز.و.ج.
to marry someone off	زوّج – يُزوّج (II)	
to get married	تزوّج – يتزوّج (V)	
to visit	زار – يزور (I)	ز.و.ر.
visit	زِيارة	
farm	مَزرَعة (ج. مَزارِع)	ز.ر.ع.
like, such as	زَيّ* = مثل	
as he was before	زي ما كان*	
to increase, to exceed	زاد – يزيد (على) (I)	ز.و.د.، ز.ي.د.
oil	زَيت	

س

will	سَ◆ = سَوفَ◆	
to ask	سأل – يسأل (I)	س.ء.ل.
question	سُؤال (ج. أسئلة)	
responsible	مَسؤول	
hour, time, watch, clock	ساعة	
reason	سَبَب (ج. أسباب)	س.ب.ب.
to swim	سبح – يسبح (I)	س.ب.ح.
week	أسبوع (ج. أسابيع)	س.ب.ع.

seventh	سابِع	
seven	سبعة	
six	ستّة	س.ت.ت.
temple/place of worship	مسجد (ج. مساجد)	س.ج.د.
coast	ساحِل (ج. سواحل)	س.ح.ل.
sixth	سادِس	س.د.س (س.ت.ت)
bed	سَرير	س.ر.ر.
fast	سَريع	س.ر.ع.
with speed, quickly	بسرعة	
service car		سَرفيس
to steal	سرَق – يسرِق (I)	س.ر.ق.
to get stolen	انسرق – ينسرِق (VII)	
to help	ساعَد – يساعِد (III)	س.ع.د.
assistant	مُساعِد	
pricing (system)	تسعيرة	س.ع.ر.
price	سِعر (ج. أسعار)	
to travel	سافر – يسافِر (III)	س.ف.ر.
embassy	سَفارَة	
close	سَكَّر – يسكِّر (II)	س.ك.ر
sugar	سُكَّر	
secretary		سِكرتير
to live, reside	سكن – يسكن (I)	س.ك.ن.
unfortunate, poor (as in oh, poor guy!)	مسكين	
salad		سَلَطة
Islamic	إسلامي	س.ل.م.
Muslim	مُسلِم	
I hope you are OK!		سَلامتك!
to allow	سمَح – يسمَح (I)	س.م.ح.
was permitted	سُمِح	
to forgive	سامَح – يسامِح (III)	
Samaritans		سَمَرة
to hear	سمِع – يسمع (I)	س.م.ع.
fish	سَمَك (ج. أسماك)	

year	سنة (ج. سَنوات، سِنين)	
easy	سَهل	س.ه.ل.
plain, meadow	سهل (ج. سُهول)	
black	أسوَد	س.و.د.
distance	مَسافة	س.و.ف.
will	سَوفَ ◆ = سَ ◆	
driver	سائق	س.و.ق.
market	سوق (ج. أسواق)	
to do	سَوّى* = عمِل	س.و.ي.
cigarette	سيجارة	
lady	سيّدة (ج. سيّدات)	
car	سيّارة	س.ي.ر.
policy, politics	سِياسة	س.ي.س.

ش

name of a meat dish	شاوَرما	
tea	شاي	
young man, youth	شابّ (ج. شباب)	ش.ب.ب.
to be full	شبِع – يشبَع (I)	ش.ب.ع.
window	شُبّاك (ج. شبابيك)	ش.ب.ك.
winter	شِتاء	ش.ت.و.
personal	شخصي	ش.خ.ص.
to drink	شرِب – يشرَب (I)	ش.ر.ب.
drinks	مشروبات	
policeman	شُرطي	ش.ر.ط.
street	شارع (ج. شوارع)	ش.ر.ع.
project	مشروع (ج. مَشاريع)	
honored to meet you	تشرّفنا	ش.ر.ف.
east	شرق	ش.ر.ق.
the Middle East	الشرق الأوسط	
company	شركة (ج. شركات)	ش.ر.ك.
to buy	اشتَرى – يشتَري (VIII)	ش.ر.ي.
beach	شاطىء	ش.ط.ء.
people	شعب (ج. شُعوب)	ش.ع.ب.

to feel	شَعَر – يشعُر (I)	ش.ع.ر.
poet	شاعِر	
feeling	شُعور	
to work	اشتغل – يشتغل (VIII)	ش.غ.ل.
work	شُغل	
busy	مَشغول	
hospital	مُستشفى (ج. مستشفيات)	ش.ف.ي.
apartment	شَقّة (ج. شقق)	ش.ق.ق.
hotel apartment	شَقّة فُندُقيّة	
to thank	شكر – يشكُر (I)	ش.ك.ر.
thank you	شُكراً	
thank you very much	شُكراً جَزيلاً	
you are welcome, don't mention it	لا شكراً على واجب	
problem	مُشكِلة (ج. مشاكل)	ش.ك.ل.
sun	شَمس	
north	شمال	ش.م.ل.
suitcase, bag	شنطة	ش.ن.ط.
handbag	شنطة يَد	
to watch	شاهد – يشاهِد (III) ◆ = تفرّج – يتفرّج (V)	ش.ه.د.
watching	مُشاهدة◆	
month	شَهر (ج. شُهور)	ش.ه.ر.
famous	مَشهور	
shorts	شورت (ج. شورتات)	
to see	شاف – يشوف* (I)	ش.و.ف.
to miss, long, yearn	اشتاق – يشتاق (ل) (VIII)	ش.و.ق
grilled food, baked	مَشوي (ج. مَشاوي)	ش.و.ي.
something, thing, item	شيء = اِشي* (ج. أشياء)	ش.ي.ء.
something sweet	شَيء حلو	
a little	شويّة* = قليل◆	

ص

soap	صابون	
to become	أصبح – يُصبِح (IV) ◆ = صار – يصير (I)	ص.ب.ح.
morning	صَباح	

good morning (Egyptian)	صباح النور والفُل = صباح الخير	
friend, owner	صاحِب (ج. أصحاب)	ص.ح.ب.
true, correct	صَحّ	ص.ح.ح.
correct, true	صحيح	
Bon appetit!	صحة وهناء، صحّتين وعافية!	
desert	صحراء (ج. صَحاري)	ص.ح.ر.
desert-like	صحراوي	
dishes, plates	صحن (ج. صُحون)	ص.ح.ن.
to wake up	صحا – يصحو◆ = صحِي – يصحى* (I)	ص.ح.و.
issue, issuance	صُدور	ص.د.ر.
friendship	صَداقة	ص.د.ق.
friend	صديق (ج. أصدِقاء) = صاحِب (ج. أصحاب)	
honestly, frankly	بصراحة	ص.ر.ح
bank	مصرف (ج. مصارِف) = بَنك (ج. بُنوك)	ص.ر.ف.
difficult	صَعب	ص.ع.ب.
difficulty	صعوبة (ج. صعوبات)	
elevator	مَصعَد	ص.ع.د.
Sa'idi, a person from Upper Egypt	صعيدي (ج. صعايدة)	
small	صغير	ص.غ.ر.
page	صَفحة	ص.ف.ح.
yellow	أصفر	ص.ف.ر.
zero	صِفر	
class	صَفّ (ج. صفوف)	ص.ف.ف.
the Crusaders	الصليبيّون	
to pray	صلّى – يصلّي (II)	ص.ل.و
lost and found box	صَندوق الموجودات	
made	مصنوع	ص.ن.ع.
sound, voice	صَوت (ج. أصوات)	ص.و.ت.
picture	صورَة (ج. صور)	ص.و.ر.
to fast	صام – يصوم (I)	ص.و.م.
to become	صار– يصير(I) = أصبح – يُصبِح◆ (IV)	ص.ي.ر.
summer	صيف	ص.ي.ف.
Chinese	صيني	

ض

to laugh	ضحك – يضحَك (I)	ض.ح.ك.
against	ضِدّ	
to hit	ضرب – يضرِب (I)	ض.ر.ب.
he beat him up, he hit him harshly	◆ ضربه ضرباً شديداً	
bank (of a river)		ضِفّة
to go, go out	ضهر – يضهَر* = راح – يروح* = طلع – يطلَع	ض.ه.ر.
to lose	ضيّع – يضيّع (II)	ض.ي.ع.
guest	ضيف (ج. ضيوف)	ض.ي.ف.
narrow	ضَيِّق	ض.ي.ق.

ط

doctor, physician	طبيب (ج. أطبّاء) = دكتور (ج. دكاترة)	ط.ب.ب.
weather	طَقس	
cooking	طبِخ	ط.ب.خ.
kitchen	مطبخ (ج. مطابخ)	
cooked	مَطبوخ	
of course	طبعاً	
road	طريق (ج. طرق)	ط.ر.ق.
food	طَعام = أكل	ط.ع.م.
restaurant	مَطعَم (ج. مطاعم)	
to request, ask for, to order	طلَب – يطلُب	ط.ل.ب.
student	طالب (ج. طلاب)	
to be able	استطاع – يستطيع (X) ◆	طوع
long	طويل	ط.و.ل.
table	طاولة (ج. طاولات)	
table tennis	تنس طاولة	
OK, tasty, good	طيّب	ط.ي.ب.
to fly	طارَ – يطير (I)	ط.ي.ر.
airplane	طائرة (ج. طائرات) = طيّارة (ج. طيّارات)	
airport	مَطار (ج. مطارات)	
'Alia' International Airport	مَطار علياء الدولي	

ع

to have		عِنده، عِندها، الخ.
to be considered	اعتُبِر – يُعتَبَر (VIII)	ع.ب.ر.
Ottoman		عُثماني
to please	أعجب – يُعجِب (IV)	ع.ج.ب.
pleasing	عاجِب*	
steering wheel	عَجلة القِيادة	ع.ج.ل.
number	عَدَد (ج. أعداد)	ع.د.د.
counter, meter	عدّاد	
several, a number of	عدّة	
moderate, temperate	مُعتدِل	ع.د.ل.
ordinary	عادي	ع.د.ي.
car (Egyptian)	عربيّة* = سيّارة	ع.ر.ب.
to know	عرف – يعرف (I)	ع.ر.ف.
knowing, getting to know	تعرُّف (على)	
not known, unknown	غير معروف◆	
tenth	عاشِر	ع.ش.ر.
ten	عشرة	
to have dinner	تعشّى – يتعشّى (V)	ع.ش.ي.
dinner	عَشاء	
juice	عصير	ع.ص.ر.
orange juice	عصير بُرتقال	
capital	عاصمة (ج. عواصم)	ع.ص.م.
thirsty	عطشان	ع.ط.ش.
to give	أعطى – يُعطي (IV)	ع.ط.ي.
to think	أعتقد – يعتقد	ع.ق.د.
opposite	عَكْس	ع.ك.س.
relationship	علاقة (ج. علاقات)	ع.ل.ق.
to teach	علّم – يعلّم (II)	ع.ل.م.
to learn	تعلّم – يتعلّم (V)	
education, instruction	تعليم	
grade	علامة (ج. علامات)	

science, knowledge	علم (ج. علوم)	
teacher	مُعلِّم (ج. معلِّمين) = أستاذ (ج. أساتذة)	
landmarks	مَعالم	
announcement, notice	إعلان (ج. إعلانات)	ع.ل.ن.
high	عالي	ع.ل.و.
on	عَلى	
at a distance of	على بُعد	
as you like, whatever pleases you	على راحتك	
I will be happy to (lit. on my head and eyes)	عَ (على) راسي وعيني	
for you, for your sake	عَ (على) شانك*	
for this reason	على شان هيك*	
I will be happy to ... (lit. on my eyes)	على عيوني	
to where (are you going) today? (Egyptian)	على فين النهاردا؟*	
as you wish	على كيفك*	
to me, on me	عَلَيَّ	
peace be upon him (referring to a prophet)	عليه السلام	
to depend on	اعتمد – يعتمد (VIII)	ع.م.د.
column	عمود (ج. أعمدة)	
age	عُمر (ج. أعمار)	ع.م.ر.
to work, do	عمل – يعمل (I)	ع.م.ل.
to use	استعمل – يستعمِل (X)	
public	عامّ	ع.م.م.
paternal uncle	عمّ (ج. أعمام)	
about		عن
we have		عنّا* = عندنا
seriously		عن جدّ*
when		عِندَما ◆ = لـّا
address	عُنوان (ج. عناوين)	ع.ن.و.ن.
to mean	عنى – يَعني	ع.ن.ي.
it means, in other words	يعني	
to get used to	تعوّد – يتعوّد (على)	ع.و.د.
normal, OK, fine	عادي	

English	Arabic	Root
family	عائِلة (ج. عائلات)	ع.و.ل.
shameful	عيب	ع.ي.ب.
birthday	عيد ميلاد	ع.ي.د.
to live	عاش – يعيش (I)	ع.ي.ش.
living	عَيش = سَكَن	

غ

English	Arabic	Root
stupid	غَبي	غ.ب.ي.
tomorrow	غَداً ◆ = بُكرة	
to have lunch	تغدّى – يتغدّى (V)	غ.د.ي.
lunch	غداء	
to find strange	استغرب – يستغرب (X)	غ.ر.ب.
west	غرب	
strange	غريب	
items, things (such as for the house, etc.)	غرَض (ج. اغراض)	غ.ر.ض.
room	غُرفة (ج. غُرف)	غ.ر.ف.
dining room	غُرفة أكْل	
living room	غرفة جُلوس	
bedroom	غُرفة نوم	
invasion	غَزو	غ.ز.و.
washing	غسيل	غ.س.ل.
to be angry	غضب – يغضَب ◆ = زعل – يزعَل	غ.ض.ب.
to defeat, to win	غلب – يغلب (I)	غ.ل.ب.
to raise the price; to make something more expensive	غلّى – يغلّي (II)	غ.ل.ي.
expensive	غالي	
dark	غامق	غ.م.ق.
singer	مُغَنّي (ج. مغنّيين)	غ.ن.ي.
cave	مَغارة	غ.و.ر.
to change	تغيّر – يتغيّر (V)	غ.ي.ر.
other than	غير	
cloudy	غائِم ◆	غ.ي.م.

ف

girl	فَتاة ◆ = بنت	
to open, conquer	فتَح – يفتح (I)	ف.ت.ح.
light-colored	فاتح	
open	مفتوح	
to look for	فتّش – يفتّش (على) (II)	ف.ت.ش.
name of a dish	فتّوش	
to be surprised	تفاجأً – يتفاجأً (VI)	ف.ج.ء.
surprise	مُفاجأة	
to burst, explode	انفجَر – ينفجِر (VII)	ف.ج.ر.
to watch	تفرّج – يتفرّج (V)	ف.ر.ج.
to become happy	فرِح – يفرح (I)	ف.ر.ح.
bed	فراش	ف.ر.ش.
furnished	مَفروش	
difference	فَرق (ج. فُروق)	ف.ر.ق.
team	فريق (ج. فرَق)	
oven	فُرن	
dress	فُستان (ج. فَساتين)	
season	فصل (ج. فصول)	ف.ص.ل.
to prefer	فضّل – يفضِّل (II)	ف.ض.ل.
please go ahead	تفضّل	
favorite	مُفضّل	
free, empty, available, not busy	فاضي*	ف.ض.ي.
to have breakfast	أفطر – يفطِر (IV)	ف.ط.ر.
breakfast	فُطور	
indeed	فعلاً	ف.ع.ل.
poor	فَقير	ف.ق.ر.
to think	فكّر – يفكّر (II)	ف.ك.ر.
idea	فكرة	
fruit	فواكه	ف.ك.ه.
fils (there are 1000 fils in one dinar)	فلس (ج. فُلوس)	
hotel	فُندُق (ج. فنادق)	

to understand	فهم – يفهم (I)	ف.ه.م.
understanding, having understood	فاهِم	
understanding	فَهم	
only	فقط ◆ = بَسّ*	
fava beans (Egyptian dish)	فول مُدمّس	
there is, there are	فيه	

ق

rule	قانون (ج. قوانين)	
grave, tomb	قَبر (ج. قُبور)	ق.ب.ر.
before	قبل	ق.ب.ل.
before (+ verb)	قبل أنْ ◆ = قبل ما	
future	مُستقبل	
to offer	قدّم – يقدّم (II)	ق.د.م.
to move forward	تقدّم – يتقدّم (V) ◆	
coming/next time	قادِم	
ancient, old	قديم	
front part	مُقدِّمة (ج. مقدّمات)	
how much, how many?	قَدّيش؟* = كَم؟	
Qur'anic	قُرآني	
closeness, proximity	قُرب	ق.ر.ب.
close, near	قريب	
relative	قريب (ج. أَقارِب)	
to decide	قرّر – يقرِّر (II)	ق.ر.ر.
piastre, 10 fils	قِرش (ج. قُروش)	
century	قَرن (ج. قرون)	ق.ر.ن.
village	قرية (ج. قُرى)	ق.ر.و.
intention, meaning	قَصْد	ق.ص.د.
economy	اقتِصاد	
economic, commercial	اقتِصادي	
story	قصّة (ج. قصص)	ق.ص.ص.
to sit	قعد – يقعُد (I)	ق.ع.د.
citadel	قلعة	ق.ل.ع.

less than	أقلّ مِن	ق.ل.ل.
independence	استقلال	
minority	أقلّيّة (ج. أقلّيات)	
little, few	قَليل◆	
scarcity	قلّة	
fried	مَقليّ	ق.ل.ي.
moon	قَمَر	
shirt	قميص (ج. قُمصان)	
consulate	قُنصلية (ج. قُنصليات)	
café, coffee house	مقهى (ج. مقاهي)	ق.ه.و.
leader, commander	قائد (ج. قُوّاد)	ق.و.د.
to say	قال – يقول (I)	ق.و.ل.
nonsense	قال..... قال*	

ك

cup, glass	كاسة (ج. كاسات)	ك.ء.س.
as if	كأنّ	
the biggest, oldest	الأكبر	ك.ب.ر.
big	كبير	
kibbeh (Lebanese meat dish)	كبّة	
to write	كَتَبَ – يكتب (I)	ك.ت.ب.
book	كتاب (ج. كُتُب)	
office	مَكتب (ج. مكاتب)	
written	مكتوب	
many, a lot, very	كثير (ج. كثار)	ك.ث.ر.
by a lot, very	بكثير	
more than	أكثر مِن	
to lie	كذب – يكذِب (I)	ك.ذ.ب.
thus, that way	كذلك◆	
chair	كُرسي (ج. كَراسي)	
hospitality	كَرَم	ك.ر.م.
to hate	كره – يكرَه (I)	ك.ر.ه.

basketball		كُرة سلّة
volleyball		كُرة طائرة
soccer		كُرة قدم
to discover	اكتشف – يكتشف (VIII)	ك.ش.ف.
to be sufficient	كَفى – يَكفي (I)، كفّى – يكفّي (II)	ك.ف.ي.
enough	كافي	
to cost	كلّف – يكلف (II)	ك.ل.ف.
cost	تكلفة (ج. تكاليف)	
each, every, the whole of	كُلَّ	ك.ل.ل
everything	كلّ اشي* = كلّ شيء	
whenever	كلّما ◆ (كلّ + ما)	
each one	كُل واحد	
college	كُلّيّة (ج. كُلّيات)	
law school	كُلّيّة حقوق	
to speak	تكلّم – يتكلّم (V)◆ = حكى – يحكي	ك.ل.م.
last word	كلمة اخيرة	
full	كامل	ك.م.ل.
how many?		كَم؟
as		كَما
also		كَمان*
amount		كَمّية (ج. كمّيات)
kinaafi (Arab dessert)		كنافة
shoes		كُندرة (ج. كنادِر)
church	كنيسة (ج. كنائس)	ك.ن.س.
Canaan		كنعان
electricity		كَهرَباء
bag	كيس (ج. أكياس)	ك.ي.س.
headdress		كوفيّة = حَطّة
to be	كان – يكون (I)	كون
I had it (it was with me)	كان معي	
good		كويّس*
how		كيف

how are you?		كيفك؟* = كيف حالك؟
kilo		كيلو

ل

no		لأ
to wear	لبس – يلبس (I)	ل.ب.س.
clothes	مَلابِس	
underwear	ملابِس داخليّة	
yogurt	لبن	ل.ب.ن.
refugee	لاجِئ (ج. لاجئين)	ل.ج.ء.
meat	لَحم (ج. لحوم)	ل.ح.م.
for that, for that reason		لذلك◆
must, should, it is necessary that	لازِم*	ل.ز.م.
still, up to now		لسّه*
nice, kind	لَطيف	ل.ط.ف.
to play	لعب – يلعَب (I)	ل.ع.ب.
player	لاعِب (ج. لاعبين)	
playing	لعب	
game	لُعبة	
language		لُغة (ج. لُغات)
the Arabic language		اللغة العربيّة
sign, billboard	لافتة (ج. لافتات)	ل.ف.ت.
to find, meet	لاقى– يلاقي (III) = وجَد – يوجَد	ل.ق.ي.
to meet	التقى – يلتقي (VIII)	
unfortunately		للأسف
but		لكِن
not, did not		لَم◆
I did not find it	لم أجده◆	
will not		لن◆
if you please		لو سَمحت = من فَضلك
color	لون (ج. ألوان)	ل.و.ن.
where to?		لَوين؟*

not	ليسَ ◆ = مِش*
why?	ليش؟*
why not?	ليش لأ؟*
evening, night	ليل
why? (Egyptian)	ليه؟* = ليش؟*

م

how beautiful!		ما أجمَل!
not one, nobody		ما حدا* = ما حد*
I did not hear anything other than,		ما سمعت إلا..
praise God, wow!		ما شاء الله!
don't worry about it		ما عليك*
there is not, there are not		ما فيش* = ما فيه*
water		ماء ◆ = ميّة*
what?		ماذا؟ ◆ = إيش؟*
appetizer		مازة (ج. مازات)
what is wrong?		مالك؟*
enjoyable, fun	مُمتِع ◆	م.ت.ع.
like	مِثل	م.ث.ل
for example	مَثلاً	
test	امتحان (ج. أمتحانات)	م.ح.ن.
period of time, duration	مُدّة	م.د.د.
school subjects	مادّة (ج. موادّ)	
to pass through	مرَّ – يمرّ (I)	م.ر.ر.
time	مَرّة (ج. مَرّات)	
another time, again	مرّة ثانية	
to get sick	مرض – يمرض (I)	م.ر.ض.
nursing	تمريض	
sick, unwell	مَريض	
nurse	مُمرّض	
wife (his wife – Egyptian)	مَرَة (مراته)*	
to jest, make jokes	مزح – يمزَح (I)	م.ز.ح.

Christian	مَسيحيّ (ج. مسيحيّين)
evening	م.س.ي. مَساء
not	مِش*
not possible, unthinkable	مش معقول!*
walking	م.ش.ي. مَشي
good	ماشي = كويس*
Egypt	مَصر
past, last	م.ض.ي. ماضي
rain	م.ط. ر. مَطر (ج. أمْطار)
rainy	ماطِر
with	مع
with us	معانا* = مَعنا
goodbye	مع السلامة
together	مع بعض
stomach	معدة
place	مَكان (ج. أماكن)
possible, maybe, perhaps	م.ك.ن. مُمكن = يُمكن
full	م.ل.ء. مَملوء
to own	م.ل.ك. مَلَك – يملِك (I)
from	مِن
for the sake of	مِن أجل
all kinds (lit. from the sour to the sweet)	من الحامض للحلو
if you please, excuse me	من فضلك = لو سمحت
scholarship	م.ن.ح. مِنحة (ج. مِنَح)
since	مُنذُ ◆
mansaf (Jordanian meat dish)	مَنسَف
prohibited, not allowed	م.ن.ع. مَمنوع
good, well	منيح* = كويس*
skilled	م.ه.ر. ماهِر
profession	م.ه.ن. مِهنة (ج. مِهن)
to die	م.و.ت. مات – يموت (I)
bananas	م.و.ز. موز

excellent	مُمتاز	م.ي.ز.
mall	مول	
who?*	مين؟*	
water	مَيّة* = ماء◆	
a hundred	مِيّة	
100%	مِيّة في المِيّة	

ن

fire, hell	نار	
to result	نتَج – ينتُج (I)	ن.ت.ج.
result	نتيجة (ج. نتائج)	
to succeed, to pass (an exam)	نجح – ينجح (I)	ن.ج.ح.
to descend, come down, fall	نزل – ينزِل (I)	ن.ز.ل.
staying	نازِل	
suitable	مُناسب	ن.س.ب.
relative, in relation to	نِسبي	
soul, person, inhabitant	نسمة	ن.س.م.
to forget	نسي – ينسى (I)	ن.س.ي.
widespread	مُنتشر	ن.ش.ر.
half	نِصْف◆ = نُصّ*	ن.ص.ف.
area	مِنطَقة (ج. مَناطِق)	ن.ط.ق.
in the view of	في نظر	ن.ظ.ر.
scene, sight	مَنظر (ج. مناظر)	
to clean	نظّف – ينظّف (II)	ن.ظ.ف.
clean	نظيف	
sleepy	نَعسان	ن.ع.س.
yes	نَعَم	
mint	نعنَع	
self; same	نَفس	ن.ف.س.
by myself	بنفسي	
the same thing	نفس الشيء	
to move	انتقل – ينتقِل (VIII)	ن.ق.ل.
daytime	نَهار	ن.ه.ر.

river	نَهر	
to end	انتهى – ينتهي (VIII)	ن.ه.ي.
end	نِهاية (ج. نهايات)	
type, kind	نوع (ج. أنواع)	ن.و.ع.
to sleep	نام – ينام (I)	ن.و.م.
the sleep	نوم	
the Nile River	نهر النيل	

هـ

this name	هالاسم* = هذا الإسم	
this (f.)	هاي* = هذه◆	
now	هلّا* = الآن◆	
telephone	هاتِف◆ = تلفون	ه.ت.ف.
to emigrate	هاجر– يُهاجِر (III)	ه.ج.ر.
immigration	هِجرة	
quiet	هادئ = هادي	ه.د.ء.
goal	هدَف (ج. أهداف)	ه.د.ف.
gift	هدية (ج. هدايا)	ه.د.ي.
this (m.)	هذا	
this (f.)	هذه	
to flee	هرَب – يهرُب (I)	ه.ر.ب.
name of a dessert	هَريسة	
defeat	هزيمة	ه.ز.م.
thus, this way	هكَذا◆ = هيك*	
whether (also used to ask yes/no questions)	هَل◆	
they (dual)	هُما◆	
important	مُهم = هامّ	ه.م.م.
importance	أهمّيّة	
here	هُنا◆	
here (Egyptian)	هنا* = هُنا◆ = هون*	
there, there is	هُناك◆ = فيه*	
engineer	مُهندس (ج. مهندسين)	ه.ن.د.س.
Indian	هِندي	

hobby	هواية (ج. هوايات)	ﻫ.و.ي.
here	هون*	
here is	هَي*	
like this	هيك*	
here I am!	هيّني!*	

و

and	وَ	
by God, I swear!	والله	
or	وَلا* = أو	
homework	واجب (ج. واجبات)	و.ج.ب.
must, should	يَجب أنْ◆ = لازم*	
to find	وَجَد – يَجِد◆ = وجد – يوجَد* (I)	و.ج.د.
found, available	مَوْجود	
pain	وَجَع	و.ج.ع.
are you in pain?	موجوعة شي؟*	
to face	واجه – يواجِه (III)	و.ج.ﻫ.
one	واحد	و.ح.د.
by himself, herself, etc.	وحده، وحدها، الخ.	
one, anyone	حَدا* = حَدّ*	
no one, nobody	ما حَدّ* = ما حَدا*	
paper	ورقة (ج. أوراق)	و.ر.ق.
State Department (Ministry of Foreign Affairs)	وزارة الخارجيّة	و.ز.ر.
weight	وَزن	و.ز.ن.
middle	وَسَط	و.س.ط.
downtown	وسط البَلَد	
middle, average	متوسّط	
wide	واسع	و.س.ع.
to arrive, reach	وصل – يصل◆ = وصل – يوصَل* (I)	و.ص.ل.
arrival	وُصول	
public transportation	مُواصَلات عامّة	
to call	اتصل – يتصل (VIII)	
to put	وضع – يضع◆ (I)	و.ض.ع.

situation	وَضْع	
employee	مُوَظَّف (ج. موظّفين)	و.ظ.ف.
job	وَظيفة (ج. وَظائف)	
to agree	وافَق – يوافِق (III)، اتّفق – يتّفق (VIII)	و.ف.ق.
time	وَقت	و.ق.ت.
the whole time	طول الوَقت	
any time	أيّ وَقت	
to be located	وقع – يقع◆ (I)	و.ق.ع.
location	مَوقِع (ج. مواقِع)	.
to stop	وقّف – يوقّف (II)* = توقّف – يتوقّف◆ (V)	و.ق.ف.
stop (bus stop)	مَوقِف (ج. مواقف)	
standing	واقِف	
boy, son, child	وَلَد (ج. أولاد)	و.ل.د.
birth	ولادة	
A.D.	ميلادي	
to be born (Egyptian)	اتولد – يتولد* = انولد – ينولد*	
state	وَلاية (ج. ولايات)	و.ل.ي.
where?	وين؟*	
where is he?	وينه = وين هو؟*	

ي

oh God!	يا ألله!
my dear, my lady	يا ستّي*
let's	يالله*
left (direction)	يَسار	ي.س.ر.
thank you (lit. may your hands be safe)	يسلموا ايديك
right (direction)	يَمين	ي.م.ن.
day	يوم (ج. أيّام)	ي.و.م.
today	اليوم	.
or	يا* = او
hand	يَد (ج. أيدي)◆
Greek	يوناني

English–Arabic Glossary

A

"Alia" International Airport	مَطار علياء الدولي
A.D.	ميلادي
about	عَن
according to, depending on	حسَب
accountant	مُحاسب
address	عُنوان (ج. عناوين)
administrative	إداري
afraid	خائف◆ = خايِف*
Africa	إفريقيا
after	بَعد
afternoon	بعد الظُهر
against	ضدّ
age	عُمر (ج. أعمار)
agree (to)	وافَق – يوافِق (III)
ahead, in front of	أمام◆
airplane	طائرة (ج. طائرات) = طيّارة (ج. طيّارات)
airport	مَطار (ج. مطارات)
Alexander	الإسكَندر
all kinds (lit. from the sour the sweet)	من الحامض للحلو

allow (to)	سمَح – يسمَح
also	أيضاً◆ = كَمان*
always	دائماً
amount	كَميّة (ج. كَميّات)
amount (to)	بلغ – يبلُغ
ancient, old	قديم
and	وَ
announcement, notice	إعلان (ج. إعلانات)
another (m.)	آخَر◆
another (f.)	أخرى◆
another time, again	مرّة ثانية
answer (to)	ردّ – يرُدّ
any time	أيّ وَقت
apartment	شَقّة (ج. شقق)
appetizer	مازة (ج. مازات)
apples	تُفّاح
Arabian Peninsula (the)	الجزيرة العربيّة
Arabic Language (the)	اللغة العربيّة
are you in pain?	موجوعة شي؟*
area	مِنطَقة (ج. مَناطِق)
army	جَيش
arrival	وُصول
arrive, reach (to)	وصل – يصل◆ = وصل – يوصَل*

as	كَما	be born (Egyptian) (to)	= اتولد – يتولد*
as he was before	زي ما كان*		انولد – ينولد*
as if	كأنّ	be considered (to)	اعتُبِر– يُعتَبَر (VIII)
as you like, whatever pleases you	على راحتك	be founded (to)	تأسّس – يتأسّس (V)
as you wish	على كيفك*	be full (to), satisfied (eating)	شبع – يشبع
Asia	آسيا	be late (to)	تأخّر– يتأخّر
ask (to)	سأل – يسأل	be located (to)	وقع – يقع ◆
assistant	مُساعِد	be sufficient (to)	كَفى – يَكفي، كَفّى –
Assyrians (the)	الآشوريون		يكفِّي (II)
at a distance of	على بُعد	be surprised (to)	تفاجأ – يتفاجأ (VI)
at all, never	أبداً	beach	شاطِىء
available (to us), we have	موجود عنّا	beautiful	جميل = حلو
		become (to)	= ◆(IV) أصبح – يُصبِح
			صار – يصير

B

		become happy (to)	فرِح – يفرح
Babylonians (the)	البابليّون	bed	سَرير
Bachelor's, B.A. degree	بكالوريوس	bedding	فراش
bag	كيس (ج. أكياس)	bedroom	غُرفة نوم
baklaawa (name of a dessert)	بقلاوة	before	قبل
balcony	بَلكونة	before (+ verb)	قبل أنْ ◆ = قبل ما
bananas	موز	built (was)	بُني ◆
bank	مصرف (ج. مصارف) =	believe (to)	آمَن – يُؤمِن (IV)
	بَنك (ج. بُنوك)	belly, stomach	بَطن (ج. بطون)
bank (of a river)	ضفّة	better, the best	أحسَن
basketball	كُرة سلّة	bicycle	درّاجة = بُسكليت (بِسكليت)
bathroom	حَمّام (ج. حمّامات)	big	كبير
be (to)	كان – يكون	biggest, oldest (the)	الأكبر
be able (to)	استطاع – يستطيع (X)◆	birth	ولادة
be afraid (to)	خاف – يخاف	birthday	عيد ميلاد
be angry (to)	غضب – يغضَب ◆ =	black	أسوَد
	زعل – يزعَل*	Black Sea (the)	البحر الأسود

blue	أزرق	call (to)	اتصل – يتصل (VIII)
Bon appetit!	صحة وهناء، صحّتين وعافية!	camp	مُخيَّم (ج. مُخيَّمات)
book	كِتاب (ج. كُتُب)	Canaan	كنعان
border (to)	حدّ – يحُدّ	capital	عاصمة (ج. عواصم)
border	حَدّ (ج. حُدود)	car	سيّارة
bother (to)	أزعَج – يزعِج (IV)	car (Egyptian)	عربيّة*
bothering, inconvenience	إزعاج	cave	مَغارة
boy, son, child	وَلَد (ج. أولاد)	center	مَركَز (ج. مَراكِز)
bread	خُبز	century	قَرن (ج. قرون)
breakfast	فُطور	certainly	أكيد
bridge	جِسر	chair	كُرسي (ج. كَراسي)
bring (to)	جاب – يجيب*	change (to)	تغيّر – يتغيّر (V)
brother	خيّ* = أخ	cheap	رَخيص
brother, a friendly way of addressing a man	أخ (ج. إخوة، إخوان)	cheese	جبن
brown	بُنّي	chicken	دَجاج
building	بِناية (ج. بِنايات)	China	الصين
built	مبني	Chinese	صيني
burst, explode (to)	انفجَر – ينفجِر	Christian	مَسيحيّ (ج. مسيحيّين)
bus	باص	church	كنيسة (ج. كنائس)
busy	مَشغول	cigarette	سيجارة
but	لكِن	citadel	قلعة
buy (to)	اشتَرى – يشتَري (VIII)	city	مدينة (ج. مُدُن)
by a lot, very	بكثير	city quarter, neighborhood	حَيّ (ج. أحياء)
by God, I swear!	والله	civilization	حضارة
by himself, herself, etc.	وحده، وحدها، الخ.	class	صَفّ (ج. صفوف)
by myself	بنفسي	clean (to)	نظّف – ينظّف (II)
		clean	نظيف
		close (to)	سَكّر – يسكّر (II)
		close, near	قريب

C

café, coffee house	مقهى (ج. مقاهي)	closeness, proximity	قُرب
Cairo	القاهرة	clothes	مَلابِس
		cloudy	غائِم◆

coast	ساحِل (ج. سواحل)
cold (adjective)	بارِد
cold (noun)	بَرْد
college	كُلِّيّة (ج. كُلِّيّات)
color	لون (ج. ألوان)
column	عمود (ج. أعمدة)
come (to)	جاء – يجيء ◆ = أجا – ييجي *
comfortable	مُريح
coming/next time	قادِم
commerce, trade, business	تِجارة
commercial	تجاري
company	شركة (ج. شركات)
condition	حالة
consulate	قُنصلية (ج. قُنصليات)
control, rule	حُكم
cooked	مَطبوخ
cooking	طبخ
Copts (the)	الأقْباط
correct, true	مزبوط*، صَحيح
correspondence	مُراسَلة
cost (to)	كلّف – يكلف (II)
cost (the)	تكلفة (ج. تكاليف)
counter, meter	عدّاد
country	بَلَد (ج. بِلاد)
countryside	ريف
cow(s)	بَقَر
crazy	مَجنون
crowdedness	زَحمة
Crusaders (the)	الصليبيّون
culture	ثقافة
cup, glass	كاسة (ج. كاسات)

D

Damascus	دمشق، الشام
dark	غامِق
date, history	تاريخ
day	يوم (ج. أَيّام)
day after tomorrow (the)	بَعد بُكرة*
day before yesterday (the)	أوّل أمس ◆ = أوّل مبارِح*
daytime	نَهار
decide (to)	قرّر – يقرِّر (II)
defeat	هزيمة
defeat (to)	غلب – يغلب
delicious, tasty	زاكي*
depend on (to)	اعتمد – يعتمد (VIII)
descend, come down, fall (to)	نزل – ينزِل
desert	صحراء (ج. صَحاري)
desert-like	صحراوي
die (to)	مات – يموت
differ (to)	اختلف – يختلف (VIII)
difference	اختلاف (ج. إختلافات)، فَرق (ج. فُروق)
different	مختلف
difficult	صَعب
difficulty	صعوبة (ج. صعوبات)
dinar (Jordanian currency)	دينار (ج. دنانير)
dining room	غُرفة أكل
dinner	عَشاء
director, manager	مُدير
discover (to)	اكتشف – يكتشف (VIII)
dish, food	أكلة
dish, plate	صحن (ج. صُحون)
distance	مَسافة

disturbing, bothersome	مُزعِج	employee	مُوظَّف (ج. موظَّفين)
do (to)	سَوّى* = عمِل	end (to)	انتهى – ينتهي (VIII)
doctor, physician	طبيب (ج. أطبّاء) =	end	نِهاية (ج. نِهايات)
	دكتور (ج. دكاترة)	engaged	مَخطوب
don't worry about it	ما عليك*	engagement	خُطوبة
door	باب (ج. أبواب)	engineer	مُهندِس (ج. مهندسين)
dormitory	بيت طُلاب	enjoyable, fun	مُمتِع◆
downtown	وسط البَلَد	enough	كافي
dream (to)	حلِم – يحلُم	enter (to)	دخل – يدخُل
dress	فُستان (ج. فَساتين)	evening	مَساء
drink (to)	شرِب – يشرَب	evening, night	ليل
drinks	مشروبات	everything	كلّ اشي* = كلّ شيء
driver	سائق	excellent	مُمتاز
dry	جافّ	exchanging	تبادُل◆
		expensive	غالي

E

English	Arabic		
each, every, the whole of	كُلّ		

F

each one	كُل واحد	face (to)	واجه – يواجِه (III)
early	مُبكِّر	fail (to) (an exam)	رسب – يرسُب
east	شرق	fall, autumn	الخريف
easy	سَهل	family	عائِلة (ج. عائلات)
eat (to)	أكل – يأكل	famous	مَشهور
economic	اقتصادي	far	بعيد
economy	اقتصاد	fare, rent	أجرَة
education, instruction	تعليم	farm	مَزرَعة (ج. مَزارِع)
eggs	بَيض	fast (to)	صام – يصوم
Egypt	مَصر	fast	سَريع
eight	ثمانية	fat	دُهن
eighth	ثامِن	father	أب (ج. آباء)
electricity	كَهرَباء	fattuush (name of a dish)	فتّوش
elevator	مَصعَد	fava beans (Egyptian dish)	فول مُدمَّس
embassy	سَفارَة	favorite	مُفضَّل
emigrate (to)	هاجر – يُهاجِر (III)		

fear	خَوف
feel (to)	شَعَر – يشعُر
feeling	شُعور
fifth	خامِس
fils (there are 1000 fils in one dinar)	فِلس (ج. فُلوس)
find (to)	وَجَد – يجِد ◆ =
	وجد – يوجَد*
find strange (to)	استغرب – يستغرب (X)
find, meet (to)	لاقى – يلاقي (III) =
	وجَد – يوجَد
finish, complete (to)	خلّص – يخلّص (II)*
fire, hell	نار
first	أوّل
first time	أوّل مرّة
fish	سَمَك (ج. أسماك)
five	خمسة
flee (to)	هرَب – يهرُب
flower	زهرة (ج. زهور)
fly (to)	طارَ – يطير
food	أكْل، طَعام
for example	مَثلاً
for men	رِجالي
for that, for that reason	لذلك ◆
for the sake of	مِن أجل
for this reason	على شان هيك*
for you, for your sake	عَ (على) شانك*
foreigner	أجنَبي (ج. أجانِب)
forget (to)	نسي – ينسى
forgive (to)	سامَح – يسامِح (III)
found, available	مَوْجود
four	أربعة
fourth	رابِع

free, empty, available, not busy	فاضي*
free, for nothing	ببلاش*
Friday	الجُمعة
fried	مَقليّ
friend	صديق (ج. أصدِقاء) =
	صاحِب (ج. أصحاب)
friend, owner	صاحِب (ج. أصحاب)
friendship	صَداقة
frightening	مُخيف
from	مِن
front part	مُقدِّمة (ج. مقدّمات)
fruit	فواكه
full	كامل
full, filled	مَملوء
furnished	مفروش
future	مُستقبل

G

game	لُعبة
gender, sex	جِنس
get stolen (to)	انسرق – ينسرق (VII)
get used to something (to)	تعوّد – يتعوّد (على)
gift	هدية (ج. هدايا)
girl	فَتاة ◆ = بنت
girl, daughter	بِنت (ج. بنات)
give (to)	أعطى – يُعطي (IV)
go (to)	ذهَب – يذهب ◆ =
	راح – يروح*
go, go out (to)	ضهَر – يضهَر* =
	راح – يروح* =
	طلع – يطلَع

goal	هدَف (ج. أهداف)
God knows	الله أعلَم
God willing	إن شاء الله
good	كويّس*، ماشي
good morning (Egyptian)	صباح النور والفُل = صباح الخير
good, well	منيح* = كويّس*
goodbye	مع السلامة
grade	علامة (ج. علامات)
grandfather	جَدّ
grave, tomb	قَبر (ج. قُبور)
great, perfect	تَمام
Greater Syria	بلاد الشام
Greek	يوناني
Greeks (the)	اليونان
green	أخضَر
grilled food, baked	مَشوي (ج. مَشاوي)
group	مجموعة
guest	ضيف (ج. ضيوف)

H

half	نِصْف ◆ = نُصّ*
hand	يَد (ج. أيدي)◆ = إيد (ج. إيدين)*
handbag	شنطة يَد
happen (to)	حدَث - يحدث◆
hariisi (name of a dessert)	هَريسة
hate (to)	كرِه - يكرَه
have (own) (to)	عنده، عندها، الخ.
have breakfast (to)	أفطر - يفطِر (IV)
have dinner (to)	تعشّى - يتعشّى (V)
have lunch (to)	تغدّى - يتغدّى (V)

have you been ... a long time?	زمان صار لِك ... ؟*
he	هو
he beat him up, he hit him harshly	ضربه ضرباً شديداً◆
head	راس (ج. روس*، رؤوس◆)
headdress	كوفيّة = حَطّة
hear (to)	سمِع - يسمع
heat	حَرّ
heaven, paradise	جنّة
help (to)	ساعَد - يساعِد (III)
here	هُنا◆ = هون*
here (Egyptian)	هنا*
here I am!	هيّني!*
here is	هيّ*
high	عالي
higher, graduate studies	دراسات عُليا
hit (to)	ضرب - يضرِب
hobby	هواية (ج. هوايات)
homework	واجِب (ج. واجبات)
honestly, frankly	بصراحة
honored to meet you	تشرّفنا
hookah	أرجيلة = نرجيلة
hope (to)	رجا - يرجو◆
hospital	مُستشفى (ج. مستشفيات)
hospitality	كَرَم
hot	حارّ◆ = حامي
hot	حامي*
hotel	فُندُق (ج. فنادق)
hotel apartment	شَقة فُندُقيّة
hour, time, watch, clock	ساعة

house	بيت (ج. بيوت)	indeed	فِعلاً
housewife	ربّة بيت	independence	استقلال
how	كيف	Indian	هِندي
how are you?	كيفك* = كيف حالك؟	intelligence service	مُخابَرات
How beautiful!	ما أجمَل!	intention, meaning	قَصْد
how much, how many?	قَدّيش؟* = كَم؟	invasion	غَزو
humid	رَطب	invitation	دَعوة
humidity	رُطوبة	invite (to)	دَعا – يدعو◆
		Islamic	إسلامي
I		Islamic month of fasting	رَمَضان
I	أنا	Islamic religion (the)	الدين الإسلامي
I came	جيت*	issue, issuance	صُدور
I did not find him (it)	لم أجده◆	it (her)	ايّاها
I did not hear anything other than ...	ما سمعت إلا..	it means, in other words	يعني
I had it (it was with me)	كان معي	it seems	يبدو
I hope you are OK!	سَلامتك!	items, things (such as for the house, etc.)	غرض (ج. اغراض)
I will be happy (lit. on my head and eye)	عَ (على) راسي وعيني	It's not right! It's too much!	حَرام عليك!
I will be happy to ... (lit. on my eyes)	على عيوني		
idea	فكرة	**J**	
if	إذا	jacket	جاكيت
if you please, excuse me	من فضلك = لو سمحت	Jerusalem	القُدس
immigration	هِجرة	jest, make jokes (to)	مزح – يمزَح
importance	أَهَمّية	job	وَظيفة (ج. وَظائف)
important	مُهم = هامّ	juice	عصير
impossible	مُستحيل		
improve (to)	تحسّن – يتحسّن (V)	**K**	
in spite of	رَغمَ أنّ	kibbeh (Lebanese meat dish)	كبّة
in the view of	في نظر		
in your opinion	في رأيك	kilo	كيلو
increase, exceed (to)	زاد – يزيد (على)	kinaafi (Arab dessert)	كنافة

kitchen	مطبخ (ج. مطابخ)
know (to)	عرف – يعرف
knowing, getting to know	تعرُّف (على)

L

lady	سيّدة (ج. سيّدات)
lamb	خَروف
landmarks	مَعالم
language	لُغة (ج. لُغات)
last	أخير
last word	كلمة اخيرة
last, latest, most recent	آخِر
late	مُتَأخر
laugh (to)	ضحك – يضحَك
law school	كُلّية حقوق
leader, commander	قائد (ج. قُوّاد)
learn (to)	تعلّم – يتعلّم (V)
leave (to)	ترَك – يترُك
left (direction)	يَسار
less than	أقلّ من
let me see	خلّيني أشوف*
let's	يالله*
lettuce	خسّ
lie (to)	كذب – يكذِب
life	حياة
light-colored	فاتح
like	مِثل
like this	هيك*
like, such as	زَيّ* = مِثل
limit (to)	حدّد – يحدّد (II)
little, a little, few	قليل، شويّة*
live (to)	عاش – يعيش

live, reside (to)	سكّن – يسكن
living	عَيش = سَكَن
living room	غرفة جلوس
local	بَلَدي
location	مَوقِع (ج. مواقع)
long	طويل
look for (to)	فتّش – يفتِّش (على) (II)
look! (Egyptian)	بُصّ* = شوف*!
lose (to)	ضيّع – يضيّع (II)
lost and found box	صَندوق الموجودات
love, like (to)	حبّ – يحبّ*
lunch	غداء

M

made	مصنوع
main, principal	رئيسي
make someone dizzy (to)	دوّش – يدوِش*
male	ذكر (ج. ذكور)
mall	مول
Mamluks (the)	المماليك
man	رَجُل (ج. رجال)
mansaf (Jordanian meat dish)	مَنسَف
many, a lot, very	كثير (ج. كثار)
market	سوق (ج. أسواق)
marriage	زواج
maternal uncle	خال (ج. أخوال)
me, on me	عليّ
mean (to)	عنى – يَعني
meat	لَحم (ج. لحوم)
mentioned (was)	ذُكِر
Mediterranean Sea (the)	البحر الأبيض المتوسط

meet (to)	التقى – يلتقي (VIII)	narrow	ضَيّق
middle	وَسَط	nation	دولة (ج. دُوَل)
Middle East (the)	الشرق الأوسط	nationality, citizenship	جِنسيّة
middle, average	متوسّط	neighbor	جار (ج. جيران)
milk	حَليب	new	جديد
minority	أقلّيّة (ج. أقلّيات)	news	خبر (ج. أخبار)
mint	نعنَع	newspaper	جَريدة
minus, to, except	إلّا	nice, kind	لَطيف
minute	دقيقة (ج. دقائق)	Nile River (the)	نهر النيل
moderate, temperate	مُعتدل	nine	تسعة
modern; conversation	حديث	ninth	تاسع
Monday	الإثنين	no	لأ
month	شَهر (ج. شُهور)	no one, nobody	ما حَدّ* = ما حَدا*
more than	أكثر من	nonsense	قال..... قال*
morning	صَباح	nonsense (lit. no study no watermelon)	بلا دراسة بلا بطّيخ*
mosque	جامع (ج. جوامع) = مَسجد (ج. مساجد)	normal, OK, fine	عادي
mother	أم (ج. أمّهات◆)	north	شمال
mountain	جَبَل (ج. جبال)	not	ليسَ◆ = مِش*
mountainous	جَبَلي	not known, unknown	غير معروف◆
move (to)	انتقل – ينتقل	not one, nobody	ما حَدا* = ما حَد*
move forward (to)	تقدّم – يتقدّم (V)◆	not possible, unthinkable	مش معقول!*
Mu'adhdhin, the one who calls for prayer (the)	مُؤَذِّن	not, did not	لم◆
museum	متحف (ج. متاحف)	now	الآن◆ = هلّأ*
Muslim	مُسلم	number	رقَم
must, should, it is necessary that	يَجب أن◆ = لازم*	number	عَدَد (ج. أعداد)
my dear lady	يا ستّي*	nurse	مُمَرّض
		nursing	تمريض

N

English	Arabic		
Nabataeans (the)	الأنباط		
name	اسم (ج. أسماء◆، أسامي*)		

O

obtain (to)	حصل – يحصُل (على)
occupy (to)	احتلّ – يحتلّ (VIII)
ocean, surrounding	مُحيط

of course	طبعاً	painful	مُؤلِم
offer (to)	قدّم – يقدّم (II)	pants, trousers	بَنطلون
office	مَكتب (ج. مكاتب)	paper	ورقة (ج. أوراق)
Oh God!	يا أَلله!	part, section	جُزء (ج. أجزاء)
oil	زَيت	partial	جُزئي
OK, tasty, good	طيّب	pass through (to)	مرَّ – يمرّ
on	على	passenger	راكِب (ج. رُكّاب)
one	واحد	passport	جَواز سَفَر
one hundred	ميّة	past, last	ماضي
one hundred percent	ميّة في الميّة	paternal uncle	عمّ (ج. أعمام)
one, anyone	حَدا* = حَدّ*	pay (to)	دفَع – يدفَع
only	فقط◆ = بَسّ*	peace be upon him (referring to a prophet)	عليه السلام
open	مفتوح		
open, conquer (to)	فتَح – يفتح	people	شعب (ج. شُعوب)
opinion	رأي	people, folks	أهل (ج. أهالي)
opposite	عَكْس	perhaps	ربّما◆
or	وَلا* = أو	period of time, duration	مُدّة
or	يا* = او	permitted (was)	سُمح
or (in direct and indirect questions)	أم◆ = أو	Persians (the)	الفُرس
		personal	شخصي
orange	بُرتقال	Ph.D., doctorate	دكتوراه
orange (color)	بُرتقالي	picture	صورة (ج. صور)
orange juice	عصير بُرتقال	place	مَكان (ج. أماكن)
ordinary	عادي	plain, meadow	سهل (ج. سُهول)
origin	أصل	play (to)	لعَب – يلعَب
other than	غير	player	لاعب (ج. لاعبين)
Ottoman	عُثماني	playing	لِعب
oven	فُرن	please (to)	أعجب – يُعجِب (IV)
own (to)	مَلَك – يملك	if you please	أرجوك = لوسمحت = من فَضلَك
P		please go ahead	تفضّل، تفضّلي
page	صَفحة	pleasing	عاجِب*
pain	وَجَع		

pocket	جيب (ج. جُيوب)
poet	شاعِر
policeman	شُرطي
policy, politics	سِياسة
poor	فَقير
pork, pig	خَنزير
possible, maybe, perhaps	مُمكِن = يُمكِن
potatoes	بطاطا
praise God, wow!	ما شاء الله!
pray (to)	صلّى – يصلّي (II)
prefer (to)	فضّل – يفضّل (II)
presently, right away	حاضِر
pretty (sweet)	حلو
price	سِعر (ج. أسعار)
pricing (system)	تسعيرة
private	خاصّ
problem	مُشكِلة (ج. مشاكل)
profession	مِهنة (ج. مِهن)
prohibited, not allowed	مَمنوع
project	مشروع (ج. مَشاريع)
public	عامّ
public transportation	مُواصَلات عامّة
public, governmental	حُكومي
put (to)	حَطّ – يحُطّ* = وضع – يضَع◆

Q

quarter	رُبع (ج. أرباع)
question	سُؤال
quiet	هادِئ = هادّي
Qur'anic	قُرآني

R

rain	مَطَر (ج. أمْطار)
rainy	ماطِر
raise (to)	رفع – يرفَع
raise the price; make more expensive (to)	غلّى – يغلّي (II)
reason	سَبَب (ج. أسباب)
red	أحمر
Red Sea (the)	البحر الأحمر
refrigerator	ثلّاجة
refugee	لاجِئ (ج. لاجئين)
refuse (to)	رفض – يرفُض
relationship	علاقة (ج. علاقات)
relative	قريب (ج. أقارِب)
relative, in relation to	نِسبي
religion	دين (ج. أديان)
religious	مُتدَيِّن
remain, stay (to)	بقي – يبقى
remaining, rest	باقي
remember (to)	ذكَر – يذكُر
rent (to)	استأجَر – يستأجِر (X)
rent	إيجار = أجرة
reply, answer (to)	جاوب – يجاوب (III)
republic	جُمهوريّة
request, ask for, order (to)	طلَب – يطلُب
reserve (to)	حجز – يحجِز
responsible	مَسؤول
rest (to)	استراح – يستريح
restaurant	مَطعَم (ج. مطاعم)
result (to)	نتَج – ينتُج
result	نتيجة (ج. نتائج)
return, go back (to)	رجع – يرجع

English	Arabic
return something (to)	رجّع – يُرجّع (II)
revolution	ثَورة (ج. ثَورات)
rice	رُزّ
ride (to)	رکِب – يرکَب
right (direction)	يَمين
river	نَهر
road	طَريق (ج. طرق)
role	دَور
room	غُرفة (ج. غُرف)
ruins	آثار
rule (to)	حكم – يحكُم
rule, law	قانون (ج. قوانين)

S

English	Arabic
Sa'idi, a person from Upper Egypt	صعيدي (ج. صعايدة)
safe	أمين
salad	سَلَطة
Samaritans	سَمَرة
same thing (the)	نفس الشيء
Saturday	السبت
say (to)	قال – يقول
scarcity	قِلّة
scene, sight	مَنظر (ج. مناظر)
scholarship	مِنحة (ج. مِنَح)
school	مَدرسة (ج. مدارس)
school subject	مادّة (ج. موادّ)
science, knowledge	عِلم (ج. علوم)
season	فَصل (ج. فصول)
second	ثاني
secondary (high) school	المَدرسة الثانوية
secretary	سكرتير
security, guarding	حِراسة

English	Arabic
see (to)	رأى – يرى = ◆ / شاف – يشوف*
self; same	نَفس
seriously	عن جَدّ*
service	خِدمة
service car	سِرفيس
seven	سبعة
seventh	سابِع
several, a number of	عِدّة
shameful	عيب
shawarma (name of a meat dish)	شاوَرما
she	هي
shirt	قميص (ج. قُمصان)
shoes	كُندرة (ج. كنادِر)
shop	مَحَلّ (ج.محلّات) = دُكّان (ج. دكاكين)
shower	دُشّ
sick, unwell	مَريض
sign, billboard	لافتة (ج. لافتات)
since	مُنذُ ◆
singer	مُغنّي (ج. مغنّين)
sister, a friendly way of addressing a woman	أُخت (ج. أخوات)
sit down (to)	قعد – يقعُد = جلس – يجلس
sitting	جالِس
situation	وَضع
six	ستّة
sixth	سادِس
skilled	ماهِر
sleep (to)	نام – ينام
sleep	نوم

sleepy	نَعسان	still	لِسّه
small	صغير	stomach	معدة
smoke (to)	دخّن – يدخّن (II)	stop someone (to)	وقّف – يوقّف (II)* =
smoking	تَدخين		توقّف – يتوقّف (V) ◆
snow	ثَلج (ج. ثلوج)	stop, (bus stop)	مَوقِف (ج. مواقف)
soap	صابون	stop, station	مَحطة
soccer	كُرة قدم	story	قصّة (ج. قصص)
socks	جْرابات	straight	دُغري*
solution	حَلّ	strange	غريب
some	بَعض	street	شارع (ج. شوارع)
something	حاجة	student	طالب (ج. طلاب)
something sweet	شيء حلو	study (to)	درس – يدرُس
something, thing, item	شيء = اِشي* (ج. أشياء)	study	دراسة
		stupid	غَبي
sometimes	أحياناً	succeed, pass (an exam) (to)	نجح – ينجح
soul, person, inhabitant	نسمة		
sound, voice	صَوت (ج. أصوات)	sugar	سُكّر
south	جنوب	suitable	مُناسب
speak (to)	تكلّم – يتكلّم (V) ◆ =	suitcase, bag	شنطة
	حكى – يحكي	sum, amount	مبلغ
specialization, major	تخصُّص	summer	الصيف
specially	خصوصاً	sun	شَمس
spices	بهارات	Sunday	الأحد
sport	رياضة	surprise	مُفاجَأة
spring	الربيع	surround (to)	أحاط – يُحيط (IV)
standing	واقف	sweets, desserts	حَلَويات، حلويّات
start (to)	بدأ – يبدأ	swim (to)	سبح – يسبَح
state	وَلاية (ج. ولايات)		
State Department (Ministry of Foreign Affairs)	وزارة الخارجيّة	**T**	
		tabbuuli (name of a vegetarian dish)	تبّولة
staying	نازِل	table	طاولة (ج. طاولات)
steal (to)	سرَق – يسرِق	table tennis	تنس طاولة
steering wheel	عجلة القيادة		

take (to)	أخذ – يأخذ	there, there is	هُناك ◆ = فيه*
take (something) out (to)	أخرج – يخرِج (IV)	there is not, there are not	ما فيش* = ما فيه*
take a bath (to)	استحمّ – يستحمّ ◆ (X)	therefore, in that case	إذَن
talk (about something) (to)	تحدّث – يتحدّث◆ (V)	they (dual)	هُما ◆
tea	شاي	they (plural)	هُمّ
teach (to)	درّس – يدرّس = علّم – يعلّم (II)	think (to)	اعتقد – يعتقد (VIII) = فكّر – يفكّر (II)
teacher	مُعلِّم (ج. معلّمين) = أستاذ (ج. أساتذة)	third	ثالث
		third (one third)	ثُلُث
teaching	تدريس = تعليم	thirsty	عطشان
team	فريق (ج. فِرَق)	this (Egyptian)	دا* = هذا
telephone	هاتِف◆ = تلفون	this name	هالاسم * = هذا الإسم
temperature (degree of heat)	درجة حَرارة	this (f.)	هاي * = هذه
		this (m.)	هذا
temple/place of worship	مسجد (ج. مساجد)	three	ثلاثة
ten	عشرة	Thursday	الخميس
tenth	عاشِر	thus, this way	كذلك◆ = هكَذا ◆ = هيك*
test	امتِحان (ج. أمتحانات)	time (occurrence)	مَرّة (ج. مَرّات)
thank (to)	شكر– يشكُر	time	وَقت
thank God	الحمد لله	time, era	زَمَن
thank you	شُكراً	tired	تَعبان
thank you (lit. may your hands be safe)	يسلموا ايديك	to	الى ◆ = ل
		to	أن ◆
thank you very much	شُكراً جَزيلاً	today	اليوم
that (relative pronoun)	إنّ	together	مع بعض
that, f. (demonstrative pronoun)	تِلكَ	tomato	بَندورة
that, m. (demonstrative pronoun)	ذلكَ ◆	tomorrow	غَداً ◆ = بُكرة*
		Torah (the)	التوراة
that's sufficient, enough	خَلاص*	total	مجموع
totally, exactly, fully	تماماً		
then, and then	ثمّ ◆ = بَعدين*	traffic light	إشارة ضوئيّة

travel (to)	سافر – يسافر (III)	visit (to)	زار – يزور
trip	رحلة	visit	زيارة
true, correct	صَحّ	volleyball	كُرة طائرة
try, attempt (to)	حاوَل – يحاوِل (III)		
try something out (to)	جرّب – يجرّب	**W**	
Tuesday	الثلاثاء	wait (for) (to)	استنّى – يستنّى (X)*
two	اثنين	wake up (to)	صحا – يصحو ◆ =
two kilograms	اثنين كيلو*		صِحي – يصحى*
type, kind	نوع (ج. أنواع)	walking	مَشي
		wallet	مَحفظة
U		want (to)	أراد – يُريد (IV) ◆ =
under	تَحت		بدّه، بدها، الخ.*
understand (to)	فهم – يفهم	warm	دافئ
understanding	فَهم	washing	غسيل
understanding, having understood	فاهِم	watch (to)	شاهد – يشاهد (III) ◆ = تفرّج – يتفرّج (V)
underwear	ملابِس داخليّة	watching	مُشاهدة◆
unfortunate, poor (as in oh, poor guy!)	مسكين	water	ماء◆ = ميّة*
unfortunately	للأسف	watermelon	بطّيخ
United States (the)	الولايات المتحدة	we	احنا*
university	جامعة	we have	عنّا* = عندنا
until; in order to; even	حتّى	we missed you	أشتقنا لَك
		wear (to)	لبس – يلبس
upset someone (to)	أزعَل – يزعِل (IV)* = زعّل – يزعّل (II)*	weather	طَقس
		Wednesday	الأربعاء
use (to)	استعمل – يستعمِل (X)	week	أسبوع (ج. أسابيع)
		weight	وزن
V		weight loss, weight reduction	تخفيف الوزن
vegetables	خُضار	welcome to you	أهلا (وسهلاً) فيك
very	جدّاً◆ = كثير	well	بِئر (ج. آبار)
village	قرية (ج. قُرى)	west	غرب
visa	تأشيرة	what?	ماذا؟◆ = إيش؟*

English	Arabic
what is wrong?	مالك؟*
what is your opinion?	إيش رأيِك؟*
when	عندَما ◆ = لَمّا
whenever	كلّما ◆ (كلّ + ما)
where?	وين؟*
where (are you going) today? (Egyptian)	على فين النهارد؟*
where is he?	وينه = وين هو؟*
where to?	لَوين؟*
whether (also used to ask yes/no questions)	هَل ◆
which?	أيّ؟
white	أبيض
who, that, which (feminine, singular)	التي ◆ = اللي*
who, that, which (masculine, plural)	الذين ◆
who, that, which (masculine, singular)	الذي ◆
whole time (the)	طول الوَقت
why?	ليش؟*
why? (Egyptian)	ليه؟* = ليش؟*
why not?	ليش لأ؟*
wide	واسِع
widespread	مُنتشِر
wife (his wife)	مراة (مراته)*
will	سَ ◆ = سَوفَ ◆
will not	لن ◆
wind	ريح (ج. رِياح)
window	شُبّاك (ج. شبابيك)
winter	الشِتاء

English	Arabic
with	مع
with speed, quickly	بسرعة
with us	معانا* = مَعنا
without	بدون
without, no need for	بَلاش*
work (to)	اشتغل-يشتغل (VIII)
work	شُغل
work, do (to)	عمل – يعمل
world	دُنيا = عالَم
World War I	الحرب العالميّة الأولى
would like, liking	حابّ* = حابِب*
written	مكتوب

Y

English	Arabic
year	سنة (ج. سَنوات، سِنين)
yellow	أصفر
yes	أيوا*، نعَم
yesterday	أمس ◆ = مبارِح*
yogurt	لبن
you (f.s.)	انتِ
you (m.s.)	انتَ
you (pl.)	انتو*
you are welcome	لا شكراً على واجب
you, formal way of address	حضرتك
you're most welcome; whatever pleases you	تِكرم عينك*
young man, youth	شابّ (ج. شباب)

Z

English	Arabic
zero	صِفر

Grammar Index

More Arabic Terms